A SOUTHERNER
DISCOVERS THE SOUTH

A Da Capo Press Reprint Series

THE AMERICAN SCENE
Comments and Commentators

GENERAL EDITOR: WALLACE D. FARNHAM
University of Illinois

A SOUTHERNER DISCOVERS THE SOUTH

By Jonathan Daniels

New Introduction by the Author

DA CAPO PRESS • NEW YORK • 1970

Library of Congress Catalog Card Number 68-16228

SBN 306-71011-0

Published by Da Capo Press
A Division of Plenum Publishing Corporation
227 West 17th Street, New York, N.Y. 10011

Manufactured in the United States of America

To

J. D.

A Better Southerner

All of the characters in this book are fictitious, though most of them will be surprised to discover it.

CONTENTS

CONTENTS

INTRODUCTION

The reprinting of an old travel book about the South may be like taking a chromo of grandma out of the attic. Grandma doesn't look quite like she did as a girl. But the changes do not make her less loved. Fortunately there is a possibility that, unlike a lady, a land may be more beautiful—certainly more worth loving and cherishing—as it ages. But the contrary is also possible. Gullies may come like the crow's-feet—but uglier. And while stretches of pine trees may be fairer to the eye than old eroded fields fit only for the production of broom sedge, the pines may cover the old home farms where men were sometimes content. "Niggertown" may be an unmentionable word today, but spreading city slums certainly deserve an ugly word expressive of indignation about the places if not the people captured in them.

Any portrait of a man's homeland is a self-portrait, too. But I can report that it is more than a narcissistic experience for an author in his late sixties to present the description of the South he tried to see with the eyes of his thirties. If highways widen, arteries harden. The story of an old journey may seem only a quaint piece of decoration. But a view in time may be set up for comparison, too. And the old view may point up not only change but continuity as well.

Possibly to understand any land, we need rear-view mirrors as well as clean windshields. I hope this reprint will help to provide both. Preparation of this small new essay to go with the old book has been an experience of mixed emotions for me. It has amounted to retracing a journey in long recollection, and that has brought feelings of nostalgia and a sense of escape—and some sense of frustration about both change and lack of change in the three decades since *A Southerner Discovers the South* was first published. Now I wonder at my brashness in daring to pose as discoverer of an ancient region. Fortunately, then I did not quite set myself up as prophet or as one who could confidently point Southern directions.

Still, if I had, I would not now have to blush unduly. The year in which this book was written was the same one in which Neville Chamberlain, umbrella in hand, ended a journey from Munich to London with the avowal that he brought "peace for our time." And as to directions, that was the same year, also, in which a young Irishman, denied a permit for trans-Atlantic flight, set out, so he said, from Brooklyn to San Francisco and with dead pan astonishment landed in Dublin. "Wrongway" Corrigan was an hilarious hero all the same.

This reprinting Southerner expects no such applause, though he may deserve such laughter for some misguiding directions he presented. He hopes not to serve prodigious illusion about the pain or the progress of the South from then to now and from now to eternity. In understanding this American region we need to look back and to look forward. For me such retrospect and anticipation is a sort of autobiographical adventure. I hope others will share it. We see because of what we are. We can be the blind. We can only hope to be perceptive.

It is notorious that we Southerners look back with pride. Sometimes like children at a party we look big-eyed at progress. But we remain a people in puzzle. Perhaps I am mistaken about that. My bewilderment may be exclusively my own. Certainly considering the number of discoverers and explorers, there should no longer be any mysteries about the South. Still, there remain some contradictions. We laugh at some of them ourselves. It was from a Georgian that I heard the line: "Please hold my magnolia while I whip this slave." And certainly today a South, which in some evident opulence cherishes antiques, seems to talk more than any other region of the New, the ever New, the forever New South.

It may be, as a distinguished Southern sociologist from Chapel Hill says, that the myth of the New South "is coming to pass before our very eyes." Also, it may be true, as a Southern economist reports, that "dynamically and dramatically" the present South is "entering the main stream of American life." Another learned Southern scholar announces that "the South appears to be rapidly throwing off its old cloak of regional distinctiveness and is moving into the main stream of American life."

Possibly all should hail the event. Still, as perhaps there should be a specter at every feast, I, as aging Southerner, would like some assurances about that much repeated phrase, "entering the main stream of American life." Frankly, it carries for me that not entirely delightful connotation of a homogenized America. If we were caught in it, I would certainly rejoice in escape from what one of our poets has termed "the fascinating nightmare called the South." But we Southerners have suffered long enough from the caricature and the calumny about us, and from the romanticism and nostalgia of our own making. Both should be recognized as imposters. At the risk of seeming a neo-Confederate, I reject the notions of the special sinfulness of a South which has covered its bad conscience with the worse cloak of hatred. The abolitionists and the Southern hotspurs are still telling their alternate tales. And sometimes today we seem impaled upon the propaganda of industrial promoters. Of course, there once was a stagnant South, even if it had waterlilies in it. But I cross my cotton-picking fingers about this "main stream of American life" which at last we may be permitted to enter. I have the perverse notion that it may be the South at last, unintentionally, even unconsciously, which is bringing the nation back into the main stream which had its source in the American dream.

It pleased me that one of the "main stream" philosophers spoke of "the myth of the New South." Certainly our greatest mythology is that which swings to band music in that phrase, "the New South." It is, of course, all around us, to be described in detail by the historian and the economist. It has become a cliché in technicolor. We sing of the glory that is Georgia and the grandeur that is Richmond, Birmingham, and New Orleans. Yet the New South is an old song.

Recently I attended a meeting in Atlanta celebrating twenty years of Southern progress, particularly in the field of higher education. As homework in advance I looked at the newspapers twenty years before that meeting. The old headlines gleamed. Out of the Atlanta office of the U.S. Department of Commerce came the New South news of two decades before: "Seven years of war and post-war activity in the Southeast brought an increase of 179 per cent in net salaries and wages." Everything was up— telephones, electricity, new businesses. Here was the up, up, up New South, even if, counting from the Depression, it was up from the almost nothing of the grim years before. We have all watched the more meaningful soaring since, and sometimes, as is our perpetual custom, we have romanticized that, too. At the same time other folks have sharpened the story of our short-comings. Whatever its meaning today, the New South is, as always, welcome in terms of its meaning for tomorrow. Still present and future, the phrase also deserves some understanding in terms of the long past as a shibboleth grown smooth from too much handling.

Like so many other things the accepted view seems to be that the term New South came with the wind from Atlanta. The great editor and orator, Henry Grady, is supposed to have invented it in December, 1886. Certainly he popularized it. But it was a quarter century old then. The honor actually belongs to Adam Badeau, a New Yorker, later military secretary to General Grant, who in 1862 established a newspaper for the convenience of carpetbaggers in Port Royal, South Carolina. He named it *The New South.* I have a writing hideaway just across the sound from Port Royal now. On a gardened island there golfers move from their surf-side villas to play in the sun. And little more than a golf shot away recently persisting poverty was pointed to the nation. In the same county Dr. Martin Luther King came for his meditations between demonstrations.

But I get ahead of my story, which is easy to do in the South. Adam Badeau's paper was not exacty the organ the Old South was seeking in his time. "We trust the paper will be a powerful organ for freedom," said one of the most militant Northern missionaries who had come to the region in 1865. That was a New South, too—that one of forty acres and a mule. It was not the first one. Actually the hope in the term—and sometimes the despair, too—was a reality before Thomas Jefferson died as bankrupt Southerner on his eroded hill of Monticello.

Before the great Agrarian President died, two centuries of tobacco farming had left Southern land worn out, washed out, unwanted. Much of it was left to the briars and the brush, the wild turkeys and the deer. And from the already barren ground of the eastern seaboard South, it was said, "an emigrating contagion resembling an epidemic disease" spread among the people. Slaves were shipped and sold "down the river." There was a New South then, tangible and geographical, which we now call the Deep South.

But hope spread again. A Virginian named Edmund Ruffin, who hated Jefferson's notions of human equality, discovered that the old lands could be revived by the application of marl. There was resurgence in the soil, but Ruffin and others were as zealous in defense of slavery as in land improvement. Early an advocate of secession, Ruffin in 1860 published a sort of prospectus for a New South which he called *Anticipations of the Future.* In imaginative prophecy, it pictured a South pushed into such ruin by the Abolitionist Yankees that secession was accepted.

There followed a short, devastating war in which the South suffered from a blockade but Northern merchants were bankrupted and their cities overwhelmed by mobs of "undigested foreigners." Finally the West broke with the North and joined the South. The end, as Ruffin envisioned it, was a South rising from ruin to prosperity, adding industries to its agriculture and trading directly and profitably with Europe.

Such fantasy entitled Ruffin to the honor of firing the first shot at Fort Sumter. As most of us are aware, the shot didn't bring him what he expected. The New South, to which he preferred suicide, was Reconstruction. Some of its history has been written in terms as overwrought as his prophecy. We miss much of the fact of the painful period, however, if we fail to understand that this was a time when in terms of both promoters and politicians, the South was supposed to be drawn, though sometimes kicking and screaming, into "the main stream of American life" as elsewhere designed.

Instead there emerged the Solid South, which some would describe as the Stubborn South. And in place of the "myth of the New South" there emerged a double mythology—at home of an Old South of grace, leisure, and abundance, abroad of a South which should be conscience stricken for its sins. Both were largely made of the stuff of legend. The rich South was always rare. The Wade Hamptons were as few as the oil millionaires now. The poor poor were the poor whites. There was cruelty under slavery as a cruel system itself. But when Southern promoters undertook dangerous projects like the draining around Lake Pontchartrain, they used Irishmen instead of Negroes. A dead slave was a thousand-dollar loss; a dead Irishman was a dead Irishman. When Frederick Law Olmsted marched the South to record the evil results of slavery, European immigrants were already in New York slums, soon to explode in draft riots which have never been equaled by any people in any fury of our times. Man's inhumanity to man was not a Southern invention.

Our sins are many, but in America we have not sinned alone. And we have not suffered alone either.

It may be good poetry to speak of the "fascinating nightmare called the South." It is good sociology to discover and reveal statistically the pervasive poverty of our region, now as in the past. But sometimes in the increasing ranks of our Ph.Ds, which we greatly need, we appear to have lost from our colleges the poets and philosophers who not always with accuracy but often with feeling and perception argued out of academic cloisters about the proper qualities of the South. I remember when I traveled as discoverer long ago, there was an intellectual debate between the learned men at Chapel Hill and those at Vanderbilt in Nashville. Compiling statistics on want and need, the men at Chapel Hill were loudly insisting that the South should throw away its chains. The men at Vanderbilt, calling themselves Agrarians, warned that the South should not forget its traditions. I took the Chapel Hill side. But I went to Nashville and came away impressed with the perhaps romantic insistence of the Agrarians that the South did not need to engorge everything which constituted what even then was called the "main stream of American life." The debate has subsided since. Most of the prophets at Chapel Hill are dead. The Agrarians are dispersed to their individual and separate writing of their poems, essays, novels.

I miss them. Sometimes today the South seems without debate save over the grisly bones of Jim Crow or who is going to get the new garment factory. We have come almost to the indissoluble combination of the promoters and the professors—both performing in a sort of mutual hypnosis by the wonderful tools they require. Research is not only respectable—far more important, it is profitable. But sometimes discussion seems entirely succeeded by advertising. Learning is praised on billboards and corporate recruiters come hat and cash in hand to enroll the young erudite on their payrolls. Hardly anything seems to be more the symbol

xv

of our opulent society than our expanding universities. That is a new blessing in an old land. But beside them poverty remains. It crowds in more and more. And the most fervent questioning about our destiny takes place not in our classrooms but on our streets. The ferment in the colleges roars sometimes like the riots in the ghettos. And sometimes our colleges seem not so much leading as besieged. Of course, this phenomenon is not Southern. Columbia, on the edge of Harlem, is not regarded as a Southern institution. Still there are some evidences that like other colleges and cities, it may be engulfed in a far from placid main stream of America which has been pouring out of the South.

It is a stormy stream. It seems often a polluted one. But navigators on the American main stream in our past never reported it to be a pellucid river. Like America's true natural main stream, the Mississippi of so much Southern legend, it has been marked by violence, sailed by rowdies. It has washed eroded shores and disreputable ones, like that at Natchez Under-the-Hill. Some of those upon it and beside it long seemed savages. And sometimes there is still a Show Boat minstrel show quality about it, as when participants in a poor people's march come in air-conditioned buses led by an overalled leader in a Chrysler Imperial. Old man river in America has always been one on which Americans moved in such combination as river boat gamblers, stevedores, missionaries, bankers, planters, poets, roughnecks, and crinolined ladies, often writers. They have moved, they hope, toward the American dream or at least toward their individual ones. Not all have found the company of the others comfortable or even safe. We will not in our time.

Yet there may be reason for thinking that the main stream of American in the future will not be one upon which the South is finally permitted to sail but one which flows out of the South itself. In this time no antennae need be lifted high to hear the panegyrics about the appeal of the South to industry today. Southern shores and hills are filled with those who have come

from other areas to enjoy the South's climate and charm. But it
may be well not to speak so much of what is flowing southward
as of what the South is pouring into America. This region does
not generally advertise that. It is not material designed for pro-
motional brochures. Actually it is the old poverty of the South
which is transforming, astounding, and disturbing other parts
of America. Much of it is black. Not many fond farewells in
the South followed it to the North and West. Many Southerners regarded it as good riddance. Yet, whatever other mis-
chief or malfeasance this mobile poverty is about, it is more
than anything else giving national dramatization to problems
which once seemed so much Southern and are at last disclosed
as the shame of dreadful destitution in the whole of an opulent land.

There was never any Southern army like this before. And it
doesn't carry the South's revered banners. But nothing is so
certain as that this force will alter the America before us and
send those alterations swiftly back home to Dixie. I say certain.
That is always precarious in a prophet. And every historian
knows that while there were New Souths before, there was also
that other Reconstruction which passed away in violent Southern
distaste and mounting Northern disregard.

So nothing is certain. Our slums may grow more crowded and
more fetid. Ignorance may continue with its old companion,
destitution. Protests may be backlashed into the rat-infested ten-
ements. This may be only a disagreeable interlude from which
the well-to-do emerge in comfort and the poor be again forgotten
sealed in slums. The old master may get back the forty acres
and the mule may die. This happened once. It could happen
again. But the last to welcome this now should be the people—
particularly the white people, among whom are so many of the
poor in the South.

The kind of New South of which the wisest Southerners have
always dreamed must be based upon the elimination of the dread-

ful contrasts between elegance and destitution. That could come most quickly by a national determination. The South, which in exodus has shown the need, could in similar determination so best serve the nation and itself. The result would be, coming perversely out of the South, a recommitment of the nation to a fair, good chance for every man. That was the American dream. That is the American main stream. It may seem a twisting river, but it could flow out of Alabama, through Harlem, back to the old loved—and the old despised—Southern land.

There will be no other New South. Our bootstraps are torn from tugging on them. We have followed will-o-the-wisps long enough, sometimes in jet planes. The only New South worth having will be one in a nation pursuing the happiness of all of its people—and, pathetically, in answer to the cry of the least of them.

I wish I could confidently prophecy the arrival of such a time. I wish I could speak confidently about the next thirty years or even the last thirty. I wish I could be as sure as some of our savants that the real, certain, blown in the bottle New South was "coming to pass before our very eyes." Maybe I am just a blind man at a fireworks display. I am aware of the pyrotechnics of our much emphasized Southern progress. But I am most aware of our continuing poverty, our ignorance, and—sometimes pathetically—our pretensions. There are still too many white columns in our minds and too many shantys in our yards. I am not sure that in times which have raced in prosperity and now perilously toward inflation, the South has advanced much on the hot, dusty road upon which it has moved so long. It is easy to see that we have moved to Southern towns—and to cities far away. Yet, sometimes the rising towers of the towns only cast greater shadows in the urban canyons beneath them. This is no time for Southern elation over the veneer of progress or deepened Northern concern about a South of crinolines and rags, magnolia and whip. This is a time for the South and America to

xviii

take stock and call up courage. We have more money in our banks and too much hideous poverty by our bayous—and today the bayous, the swamps of our civilization, are often only across the town from the banks. Today new factories gleam just across the broom sedge from the cabin where the old door hangs on one hinge. Our greatest universities are often only up the hill from our vilest slums. And sometimes it seems less certain that the New South has arrived than that the once supposedly revolutionary New Deal is out-of-date, and perhaps most antiquated in the South which it seemed to serve most and best.

Of course, we have reasons to thank God as well as to take courage. But there have been New Souths aplenty. Also there was a Reconstruction once before. Both New, New Souths and the provocative second Reconstruction of recent years could pass. I leave that to other witnesses. I don't ride so brashly as once I did. I don't knock on as many doors. It is difficult to draw a graph of greatness. But regardless of our statisticians and our computers, I am sure we can count on no New South as the fulfillment of an ancient dream unless it steadily better serves the needs, the hopes, and the happiness of all. Once it was easier to dream. Henry Grady saw the image of contentment he hoped might come in a New South in terms of every man by his own vine and fig tree with plenty on his table and peace on his mind. That image is changed forever. Our task may be more difficult, but we shall enter the American main stream, or bring the nation back into it, only when we insist upon solutions which will suffice for the chance, the decency, and the dignity of all men.

We cannot wait for that day's arrival to nourish and cherish the dream that it will come. And only all together shall any of us overcome.

The News and Observer　　　　　JONATHAN DANIELS
Raleigh, North Carolina
October, 1969

A SOUTHERNER DISCOVERS THE SOUTH

1

"WE GO FO'TH"

WE SOUTHERNERS are, of course, a mythological people. Supposed to dwell in moonlight or incandescence, we are in part to blame for our own legendary character. Lost by choice in dreaming of high days gone and big house burned, now we cannot even wish to escape. We may not even be found. Certainly, the land called South is no realm for geographers. I know. There are two old ladies in Sussex County, Delaware, who are as certain that they are Southerners on Southern soil as are any four persons who live on Bull Street in Savannah. There is a dirt farmer deep in Texas who preserves the plantation pattern with a fidelity impossible in Virginia. And I have talked with men and women fixed in big houses on Red Mountain at Birmingham and on Paces Ferry Road in Atlanta who never in any true sense could be Southern. They make the land Yankee by stepping on it. The Gulf and the Atlantic are fairly dependable borders. But the Potomac and the Mississippi cannot with the slightest accuracy bound a Dixie which, if it contains anything Southern, must include a yellow fellow who roasts oysters on the Eastern Shore of Maryland, the Boston Club in New Orleans and a well-advanced case of pellagra which I had the privilege of observing in southeastern Arkansas.

All this I know as discoverer. And the South has been wanting discovery for a long time. Natives and foreigners, first depended upon to present the South, broke it instead into fragments of local colors as diverse as the cheeks of colored girls, all the way from chalk to chocolate. Perhaps it remains fragmentary. But as one, Southern as far back as there have been Europeans in the South's lost woods and waters, I set out to find out. I began unaware how much stress in knowing this South should go on climate or on Negroes, lost grandeur or present poverty, the unique proximity of the equator to a Northern breed of people, the fact that life was so easy it was taken too easily, the meanness or the jealousy of the Yankees, semi-tropical diseases, slavery or the shade. Such a quest obviously did not run from the luncheon table in 45th Street where Amy Loveman, James Putnam, George Stevens and I talked about it, to Raleigh to Little Rock to New Orleans, but straighter from tobacco to TVA to tenant farmers, from the prancing power of the demagogue to aristocracy to shrimp seining, to lynchings, to high birth rate, to heat, to politics, to hot biscuits and cool evenings, to poor whites and rich Yankees. Indeed, the truth is that the journey began a long time ago. Precisely at the moment when "Old Doctor" Haywood (not to be confused with "Young Hubert") spanked me smartly with the flat of his hand and set off my initial bawling in that front room with the bay windows over the rose garden, this Southerner began to discover his South.

My first guide was Harriet, yellow and wise, who could look all that the conventional Mammy was supposed to be but who possessed knowledges and interests which made childhood under her guiding a dark excitement of endless variety. I still remember being introduced to Death in the stringy guise of Pink, an ancient Negress who went to Heaven by the processes of desiccation. Harriet and I went to see her, laid out in her brass bed, which Harriet inherited, in the unpainted two-room house, which she and Harriet shared. I still smell the wood smoke, the pig fat, and the perspiration which together remain for me the by no means unpleasant smell of Negro. And I recall, with a vividness which none of the mir-

2

acles recorded in Old or New Testaments ever possessed for me, the story of the angel who came and sat on the shining foot of Pink's brass bed. He was only as tall as a slop bucket, but he had a crown on his head, and he straddled the brass tubing of the bed as a man, or an angel, might straddle a golden horse. Pink had died quietly in the midst of reporting his visitation and the unutterably sweet music which accompanied him. That others in the room had been blind to his presence was as it should have been. Pink, when she saw, was half way from Lenoir Street to Heaven and simply and naturally beheld what one day we should all pray to be able to see. "Amen, Sister. Ain't you right!"

But when we went home with my hand still wet with excitement I knew better than to share my adventure with Mother or ask her questions about it.

"And where has my big boy been?"

Harriet had instructed me well in my unshakable answer: "Down in the low ground to jump Jim Crow."

What a childhood of discovery it was! My grandfather had built our house in Raleigh to endure, but he could not do as much for the neighborhood. The grounds of the old Governor's Palace were a block away. But the new Governor's Mansion, towered and twisting and ornamented, rose on the increasingly more fashionable Blount Street. The old palace became the Centennial School. And all around our house Negroes and questionable white people came more and more to live. Across the street was Shaw University, important to us because of the story, which each older brother in turn told to each incredulous younger one, that the iron dogs there would rise from their pedestals and run when they heard the thunder, and because in the spring under the wooden fence around it a pocket-sized species of ground snake could be easily caught. At least one of Booker T. Washington's sons went to college there. And next door to us lived Wesley

Hoover, as dignified an Anglo-Saxon gentleman, for all the little Negro blood in him, as I ever saw. He had daughters whose skins really were the color of magnolia petals. But Wesley Hoover had made his money, a great deal for a Negro in Raleigh in those days, running a saloon. That was an occupation which we understood was a special service rendered in assistance to the Devil. Yet he was a good neighbor and man. The South was not entirely simple even then. But from us and from the Hoovers and from Shaw, the neighborhood fell off precipitately. It was the only world we had seen and so, if not simple, not strange. We lived as children close to life, innocently and uncritically. I remember the bewildered weeping of poor Frank, my younger brother, when he entirely overturned a Sunday afternoon. My uncle and aunt had some very special guests one winter Sunday and they decided that it would be fun to share with the children the joys of one of our infrequent snows which then lay upon the ground. With us they went to a little hill a block or two away. Frank, who was just beyond prattling, was being helpful and conversational, pointing out the places of interest in his restricted world. In the sense of knowing his cosmos, he was a true cosmopolitan.

"And that," he said to the pretty lady visitor as he pointed to a weather-beaten house among the items of his known world, "is a whore house."

He was right. It was. But those were Taftian times when even in this land Victoria's spirit, or at least the spirit labeled with her name, lingered on. My memory is that my uncle, as angry red as his guest's blush, thought that Frank should be soundly whipped but that Mother refused. Frank, she held, had said only the truth and said it innocently. He was not yet responsible for what existed in his world. Mother was as ready a woman with the rod as I ever knew. Father turned over his responsibilities in that regard entirely to her. But

4

she sought as she could to keep clear always the relationship between punishment and justice. She seldom, if ever, sent us out to the Spirea bush to get switches without the culprits being convinced of the full justice of the forthcoming flagellation. But as I remember it, also, we always bawled like the innocent victims of merciless wrath.

On Christmas night every year Father had an empty ink barrel brought from the office and put in the middle of the street in front of our house. That was before automobile traffic and before they began to ship ink in iron drums. Father lit the barrel like High Priest and all the rest of us, white and black, ran with our fireworks like savages about it. It was bedtime when the last hoop dropped and all the stays fell across themselves in bright coals. Even when only kin gathered at one table, it took the conversational genius of Uncle Herbert in lyricizing Peanut Pig and Muscavado Molasses to fill both the finicky and the voracious. But children and adults, too, were expected to eat in those days. Our cook had a slab of marble and a baseball bat for beating the biscuits. In the winter, black and bearded Buffalo came without failing, with strings of partridges. Mother broiled them on Sunday nights. Men brought Father strings of fish all the way up from Morehead. And in our garden there seemed to be under Uncle Ricks' tending all the berries and all the fruit trees, plentifully bearing. How low the branches of the fig tree hung under its fruit! And pleasant above eating were oak and myrtle and mimosa. The leaves of the magnolia made excellent sandals to protect bare feet from the ubiquitous unpleasantness of chicken doos.

Down the culvert (a storm sewer five feet square through which we used to go for blocks with lightwood torches) and along the bed of the shallow stream which ran from the culvert was the tumbling house of the Smathers family. They were our local duplicates of the Kallikaks, po' whites in

Raleigh, poor human material anywhere, but interesting. Certainly I shall never forget one Sunday afternoon spectacle: Ma Smathers sprawled drunk and sleeping on her front steps and her dirty youngest seeking unaided the vast breasts and the milk they contained. I watched him; he succeeded.

Finally, when Aunt Elvira sold her block with the house in the middle of it, the mulberry arbor and the corn field where we dug Jerusalem artichokes, our neighborhood was lost forever to the world of white gentility. But not to us. We stayed on for years, happy and joyous. Legislators and judges, authors and politicians from far away came down to Father's dinners. They meant special ice cream—the dasher in the afternoon and saucersful after the guests were served at night. Harriet smuggled them in to Frank and me. Also, in the cotton warehouse, which was built back of our block, the Holy Rollers came and rolled. I remember hearing them shout as I went to bed and Harriet's yellow sneering when I spoke of them. In the same warehouse other Negroes came and danced with no more and no less noise. And one summer when we were a little older we hid in the weeds and watched them: A Negro man slapped a woman and she went off screaming louder than the music.

All that seems far away and long ago and yet essentially all of that Southern childhood was a part of my journey in discovery of the South. Nearer now than the depths of that childhood, my discovering is marked by the angry concern of my mother and the fear of the servants when in Washington race riot swept so close to the Capitol. In Washington, too, I saw the Ku Klux Klan in its last fatuous march of masked men down Pennsylvania Avenue. More revealing than the marching I saw the unmasked faces in the hotels. A good deal earlier I saw the South as law student in New York, and as a callow, often sleepy, reporter in the basement of the city hall in Louisville, Kentucky. I did not leave the South—no

6

Southerner ever does—though I went living and working to New York and Paris and Territet and Florence. And I am happy that I came back to it from New York to edit *The News and Observer* in North Carolina.

And I read books. I met a young fellow waiting for a ferryboat at Greenville, Mississippi, with a truckload of love stories and Westerns who said Southerners did not read as many books as they should. Perhaps not. But for nearly ten years now I have been reading books about the South for *The Saturday Review of Literature*. And that decorous journal has sent me down some dark and green-scummed bayous of the Southern mind. I remember when I first read Erskine Caldwell that I recalled with familiar delight Ma Smathers sprawling on the Sabbath with her baby fumbling greedily for her big breasts. It did not occur to me then that anybody would regard Ma Smathers as a typical Southern woman in a typically Southern condition. But they did. Put a slut in a book about the South and there are patriots who will regard it as a slander on the whole region and every female in it and there are non-Southerners who will accept it as a panoramic photograph of Dixie. Of course, such people on each side of the Mason-Dixon line should be disregarded as unimportant to life and letters, living and dying, but in the aggregate these two masses of literate humanity provide bulk to obscure vision even when they talk loud and long of the seeing of the truth. It is not so much that literature confuses as that the easily confused are able to read.

The South does sometimes seem lost even to those who live in it. I believe I know a little about the land and people though I refuse to qualify as expert. Indeed, my virtue, if any, as commentator lies in my comparative ignorance. Here I am, Southern bred and born, educated at Chapel Hill, making my living in Raleigh by commenting on the variations and the vagaries of the Southern scene and seeing to it that all respectable North Carolinians are born, married and buried in the columns of *The News and Observer* as in the Church. But, except for the briefest and swiftest passages, all my excursions and explosions have been North and East and until this trip I had hardly been south of my own State of North Carolina which is regarded as far north by some who live deep in Alabama. I think, therefore, that I can look at the South with some detachment. Howard Mumford Jones of Harvard, after he left the University of North Carolina on the way to Michigan, wrote a piece for *Scribner's* in which he said that Southerners never accept the outlander.

"Hell, Howard," I complained. "I accepted you. I may have made a mistake. Still . . ."

"You're not a true Southerner," he said. "You've escaped."

I hope not. Escape is to the South, not away from it. Watch the trains and the roads, the trailers and the new gentlemen on the old plantations. For good or for ill, being a Southerner is like being a Jew. And, indeed, more needs to be written about the similarity of the minds and the emotions of the Jew, the Irishman, the Southerner, and, perhaps, the Pole, as a basis for the better understanding of each of them and of them all. There is, of course, the sense of exile; homesickness is entirely possible to those who remain on the homeland. All of them have mastered the art of breast beating. All of them hold up history between the world and their personal deficiencies. And all of them have succeeded in making themselves fascinating to other folk, even if sometimes the fascination borders upon the reptilian.

The South naturally, like each of the others, deviates in details from the common pattern. In the first place, the South is two races. Uncle Tom is as essential as the Colonel; burrhead is as indispensable as redneck. The South would not be anywise what we feel and mean when we say the round word "South" without the Negro. Without the white man,

it might be Africa. I know that I should not be what I am but
for Harriet. The white Southerner without the Negro might
be something different and better; he would certainly be
different. Perhaps a warm Kansan. Fortunately, I think, both
of them are what they are, though each of them is a long way
from perfection. Like Siamese twins they can be cut apart
only with the possibility of killing.

Such a Southerner, then, I am. And such a South as I
found! Mountain and Piedmont and Coastal Plain, I rode it.
I ate Oysters Rockefeller in New Orleans on the very day old
man John D. Rockefeller died in Ormond, Florida. I lay on
my belly in the Arkansas dust and changed a tire on the
hottest summer day. I waited at night, while the tree toads
sang, for the ferry to come following the Mississippi up an
avenue of forest through which the waters of the spring rise
had spread. I talked with Governors and professors, with
male and female patriots, with labor leaders and industrialists, educators and uplifters, engineers and chemists, and
foresters and physicians. They told me solemn things, true
things maybe. But I also talked to hitch hikers and tenant
farmers, to filling station operators, hill billies and Delta
planters, to poets, and bartenders, to Syrians in Vicksburg
and Cajuns in Louisiana, to a lovely, starry-eyed, aristocratic
young woman in love with a liquor salesman, to a drunkard
who lives and buys his liquor on the quarters which tourists
give him for seeing the big house which his ancestors built,
and everywhere to Negroes. These told me the South: As a
Negro may know it who has lived all his life on the plantation on which he was born, as a truck driver may find it
moving and selling meat within the range of the refrigeration
in his ice box truck body, as a little man may discover it who
has grown too old to get a job, or who may, working hard,
fail to make even a living trying to grow cotton out of buckshot land. There are as many Souths, perhaps, as there are

people in it. Maybe the only certain South is the addition of all the Southerners. Here are no more than a comparative few of them. And, since the traveler is generally the same man at the end of his journey, here may be only one man's South.

But I get ahead of my story. I began my tour of discovery at the commencement exercises of the Abraham Lincoln High School. One voice rose like a boat whistle through the stirring music the Girls' Glee Club made of Handel's "Hallelujah Chorus." The colored girls swung in their organdy dresses below the swinging music. And the graphite curls of one brown girl moved like a baton, keeping the beat. They made music and one weird voice gave strangeness to it. I liked the difference in the colors of their skins, multicolored as their dresses. I liked the shrewdness with which they had dressed themselves for commencement prettiness and most of all I liked the sense of rhythm in joyousness which they put into their singing.

The black valedictorian, the principal told me, was entitled to great credit. He had helped educate his brothers and sisters and then come back, older than usual, to take for himself the precious thing he had so gladly given. And he made a good speech solemnly:

Self-reliance, perseverance, faith and service are the four avenues to the city of success.

To strive, to seek, to find and not to yield.

Onward and upward forever.

Labor may be a burden and a chastisement but it is also an honor and a glory.

We go fo'th!

But after his solemnness the girls came again, slim creatures of taffy and chocolate wrapped in yellow and lavender organdy, singing, singing, and the one queer voice among them. He sought so solemnly through his blackness. He grabbed so confidently at the old familiar rungs on the ladder of success. He clung to the old promise and answered with the old pledge. But he was already beyond thirty. And all his learning merely led back to the broom and the shovel, the plow and the hoe. He was too late or too soon. The shining promises were rusty and dull.

But the girls were young and they sang and somehow Africa, always in that queer voice, slipped through their singing. The solemn student, who had learned all the old phrases that were to his race too often the parts of an old joke, looked like a stupid black satyr, and the girls, whose very skins wedded voodoo and pagan, sang around him. But he looked beyond their brief, slim youngness to quotations from Lincoln and Milton, Andrew Jackson and Carlyle, Kipling and Tennyson.

"We go fo'th," he said.

So also I went forth: a trifle less confident, a little less certain of Lincoln and Milton as guides, but with an alarm clock set, a tank full of gasoline, a suitcase full of clothes, a suitcase full of books, maps and letters of introduction to the best—the very best—people, and a high heart above the first signs of paunchiness upon a disappearing youth. And in my ears like the South singing rang that whistle voice which took Handel's "Hallelujah" into the heart of Africa and flung it back again at our South where the Northman ultimately met the Negro and built what some have called a civilization. I rode to find it.

BEGINNING IN A GRAVEYARD

HERE is the way: You come south from anywhere through Washington and across the green mall which the wealth of America has pulled out of the river swamps. You turn into the long Memorial Bridge. Look up, then, and see it upon the hill. Arlington by any seeing must be the façade of the South. Grandly and sweetly and green the hill runs up to the great house from the river. Certainly lovely enough, seen far off, from far below, is this Custis house where the South's Lee lived: white columns before a square house, the pattern colonial builders loved so dearly in Virginia, which new rich cotton snobs followed in Mississippi, and which small town money lenders in every agricultural town below this river cherish to this day.

I stopped on the bridge and got out of the car to see it better and an old gentleman, fishing, turned his head with mine.

"Nice," he said.

"Beautiful."

"I like to fish where I can see it."

"I was thinking of it as the door to the South."

"Of course, it is."

And a pity, I thought. Now it sits among the tombstones, high over Washington, the most easily seen thing on the whole road south. And beyond it nothing is simpler for the simple than imagining a whole succession of Arlingtons in which good masters in the tradition of Lee live and preside

over the pleasant destinies of the happy colored folks. Or else this legend is seen as so glamorously false that it has led all the way to equally wonderful legends in repudiation. And then sometimes the Southerner seems a fetid frog capable only of ejecting the brown sputum of snuff or tobacco into the deep sand of the twisting road.

The house is too full of big ghosts. And particularly the ghost of Lee. At least part of the trouble with this door to the South belongs to General Lee, who was master there by marriage long before he helped make the men, whose crosses dot his lawn, what they are now. The matter with Lee is the very monumental quality of his virtuousness. And, strangely, as such a man he is still the South's model. Perhaps, it was characteristic of us as a people living in the hottest sun ever borne as native by a northern stock of people anywhere that we should have chosen Robert E. Lee as our idol. This conjunction of a sun-warmed people and white marble hero has not always been entirely beneficial. It did not take us long to discover that few of us could approximate the elevated ethics of General Lee. And, not being able to approximate General Lee, we scorned any intermediary standards. Proudly Southerners held to Lee or nothing. And it is no longer a secret that in the South nothing has had more completely faithful adherents than General Lee.

Suddenly the old gentleman next to me stirred over his tackle. Hand after hand, he pulled in his line and at last drew from the muddy river a twisting and quivering hardhead less than six inches long. While he took the fish from his hook, I could see him considering its disposition, bucket or river. The river won and perhaps the fish. Then he turned his eyes again across the river to the Virginia hill.

"I'm a retired army officer," he told me abruptly, "with no special capacity and a great deal of time. I like it here." He fingered his line without taking his eyes from the hill. "It is beautiful. It symbolizes for me life when it made sense. Long ago."

We smiled together. Actually I thought the captive Arlington, turned into a lodge in a cemetery, ought to be symbol of the fall of that always imaginary realm called Dixie. But that cannot be seen from the bottom of the hill. From where we stood no tomb showed and Arlington might still have been the Great House peopled by the Gentry and not alone by the Dead. No people have ever spent so much time and trouble denying the facts of their victory as have the incurably romantic Yankees. The House stands to keep legend alive. The Yankees have preserved it. And behind Arlington anything may be believed. Anything is.

I wished my acquaintance good fishing and rode away. This was undoubtedly the front door of the South but it ran directly into the past and a graveyard though I knew that somewhere beyond it were the living. I sought them. I had nothing against history but I was more interested in the mixture of hunger and hilarity from which has been compounded so much of the life and drama of the South. I pressed on the accelerator, hastening through the parkways and suburbs below Washington, deeper into truer Virginia. I found it certainly as it seemed to me just before I rode into Williamsburg. There it was at the roadside, a sign: "Antiques: Curb Service." So I drove into the ancient city and stopped my car and gave up my bags at an air-conditioned hotel, before which a colored boy in the open air of Virginia was sweating good-naturedly in the sun.

The Scene

Beyond the columned door the undoubted place to begin the discovery of the South is Williamsburg in Virginia. There a millionaire, archaeologists, architects, historians, builders

14

and ladies in billowing 18th century dresses over fair 20th century skins present a patterned South all fixed in a moment. It would be pleasant and comfortable to let this be the South. As such it fits snugly into our heads. Here once was an auspicious village, palisaded against the Indians, then a town with a big capitol and a rich palace, and giants walking in it unaware that they were giants. Here were Jefferson and Henry, Mason and Berkeley as unaware of their own dimensions as they were of John D. Rockefeller, Junior, and gasoline engines and the meaning of mosquitoes.

A start here in discovery of the South has one sure stage set, scene for the South: long sweet Duke of Gloucester Street, and, back of that street, away from palace and gaol and capitol and Raleigh Tavern and Paradise House, grass under a hotel window, new grass but bright and green. There was wisdom in that Williamsburg, which, preserving the past, built a hotel preserving the best of present and past together, with shining plumbing and the covers to the beds turned back, air-conditioning and black boys to bring soda water and ice. It was pure good fortune that the restorers were aware of the belief of Dr. Samuel Johnson that "the finest landscape in the world is improved by a good inn in the foreground." Here it is. It does. The hiatus from the burning of the Raleigh Tavern to the nineteen thirties is over. Once in that time the slanderers said that you could always tell when you were in the South by looking to see the dust swept under Virginia beds. The slanderers themselves are dust now. And in Williamsburg sensible folk look instead from the windows of the inn to see how white the pebbled paths run between the box hedges.

"It is a curious thing," said the talkative physician, "but history, set up to be seen, requires a great deal of box."

In the moonlight I had walked up Duke of Gloucester Street with them from the inn to the center of the town

15

where even the grocery stores masquerade in the brick and board costumes of old Williamsburg. The doctor was fifty, if he was a day, but his wife was young and, I gathered, new. She seemed bored with his long talkativeness, but her loss was my gain. When old Samuel Johnson spoke of a good inn in the foreground of every landscape, I know he meant good company and those adjuncts of the good talk of good company, good wine and good food. We had eaten well before we began to walk. And the doctor had insisted that I help them finish a very potent and pleasant bottle of wine.

"Look at those hedges," he said pointing at the black bulk of box in the dark. He laughed suddenly. "I wonder where it came from. I know a town in which they tell a rare tale of box bushes."

I thought the young wife sighed. I wondered if this were her honeymoon.

"Well, this town I'm talking about is an old town but not a big one," the doctor said, hearing nothing. "And nothing very much ever happened there except that people lived there—as we count in America—a long time ago. Nobody, as far as I know, ever considered restoring it. But in that old town for generations and generations they buried the rich and the poor, the doctor and the planter, the merchant and the school teacher and all their wives in a walled square. And above their bones the women"—in the darkness he flung his arm around his wife's shoulder—"the women, who are forever concerned with bringing forth the living and remembering the dead, planted shrub and flower, oak and oleander, flowering myrtle and especially the green, slow-growing box."

His wife spoke: "That's what women were concerned with a long time ago."

"But time crowded the cemetery," he went on, unwilling to be interrupted, "and the town surrounded the graves. So the old graveyard was left to hold the past and a new one

16

received the new dead. Then the keeper of the old City Cemetery had little to do beyond seeing that the Negroes cut the grass and that the living behaved themselves among the graves. This was fortunate because his qualifications as cemetery keeper had only been demonstrated as poll holder in the city elections. But his job was a pleasant one, not lucrative neither pressing, but pleasing behind the old walls where bees hummed over the gray marbles and only an occasional genealogist came to read names and dates cut in stone. Poor fellow, I'm afraid the security lulled him."

He paused then so long that I asked, "What happened to him?"

"The scamp," he said, "he's gone now, no one knows where. Some ladies went to the cemetery one afternoon—it was garden week or clean-up week or something—and the keeper departed between dark and dawn. It took a wagon to carry off the empty bottles he had hidden in the vault of Montague Mason, 1786–1851, or thereabouts, the richest man who built the biggest and most ornamented vault to hold himself and, ultimately, the bottles. The cemetery keeper, it turned out, had plenty of money to buy his booze because he had sold all the boxwood in the cemetery to the wicked agents of the rich and the living to make so green and so sweet, antique and formal, the gardens along paths where feet move, wearing still not only shoes but flesh. Like yours, Mrs. Presley."

He laughed but she said, "It's bedtime," very solemnly. I told them good night and watched them turn back toward the inn. Then I walked on to the campus of William and Mary where boys in the old college were playing very modern music on a piano that was out of tune.

Certainly none of the doctor's fabled box was in Williamsburg, I am sure. But if it were there could be no better place for it. Mr. Rockefeller has not so much found the South as made it. He and his associates have performed such miracles of restoration that I half expected to find crazy Lucy Ludwell Paradise looking over my shoulder at Mrs. Rockefeller's collection of American folk art which is now displayed in the house from which they took poor, pretty, crazy Lucy to be confined. I should not have been surprised had the champagne bottle, with which President Tyler was hit on the head, been set up solemnly in the undoubtedly charming remaking of the gay old Apollo Room in Raleigh Tavern. Lucy and the bottle are but details missing. I missed, too, such details as John Vidal, the convicted pirate who pleaded that he "never intended to go a-pirating" and Peter Pelham, the admirable gaoler, who supplemented his salary watching the wicked by playing the organ at Bruton Church, providing music for the playhouse, teaching young ladies to play the harpsichord and spinet, and perhaps, as the anonymous author of the admirable *Handbook for the Exhibition Buildings* suggests, by permitting for a price convicted prisoners to escape. Much as I miss them, I can spare such details. I missed without resignation, however, such a detail as Henry Wetherburn's Arrack punch which was served under the sign, *Hilaritas Sapientiae et Bonae Vitae Proles,* in the Apollo Room where Jefferson danced so gaily with Belinda. It ought to be possible to restore that. Coca-Cola in the colonially reconstructed drug store was no substitute. I recognize difficulties; though Williamsburg has taught the visitor to expect much, it is entitled to forgiveness if it occasionally lets him down. Thus the Restoration has caught the South and fixed it in terms of the 18th century costumes which the Negro waiters wear in the Travis House but not even the Restoration has been able to get the 20th century dirt from beneath their fingernails. Some present serves the past. Certainly there never were any softer, sweeter voices in any past than those of the ladies, as 18th century as their pseudo-slaves, who lead the Yankee maidens and the tourists from Birmingham through the halls, which are in every microscopic detail like those halls through which men walked so long ago. Those gentlemen were founding a land then but even the most sanguine among them would have been surprised to know that it was to flower to such wealth as would be both willing and able to buy chairs like their chairs and build houses, even a capitol, like their capitol. For us all they legislated and judged and ruled and hanged and were hanged, sang and danced, loved and slept, and watched the fires—water seemed to have been scarcer than Madeira—too often burn up their houses and our history.

But the fires did comparatively little harm. If fire burned, Rockefeller restored. And it is all now perfect, perhaps even a little more than perfect. The historical sometimes looks a little like tomorrow morning. But the South in its moment is caught. Here is not only American history but the Southern legend captured and fixed by Mr. Rockefeller as a younger Rockefeller (if any are ever younger) or a young Smith or Jones might transfix a beetle on a pin. Somehow the pin is more convincing than the bug.

Escape from History

It is not always necessary to restore the Old South to see it. History is not altogether hidden by the fields of clover with heads like strawberries which grew the day I rode across the land, nor is it entirely erased by such processes as the tree chopping which leaves small town main streets hot and naked. The two-wheeled carts still roll in Tidewater Virginia between the old houses with the two-storied piazzas. The tourist cabins are in themselves unconscious restorations of the disappearing slave quarters. And that life does not entirely alter is emphasized by the tourist cabin proprietor who advertises in old-fashioned righteousness that he wants only tourists to sleep in his beds. Of course, the South is changing and the South can be seen in process of change. The cities are changed. But in the little towns remains the tideflow of borning and dying, building and decay. All processes are stayed and slowed or seem to be. And in such a little town the South may sit as if time, and not Mr. Rockefeller, had caught and held it in the sun: Warrenton and the Courthouse Square and Saturday afternoon.

Life goes on off the railroad, even off the main highway. The high road, a ribbon of white concrete built to move millionaires without jolting from Manhattan to Miami runs six miles west of Warrenton. The Seaboard's tracks run close beside this road. But around the Courthouse Square Warrenton lives without them. To some casual-seeing, quick-talking city riders it may seem that nobody ever goes to Warrenton any more except to be tried for murder or to sue a neighbor for a long overdue bill, or to call on such pleasant people as the Arringtons and the Polks. One crowded Saturday afternoon might teach them better. All around the square are the Dime Store, the Salvage Store, the Ford Sales and Service Company, and Intelligence Row where the lawyers have their offices. The movie is up the street and the rumor persists that soon a shirt factory may be opened on the other side of town. And yet somehow even on Saturday afternoon when the Courthouse Square and the streets about it are crowded with people and their talk and laughter Warrenton itself still seems as ended as the dark store behind the window wearing the legend: Miss Lizzie Yelverton—Millinery and Notions. The spider lives in this window now and beyond the spider's web the hat block and the old form adjustable to bust measure sits like an old, rusted and outmoded weapon in the economic war. How many Miss Lizzie Yelvertons have shut their doors in the South before the pressure

20

of machine stitching and the clamor of yellow front salvage stores. And what a brave race of virgins they were! Their poverty from one war to another was too often their only qualification as milliners and their virtue was too often the only reason they were patronized. Those matrons and maids who wore the hats they decorated and the dresses they adorned were brave, too. But they did not remain long faithful when better, cheaper hats and dresses were offered to them by the chains and the ready-to-wears. The Miss Lizzies were everywhere the first victims of change. Like old soldiers they disappeared and a better looking South emerged in escape from their ministrations. Farewell and pity, but escape, too. Beauty never had any business in their grim fingers. And yet, poor girls, to how many bridegrooms they submitted themselves in vicarious ecstasy! Did they not make the gowns and bind lace with old red fingers for young fingers to feel— for trembling fingers to undo?

But life on Saturday afternoon around the Courthouse Square sweeps past the abandoned virgins. Somebody has spread a multicolored array of second-hand clothes on the courthouse lawn. Perhaps it is a church sale. Colored girls are picking up the pieces of clothing from the grass and looking at them. And on the benches and the steps of the courthouse Negro men are sitting as still and dark as that young Confederate soldier who stands in bronze, forever defending a homeland from an enemy increasingly indistinguishable from his own sons—grandsons now. His Southern womanhood, too, belle and matron, sweet slips and sour maids, are in rayons and prints and ready-to-wears uniformed like their sisters in Schenectady. These are surfaces. Surfaces too are the movie posters and the radio blare which are seen and heard on Main Street. Before them all the South has retreated around the corner, it has slipped up a driveway or an alley, down a dusty infrequented road. It may be where William

Polk reported that poker game to be which has continued without interruption since "the War"—with hands descending from fathers to sons (Was the game interrupted when Lee visited Warrenton, or did the General take a hand?).

The South certainly may sit at ease behind the iron fences of Kate Arrington's garden. It may rest under a crepe myrtle. It may hide in a mob (though not in Warrenton), it may run breathless and screaming. It may rot in shiftlessness and die of ignorance. It may, God help it, in cold blood lynch a nigger with a blow torch, and it may cherish a dangerous Killer Negro as a man elsewhere might keep a blooded, dangerous dog. With history other things slip into hiding even in Warrenton. But the sun and the Negro remain. And as long as they remain no external mold will quite confine or force into conformity the queer, pleasant land of Courthouse Square and Saturday afternoon.

3

GOLD AVENUE

"WE CALLS it mikal," said the dirty old man, grinning and pleased to be asked an old question. "It's same as ison glass."

But the late sun makes it gold. For miles about King's Mountain, where the Carolinas meet and where there was some time some kind of a battle with the British, the sun strikes the earth and sets it to gleaming as if the whole land were afire. The mica is broken into too many infinitesimal pieces to make it worth the labor of mining, but that very shattering has cast it across whole fields like sparkling powder spread above the formal decorations on a Christmas tree. Certainly it is a nice coincidence that this gold-shining land is the middle of that Gold Avenue which runs, bounding riches roughly, from Danville in Virginia to Atlanta in Georgia. Briefer and richer it extends from Greensboro in North Carolina to Greenville in South Carolina, one almost uninterrupted succession of mills and mill villages and mill people, great and small, along the Southern Railroad and along the towered procession of James B. Duke's power lines which he delivered before he died to the new, shrewd mortmain of benefaction.

Here I saw full grown what the rest of the South, with the exception of a few poets and philosophers, old ladies and old gentlemen, wished to be. When I rode, it had been more than half a century since the elder Cannon of the towel family came into Concord in the back of a wagon with his bare feet trailing in the dust. It was not until the nineties that Caesar

Cone began planting trees in the villages around the denim mills which Duke had helped him and his brothers build. But Gold Avenue had so grown that it had begun to eye distrustfully the deeper South, grabbing hungrily for a share of its development, while it still looked back fearfully at the senility of New England mill villages as at a fate not far from its own. Between the two it was touchy and afraid. And there were two other fears more immediately terrifying: Jap and union.

In such an uncertain world, Jews in Greensboro seemed to put their hope in the more fundamentalistic brands of Christian denominationalism: Holiness folk and Y.M.C.A. youth, they hoped, might reject both liquor stores and unionism. Charlotte, which had grown metropolitan quickly as the capital of the spinning kingdom without ever outgrowing its ancient Presbyterianism, clung to faith in the predestination of what its manufacturers and bankers wished to be. But Greenville showed signs of a transfer of faith to the New Sociology and had employed my classmate at Chapel Hill, Dr. Marcus Cicero Stevens Noble, Jr., one of the most persuasive abbés of the new cult, to coordinate under dependable Ben Geer its social activities and so create, with the aid of the General Education Board, contributions from manufacturers, and the soundness of Furman University, a new industrial Athens in an undisturbed industrial South. But in all three towns as in Gastonia, Gaffney, Spartanburg, Kannapolis, Concord and the other almost private towns along Gold Avenue, industrialists felt much as planters felt just before the crazy incident at Harper's Ferry in 1859. Certainly they considered John Lewis no less menacing than John Brown had been. In the area, in which had arisen a decade and more before North Carolina's tobacco-chewing Cam Morrison with his Program of Progress, men now began to consider again

24

that everything that grows holds in perfection but a little moment, and Carolina manufacturers in the midst of prosperity were secretly fearful that that moment was ticking rapidly past.

But my friend, the dirty old man looking at the shining earth around King's Mountain, was not disturbed. He grinned at the gleam. "It ain't gold at all, but lots of folks think it is. But it ain't. I wish it was." He paused and then added in devout monotone, "God A'mighty I wish it was."

"You sound like you need it."

"Naw." He spat. "I don't need it. But if it was gold I wouldn't have to worry or work at all. I'd have a car and gasoline in it and I'd ride and ride. Everywhere. Why, Lord have mercy, I'd even go down where my sister lives in Lindale, Georgia. She sho' would be surprised if she seen me ride up."

I laughed, but what the old man said was important. Nobody will ever understand either Gold Avenue or the South who does not recognize the itching will to go riding and speeding. Perhaps it rises from that restlessness that was left behind when the pioneers went on. Now the automobile has armed it. I realized that as I rode, feeling a little the restlessness myself. I had set out from Raleigh on my own riding with the omen, good or ill, of seeing a peg-legged Negro mowing a lawn. I had discovered the loss of the key to the spare tire at Chapel Hill, and in Burlington, where I stopped to pull an unwilling mechanic from toying with an outboard motor long enough to cut me a duplicate key, I found myself in the mill country which takes its colors from red brick and blue windows, panes painted blue to keep out the shadow-making sun and protect the quality of the superior synthetic light within. I passed one mill that had beds of iris before it as blue as the windows behind which men and girls work in clatter and lint all day long and sometimes through the night. Then the lighted blue windows make one of the too few additions to beauty in the South which industry can claim.

I had felt that night-loveliness first, years before, when I rode through this same country at a time when brightened blue windows of mills at night generally meant not only operations but lines of soldiers, and sometimes the blustering noisiness of Flying Squadron. Those cars and lines of cars were something new and strange, wicked and terrifying. Or at least so manufacturers thought. But I remember particularly the young women taunting the soldiers and the high laughter. Like war, the people loved it. The prettiest girls and the handsomest boys like it best. Beauty is no advantage in the operation of a loom; but it has its effect on soldiers as on strikers. A girl knows that. And those girls, so long the mechanical adjuncts of spindle and loom, enjoyed the opportunity which strike gave them of holding excitement in their hands, of riding at night with their hair flying, of shouting at soldiers, of picnicking around night fires, and sometimes of slipping off from the fires into the darkness with men equally stirred in industrial war. It was good to be young then, good to go in tumultuous crowd and shout at the fence of the Old Man's House, good to climb into Fords and rush across counties to join other familiar-unfamiliar young people in clamoring at the mesh wire of mill gates. It was excellent even to be very sad at the great funeral for the man who was split open by the bayonet of a frightened boy in National Guard uniform. Oh, certainly it was dangerous business! But Governors and mill managers sometimes played at the equally dangerous and exciting business of exerting simple force. Even Governors stir to being Field Marshals instead of clerks. And in the Carolinas, at least, there were then plenty of mill owners whose sluggish blood began to pulse again in the faith that they were having a part in saving America from Red Revolution.

Much quieter the road was when I rode it this last time. But the cars have multiplied in the mill villages. I saw them everywhere. Row on row, immaculate and gleaming, rusty and broken, they sat before the best brick houses in Proximity close to Greensboro and the oldest dwellings in Conestee south of Greenville. Before houses that need to be painted, men rubbed new cars with chamois to bring out the last gleam or tried to fix clattering old engines with pieces of wire. Along Gold Avenue a man apparently must be mobile or he is nothing. The children can go hungry and dirty. The doctor may not be paid. The grocer may be complaining, but somehow—certainly on Sunday—the family will move on Gold Avenue.

Among the blue windows and the automobiles I wished I could think the significance of the Cone trees equalled my appreciation of them. They are lovely and they represent an intent to grow and flourish on a certain happy land—for me and my children and theirs. Old Caesar Cone, who lies buried beside the mill village at Proximity, close to Greensboro, which he and his brother, Moses, made, planted them long ago. Few North Carolinians would have bothered planting them. But Caesar Cone was not many generations out of a German ghetto where there were more Jews than trees, and trees were therefore precious, particularly as they might grow out of land that was his own. But much as the trees now add in dignity and decency to the Cone villages, in the houses under them live a people who cut down the forests to such an extent that tobacco growers must import from other counties the wood with which they cure their crops, to such an extent that the Piedmont fields are falling open in red gullies. Movement in freedom means more to them than tree or shelter—even, I sometimes think, than safety or security. From this country long ago the restless went on over the hills to fill Tennessee and Texas—it was easier to kill a bear than to grow corn—but the blood of restlessness was left behind. To that blood now garages mean more than trees.

And looms certainly are more important than trees. Even sometimes—not in Proximity—they may seem more important than people. The Cones themselves think less often of the trees than of the great hall, approximately the same length as the hull of the *Queen Mary,* in which closely spaced ranks of looms turn out steadily and with a minimum of human intervention and a minimum of need for human watching the thousands of yards of heavy blue denims out of which the Cone millions have been made. The very air is blue with the blue lint, and tinged with blue is the golden hair of the Carolina girls who watch the looms. Some wear caps to cover their permanents. And all the young ones of them seem somehow captured by the machines; but this is poetry and these girls are no more poems than the rest of us. And, like the rest of us, some were sitting chatting in comfortable idleness when Ben Cone and I came in, but most busy girls they were when we went by. It struck me that some of them, now so solemn at their tasks, looked like some of those girls I had seen, so loudly joyous speeding in Flying Squadron, when I rode on Gold Avenue before.

There is no time among the looms now to wait for trees. The pace is faster all along Gold Avenue. As the Flying Squadron was new technique, so the mill has the new machine. The mill must be more and more mechanized—or die. The big mills grow not for greater and greater markets (the Japs have intervened there) but to take the markets of out-of-date mills which, dropping behind the new pace, can only operate in the best times. In bad times their villages become idle, stagnant pools of human breeding and hunger, irritability and death. The whole process is puzzling: the newer the machine the fewer the workers needed in its operation, but without the newer machine the jobs of all the workers in the plant may disappear. Men and women angrily shout, "Stretch-out!" and stretch-out exists. Avarice hides behind the pretense of efficiency and exploitation often talks big of progress. But the worst stretch-out is that which workers, paid on a piece basis, put upon themselves. No foreman could drive them so fast. No system could spread their work so far. But in thirst for things they can drive themselves like mechanisms of flesh and blood at full speed all day long. Gold Avenue is not where money is picked out of the road. It is seized or squeezed out bitterly. And the young now joining unions and riding to form unions are as determined to have the good things of life and as careless of the means used in attaining them as were those who first got the gold of this golden road.

No wonder manufacturers cry, "Agitator," as they would cry, "Snake," at every union organizer. Most of the manufacturers came originally from the same red hills as those from which their workers come. They know a secret which they have steadily and loudly denied: they know there is no dependable docility in their cousins at the looms. These cousins are the grandchildren of those who opined that it was a rich man's war but a poor man's fight and who fought like lank and indestructible devils just the same. Dig McClellan up and ask *him* if they were docile. Once hookworm may have wearied them; sometimes hunger and children and a worn, washed soil made them glad to have even the least wages in the villages. But the looms are not the only machines they can see. Their secret concern is with wheel, not shuttle. They mean to move.

The high road of the industrial South goes on from the Cone trees, past women with fingers flying at spools of yarn, past High Point, where the Flying Squadron began, through towns straddling the railroad, Lexington, Salisbury, Thomasville, where "the Lambeths wear the brass buttons," as the filling station operator said, to Kannapolis where the Cannons have a private town in which they make a good part of the towels that wipe the face of the world. As members of it, Cannons understood the Carolina race better than the Cones and spent no time planting trees for a people who too often have considered them only as things to be cut down. The Cannons did their planting in one pretty little park about the mill offices and left the village itself an ugly community of dirty clapboard and asphalt shingle. One house there, I remember, sat so close beside and below the unpaved lane that its whole side—even its windows—was painted with splashed yellow mud. But around the Cannon mills, row on unbroken row, sat the new Fords and Plymouths and Chevrolets and a respectable portion of more expensive cars. By no material standard could Kannapolis be called a pitiful town; but by any aesthetic standards it is a hideous one. And the ugliness is as much product of workers careless about their living as of careless mill. The Cannons know what beauty is: see their own cool and spacious Union Street five miles away in Concord. There big Negro gardeners gossip softly while they clip the shrubbery on one of the greenest and sweetest streets in the South. But almost any Cannon employee apparently would prefer a gallon of gasoline to a gardenia. By his needs he may be right.

Trucks roll over this Gold Avenue carrying denims and yarns, prints and calicoes and cotton bales down what the road officials call U. S. Route 29. No line of communication was ever clearer. All along it from Danville to Atlanta many little men with every kind of car may be slaves to the finance companies but they know, and the mills know, that they are equipped for flight or Flying Squadron. In industrial warfare John L. Lewis or F. J. Gorman or any other labor leader in power could move men in automobiles in menacing show of strength from mill to mill. A mill owner may be forgiven if he is disturbed by the vision of hundreds of strange men and women clamoring at his gates. Miles would be nothing and not all the highway patrolmen in the Carolinas could stop all those cars if their owners once wished to move. Hence perhaps the fences. And perhaps the fences nevertheless are a mistake.

Of course, there have always been fences. But longer and longer, higher and higher, they grow everywhere along the road upon which so many more little men—and women— have cars than had them five years ago. The fences are everywhere the same: On steel uprights set in concrete is a mesh wire fence that would resist the weight and strength of elephants. Across its top, on prongs tilted outward, is strung a strand or several strands of barbed-wire that would tear the flesh of a man or a mob. Such cyclone fences may be necessary. But it would be hard to devise a better advertisement of mill fear in this land where for so long it has been sworn that labor is "cheap and contented." Sometimes, indeed, the fences seem to extend to hysteria. One huge mill—several blocks long and four or five stories high—has not stopped with running the impregnable steel fortifications about itself. Across the street, between the textile mill and the company club, it has provided a small but well-equipped playground for the children of its workers. In it are slides and swings and a wading pool. And around the little park the cyclone fences run, high and tight enough to turn a playground into a fort or a prison. High enough, perhaps, too, to teach the children that property is afraid of people—their people.

In Greenville as on all Gold Avenue, some mills are almost incredibly big in a South of little buildings. I remember one in particular and how it loomed in the darkness. I had suddenly wanted to go into a mill operating at night. It was already late then. I had gone with two newspapermen to a Greek's place for a bite to eat. They thought it might be arranged at that hour, late as it was. But riding all around Greenville we could find but one mill in operation and that apparently in only one department. Between us and the mill the big fences rose and their gates were locked as against an army. Flood lights illumined every entrance. But while we wandered about looking for a way in, a man came, walking softly in the darkness, out of the mill. He did not see us where we moved in the shadow until he let himself out of the gate and then locked it behind him. He saw us and was afraid. The gate swayed behind him as he backed against it. Smith asked him if we could get in.

"No," he said, as if he were pleading with us. "No."

There was no superintendent, he said, or assistant superintendent on hand who could let us in. He could not. No one could. It was not permitted. He slipped away quickly, glad to be gone, almost scurrying into the darkness across the street.

"He probably slipped out," said Cantwell. "Maybe he thought he was caught. He's probably going home to a hot meal or a new wife or something."

We looked a little longer. The lights continued to burn over the moving machinery in the mill but no one else came out. At last we went back to my room in the Poinsett Hotel. There we sat a long time talking, about all things and particularly about South Carolina. Smith said the people had hated the newspapers since the papers fought Tillman. Cantwell spoke of the change in Charleston when his Irish ancestors came to outnumber the aristocrats. But, while I wanted to hear about South Carolina, about politician and aristocrat and Irishman, my mind kept going back while we talked to the more and more automobiles and the longer and higher fences—higher than horse-high, stronger than bull-strong—and the timid man who came out of the mill. He had seemed so lost, but where there were so many cars, old ones and new ones, not everybody could be lost in the mill villages. They were ready to move anywhere anytime.

"And that readiness," I told myself—I think I told them, too—"that readiness indicates a faith that there is still somewhere to go. And maybe a determination to go there."

In the darkness Gold Avenue lay paved for their moving and I wondered how the mica would shine in the darkness of their moving under the moon.

4

OVER THE MOUNTAINS

1. The Margin

OBVIOUSLY not everything is golden even on the golden road from Danville to Atlanta, and they told me in Greenville that if I were really perverse enough to wish to see the mill village in its less idyllic aspect I ought to go to Cotswold (which is not the name of the town). I had seen the other end from Eden in mill villages before. Indeed, I had seen cotton mill villages cease to be even cotton mill villages and become mere huddles of habitation around a shut mill that provided no employment nor sustenance. After such, Cotswold was a disappointment. But I am glad that I began there, far away from beauty, the trip over the mountains in May.

South of Greenville in the direction of Honea Path, where mill workers and mill guards punctuated strike in '34 with gun shot wounds, Cotswold is one of several similar places, an old brown village about an old mill sitting in ancient fashion beside a stream. Around each of the houses there is plenty of room for home gardens about which so many planners have talked so much but I did not see even a collard patch. Remote from any town, the only place close at hand where the workers can buy is the company commissary. The cars parked before the houses were less shiny and seemed less reliable than those I had seen at Kannapolis. They made me think of people seen working, hot and sweating, in best clothes on roadsides on Sunday afternoons. But I saw no evidence of hunger

34

in Cotswold. Indeed, I gathered that the old mill was fairly shaking then with work and wages.

At a store a few miles away from the old houses, the old church and the old mill, I stopped to get a Coca-Cola. And a man who sat beside me in one of the chairs before the roadside store and who looked as if he had been sitting there for years said that the mill was running 24 hours a day.

"They would run on Sundays if they could," he declared, "and one while they did start at 12 o'clock Sunday night."

Only by moving every minute could the old mill with its old machinery hope to meet the competition of the modern mills in Greenville. And only in the best times could this old mill manned by the least skilled workers in the Greenville country hope to operate at all. Here was the margin. In the cool May morning nobody on the porches in Cotswold, none of those loafing about the commissary or busy in the mills seemed aware how short the distance was from eating and owning, in a manner of speaking, a Ford, to not eating and burning up the porch railings for fuel. The almost desperate clatter of the old machinery seemed to indicate that it was aware that it must hurry, hurry before the time when it could run no more, when the windows would be broken in the mill and the spiders would repair the broken panes with webs.

The whole place made me think of old people running for their food. But not all Cotswold is old. Not by any means. In the company commissary a pretty blonde girl, almost incredibly pregnant, went heavily past me. My hat was already off but figuratively it came off again in my heart. I recognized her as omen. I never saw a dying cotton mill village that was not heavy with child.

2. *View from the Mountain*

Read the roadside sign south of Caesar's Head: Welcome

to Happy River Baptist Church. Listen to the cackle of the hen and the sound of the cowbell. All along the turning, rising road the dogwood, the mountain magnolia, the azalea and the tiny nameless wild flowers bloomed in profusion on the May highway. The road rose almost precipitately from Greenville. From making textiles the country turns abruptly to taking tourists for a living. And at Caesar's Head, fenced off, is the eminence from which tourist or traveler might look back upon the green South Carolina lands below: Adults 25¢ —Children 10¢. It was neither the first nor the last such sign I saw. And I wondered who, in any sensible system of property, owns the loveliness that here and in too many other places is purveyed as view for sale. Does view belong to the owner of the point of vantage or the owners of the properties seen? Is view mountain top or hill and dale and winding river, plowed field and precipitate meadow where cows with legs shorter on one side than on the other graze to the wonder of the lowland traveler? It was solemnly and long ago held that I may pay with the ring of my money for the smell of your roasting goose. We hurry in this auto age to the time when something similar should be decided about views, before fence builders with the side show keeper's attitude toward outdoor aesthetics shuts off the sight of wonders which do not belong to him and collects from the traveler for the looking at other men's property.

But I would prefer a fence between the road and one view I passed: a mill village for lumber, a community of houses made of rough boards with tar paper roofs, a sooty peninsula, soiled by human living, in a sparkling stream.

3. *Private Paradise*

Not far from Highlands in Cashiers Valley I rode beside the long picket fence and came to the gate of Sapphire Lodge. I looked righteously for a No Trespassing sign and, not finding one where I knew it should be, I drove boldly and happily in. One day I may write a work on the Pleasures of Trespassing. Visually the invasion of Sapphire Lodge will not be the least of them. I never saw lovelier and wiser planting. Millionaires, from the Roman procurators down, have indulged in pretentiousness with trees and shrubs and hedges and shears and stones and fountains. But Sapphire Lodge has been planted with that addition of sweet shrewdness to nature which makes nature look more naturally lovely than ever. The same sort of distinction is often observable in women. But I stick to the land. By lake and water lilies, laurel and rhododendron, the road runs through a wood and over a hill. There, set down in a green glade in a fairy tale forest, is a house and pavilions.

The house looked as if it might have been designed for little German princesses long ago. And from it the lawn ran (smooth enough for their long skirts) to a lake. I don't remember whether there were swans on it. There should have been, but at the moment for swans I was facing the caretaker. Mountain man, he looked like such a Prussian as might be retained to guard princesses or their pavilions. And he did not look as if he cared for me. The road widens in white concrete before the garage. I rode straight up to him there and spoke first. Speaking first to caretakers is a primary rule which all well-trained trespassers follow. Some of the best I know, indeed, always ring the door bell or halloo between their hands and call the fellow up. In this case I spoke with no particular skill.

"Is this a private house or a hotel?"

He looked at me long enough to let me know that my guile was not deceiving him. "A private house," he said.

"Whose is it?"

"Mistress Lupton."

"And very nice," I told him as I turned around, in such a

37

tone as I hoped suggested that such private paradises were familiar enough to me.

It was not until later that I discovered in discovery of the South that this was the first of the Coca-Cola palaces. It was by no means the last one.

4. American Plan

I don't place Mr. West's nativity. He is one of those Americans, I think, who move from Florida to the mountains, from Miami to Massachusetts, or round about, with the weather and the seasons. He is—or seems to be—a migratory bird who does the talking in the front while his wife does the cooking in the rear. Usually he wears long, tasselled knickerbockers or some such country club garment. His voice is high-pitched and his once yellow hair is parted neatly in the middle, but there is a rugged masculinity about the gray stubble on his chin.

"Oh, no, tourists are not all there is up here. The season is too short. Why, last night I slept under four blankets and two comforters and was cold in the bed. Summer folks are not coming while it's that cold. So up here they grow cabbages. Cabbages around here get ripe at a time when there's not any other cabbages to be had. I saw a man give $350 for a truckload full last year and then he went out and helped cut 'em himself."

A girl beside me at the counter came eagerly into the conversation. She wore spectacles and her teeth were so close together and so shaped that they gave her the appearance as she talked of having a bill like a bird's.

"The cabbages around here have a special flavor."

"And cabbages can be kept as sauerkraut, if you want to," Mr. West added.

38

"My sister who lives over by Blowing Rock grows cabbages," the girl went on. The thought of those cabbages seemed to excite her. "When we were children we all helped to grow cotton. My father never would grow anything but cotton." She added apologetically, "That was bad."

"Yes," agreed Mr. West. "It was a mistake."

"Undoubtedly," said I.

We shook our heads together in a community of wisdom. But I went on eating heartily. For 40 cents Mr. West served eggplant, spinach, potatoes, rib stew, custard pie and coffee. I took two cups of the last.

"Good coffee," Mr. West observed as he brought me my second cup, "is important. People often compliment us on our coffee."

As I stirred it I asked him about the Lupton place. I could feel that I had touched a rich and familiar subject of conversation.

"She's a widow and her husband had the Coca-Cola franchise for Tennessee. You ought to see her son Cartter's place. It's the best. She lives in Chattanooga."

"It's beautiful," the girl said. "The caretaker showed me the house. The furniture in the dining room cost $10,000. That in the living room cost $20,000. It's pretty. It's beautiful!"

Mr. West was not to be outdone: "Last winter Mrs. Lupton was in an automobile accident down in Georgia. It shook her up so that it knocked a $7,500 diamond out of a ring. The insurance company strained all the sand around the accident. Every bit of it. But they didn't find the diamond. Then one day a high school boy was walking down the road and he looked right at it, shining at him, and he picked it up. I heard Mrs. Lupton gave him a thousand dollar reward."

"Yes," the girl said, "that's what the caretaker told me."

I might have heard more if Mr. West's custard pie had been as good as his coffee. And I had a long twisting way to go. One piece was enough.

5. *Madame of the Mountains*

In Franklin, North Carolina, remote and pleasant mountain county seat about an amazingly dirty courthouse, I came upon a lady reading proofs in a country newspaper office. No ordinary lady. Here off the hot square before the courthouse was the Grand Manner in the Hills. There was not a false tone or note in it. Mrs. Johnston in happy and energetic exile built for me within the world of little mountaineers a picture of an almost credible island of gentle exiles brought together by ill-luck or ill-health who made that group of the merry and the wise which we all seek and never find anywhere on the earth except in the reports of enthusiasts about people like the excellent, spirited Mrs. Johnston.

Widow of an Episcopal minister, Mrs. Johnston who helps her son with *The Franklin Press* and welcomes the summer visitor at the Tremont Inn is a creative artist making drama out of all of her life, characters out of all of her people, however dull the life may be and prosaic the people in it. Another woman in the same position might make a drudgery of other people's personal items in the paper and their personal requirements at the inn. Mrs. Johnston makes of them materials for the marvelous and the amazing. People who enter her inn or her editorial sanctum are forthwith furnished with fascination. The callow college graduates, calling themselves, as the college called them, engineers, somehow seem under Mrs. Johnston's reporting booted builders of the earth, first generation after the soldiers of fortune, figures all for romance. Men on relief teaching mountaineers—or begging mountaineers—not to get their water supply from under the pig pen or the privy seem as Mrs. Johnston draws them, men against the microbes in the new thrilling battling of science. And she can make villains, too. How dark and sinister, cheap and unpleasant seem those men who have made a sweatshop industry out of the making of the candlewick bedspreads which hang multicolored from North Carolina half way across Georgia.

Mrs. Johnston talks. There is no question about that. But so did Madame De Staël. Indeed, the probability is that every woman who has long held the interest of people has had something to say to people. And a personality with which to give words distinction. The season had not begun when I was there. The inn was empty save for some permanents, like the college boys, and myself. But I remember holding Mrs. Johnston's chair for her as we sat down to dinner. And I had a sense of dining in state. The food was excellent. But the conversation was better, and good conversation is rarer than good food even in the South.

The Tremont Inn is not new. Nothing in Franklin seems very new. The room I had was ceiled with boards and across them on little porcelain bridges the electric wires ran. In May it was as cold as Iceland and I rejoiced for every blanket on my bed. When I dressed in the morning the lilac bush blooming just outside my window did not warm the room.

I left Franklin and Mrs. Johnston with something of the sense that I had spent the night not in an inn but a castle.

As for the bill—

Would I send her *The News and Observer* for the summer? Her guests who came up to the mountains would want to read it.

I bowed from the hips and my hips are getting a little big for bowing. But neither in Natchez nor Charleston, Savannah nor New Orleans did I find again a lady, old or young, who in every pleasant particular played against a better set any better the part that has been written for the Lady of the South.

6. Mountain White

When the Connecticut Yankee put two horse pistols, one extra celluloid collar, a bottle of Jamaica rum, and a certificate of good standing in the Republican party in his carpetbag and set out south in the summer of 1865, he was not alone. There were the other carpetbaggers, those gentle ladies of gentle families, Christian almost to the ascension point, whose carpetbags each contained a Bible, a bottle of arnica, *McGuffey's First Reader,* and a letter from their pastor. As the gentlemen went south to strip the dead body of the South of whatever valuables might still adhere to the corpse, the ladies bent on resuscitation hoped to blow a sweeter breath into Southern lungs, set to beating a purer Southern heart and so revive a South reformed and grateful for reformation. Of the two, the ladies were the more difficult to bear. They still are and it makes no difference whether they are male or female, Congregationalists or Communists, representatives of the Freedman's Bureau or the International Labor Defense. They have done much real good in the South from Appomattox to Scottsboro. They have educated the ignorant, fed the hungry, cared for the sick, buried the dead and secured justice for the oppressed. They deserve great credit, but they will get little affection. As a people we would rather be robbed than improved.

But nobody was ever able to rout any of them so completely as once Miss Elizabeth Kelly did. Miss Elizabeth lies in the cemetery at Franklin. I remember her, a few years before she died in her fifties when her mind was strong and keen, and her sense of humor turned people laughing to do what she wanted them to do. She went on afterwards stricken, a great elephantine power dying of cancer. It is more pleasant

42

now to think of her in times long before those days. She was born near Franklin and grew up, knowing every creek and cove in Macon County, to be six feet three of bone with flesh and strength and sinew in proportion. She went up the mountain roads and back into the roadless coves teaching— or trying to teach—children to read and write. But she discovered that it was foolishness to try to teach the children of Macon so long as their parents could not read and put no value on the reading of the young. So because she loved the people of Macon County she became the scold and driver of Macon County. She made the old folks learn to read with the children and in the process so won the respect of the people that before the women had the vote she was the boss of the county. Naturally enough her adult education work won attention and the State asked her to do for the adults of North Carolina what she had done for those of Macon County. And it was in the work for the State that she came to that meeting where the skinny little over-educated Yankee woman with the shrill voice with sharp edges in it made her speech about the poor, scrawny, runty, undernourished, pitiful mountain whites. Miss Elizabeth heard her through. Then slowly she rose, unfolding in huge dignity, until she stood vast and erect. Then she said very gently, "I just wanted to get up and show myself as one of those mountain whites."

7. *Items*

I saw a huge Negro plowing a team of oxen in the valley of the Oconalufty River on the borders of Swain and Jackson Counties in North Carolina.

There are mountaineers who talk an archaic language, but it does not run quite as uttered to blank verse. I gave a ride to a little man with very fair skin and a very black young beard. At first he declined the ride I offered despite the

43

heavy sack he was carrying. Then he took it and rode two miles. "I shore do thank ye," he said. I still half wonder if he wasn't a novelist in hiding.

The Indian postmistress at Cherokee, N. C., in the reservation for that tribe, said "All righty" when I asked for a postcard, and one of the three Indian men who were playing the one-armed-bandit type of slot machine in the Ocona Cafe said, "Oh, hell, it's a gyp." But he put another nickel in the slot.

I saw dogwood growing from a field of red clover.

And I saw at the turn off into the park such piles of new sawdust and new lumber as to make it clear how badly needed is a park set aside so that some of the trees can be used for the future and not all for planks and pulp.

8. Beauty for Sale

Ride up the mountain past the Indian reservation through New Found Gap (or perhaps in addition the road to the top of Clingman's Dome and back) and down the steep grade of the Smokies, and a rider can understand how two states might fight over access to loveliness there. I remember the fight. I rode to Washington on one of the special trains and there were several of them full of angry men, and liquor and oratory. Everybody wanted to make a speech. One time the men of Carolina and Tennessee settled their differences with squirrel guns. Now they use Congressmen. The question for anger was whether there should be two official entrances to the new Great Smoky Mountains National Park or only one. Park officials had said one, and they had chosen Gatlinburg. We North Carolinians, insistent that the loveliest parts of the park and approaches to the park were in our State, demanded at least one entrance, too, for North Carolina. The Secretary of the Interior listened and ordered that we be given an entrance, too. But I never realized how just our cause was until I rode down from the Smokies into Gatlinburg.

The mountains were behind. A flat country and a series of tourist camps along an unremarkable stream was Gatlinburg. But business is moving on. There is a hotel now. And I bought a very decent ham sandwich at a café there. Beauty is business and business is beauty. I suspect that beauty is the oldest profession in the world. Maybe one day, if properly advertised, even Gatlinburg will be world renowned for its beauty. But there are now forty towns in East Tennessee that surpass it. Indeed, it was not necessary for me to go any further than Sevierville on the road to Knoxville and the TVA. There I saw a sluggish stream full of white geese. And the sudden view of them was as lovely as any mountainside the CCC boys have carefully tended in the park.

5

KNOXVILLE IN THE VALLEY

No LESS strange than all the rest was the wide road. Concrete is simple to look at, easy to ride upon, but in this Tennessee Valley country the pyramidal pile, flung across the Clinch River to make Norris Dam, seemed little newer than the three lane highways which have succeeded the paths cut through the forest. There is significance in the succession: If anywhere in America there has been an uninterrupted continuity, it is in the South. Only now is the machine intervening to supplement the labor of white and black hands. No tide of immigration has changed racial patterns since the first white and black striping. In no real sense did the Civil War alter the South. Indeed, in the South generally, America, under a thin surface of modernity, goes on as it began. And sometimes I think that the interest in the South and in books about the South has been due to a sense of a simpler succession in the American's story there. Machine-made problems are too puzzling and in the South (as I found among the Agrarians) as out of it men and women have rejoiced in mental retreat to an Old South which now seems a great deal simpler than it could possibly have been. There is similar retreat to a living South in which even the so-many faults seem the simpler ones of a more direct if also more violent day. A man may be shot in a Shotgun Civilization but his friends and relatives need not be puzzled as to what hit him, as he and friends and relatives may very well be in a Corporate One.

46

So I rode along thinking on the wide road to Knoxville and the TVA. Here in Tennessee was supposed to be, fixed and armed, a governmental opposition to private exploitation of public resource in flowing river in the South. But I wondered if the truth were not that the engineers (thirty different kinds of them) employed by TVA were not in addition rather than opposition to the earlier-other engineers in the transformation of the South. And what a transformation might not be wrought if the army of 15,000 men officered with every technical knowledge from that of malariologists, to those knowledges of geographers, of chemists, of agronomists, of archaeologists, of soil technicians, of ceramists, and of photogrammetrists, should move not merely against one river valley but against the whole strange South! Perhaps that is exactly what it is doing.

Like any well-equipped traveler I had come over the mountains with a nice set of preconceived ideas in my head: Some of them turned out to be true. These East Tennessee people had been pioneers (the next step in restlessness beyond Gold Avenue) and Tennessee had been the Free Forest, but it had filled up to the point where a man on windy days could almost hear his neighbor's dog bark, and that was crowded. The restless went on West again, but some remained. Maybe they were the sensible or the timid, maybe the lazy. They let the frontier go on beyond them, but the frontier which they ceased to seek came in our own times straight to their doors, transformed now from geography to hydro-electricity, to an earth planned instead of an earth sought.

These people in the Tennessee hills had trusted themselves and hated government. The feuds and the revenuers have been badly worn in fiction, but in life it was interesting to discover that in the land where the representative of government was a foe to be watched and perhaps shot, government had become something else altogether, the light bringer and the food bringer, or, less poetically, the hirer and the buyer. Social planning has succeeded an individualism which once made every mountaineer an underfed king on his side of the creek.

Before TVA's two Morgans and one Lilienthal came to the valley representing the USA, the last earlier and significant representative of the USA, General William Tecumseh Sherman, had passed the valley on a destroyer's errand. The movement in occupation in 1933 was perhaps no less invasion (listen to the power companies) but a strange new blessed one for a South which is nearly always late in being lucky. Strange, though: This invasion in the reverse of Sherman's purpose seeks to serve especially a section which was Union in its sentiments during "the War," and a Democratic Administration at Washington has set up its headquarters for new Southern invasion in one of the very few Republican Congressional districts in the South. And it remained Republican despite TVA.

But as Sherman was not the discoverer of Atlanta, so the exploiters found the Tennessee Valley's potentialities long before the planners. And the old exploiters continued in angry resistance to the social experiment for public good and not private profit. Even the once exploited have sometimes regarded the planner with suspicion. This was not entirely surprising: In the early days some of the secondary officials of the Authority played God in public and announced out loud the miracles by which they proposed the transformation of valley and valley people. The transformers are chastened, I think: that they are completely forgiven I am not sure.

Indeed, as I came first to TVA I was not entirely sure that they should be forgiven. I came, carefully conscious of my prejudice in TVA's favor as a result of the lower and lower power rates in the Southeast which had clearly resulted from its policies. But first view of TVA and first talking about TVA to people on the scene left me a good deal less enthusiastic than I had been as I rode across the Tennessee River into the crowded town, past a series of parking lots, a thriving city market for flowers and potted plants, down stirring Gay Street to the Farragut Hotel. Perhaps the trouble was that in the midday change from Eastern Standard to Central time I got my lunch too late or too soon. But I still wonder if there was not involved some lingering aspect of that feature of TVA about which Marshall McNeill, the tall, good-looking Scripps-Howard editor, spoke:

"You remember that TVA was created in the Hundred Days back in 1933 when Congress seemed to amount to nothing. And for a while if a man came out here with a letter from a professor he was clasped to the bosom, but if he came with a letter from a Congressman he was about as welcome as a kick in the pants."

Fortunately, I did not have a letter from my Congressman. But neither did I have one from a professor. Looking back I can recall nothing but helpful courtesy in the Knoxville offices of the TVA except a certain attitude, probably entirely imaginary, of weariness and superiority before an inquisitive visitor. If such an attitude existed and it probably did not (Maurice Henle, information assistant, made every arrangement for me that I could ask), it would be easy to understand. Beyond the hordes of tourists, I gather that there are two primary types of visitors at TVA. One: Those who come sighting down their superior noses for the sins of the Democrats and the insanities of the intellectuals. And, two: Those who oo and ah at the new heaven in the old earth. One, I should imagine, would be about as hard to bear as the other. I considered myself one who expected to find in Eden both fruit and snakes, but I have often wondered in which camp T. Levron Howard (It should be Dr. Howard, I think) catalogued me. I regretted that no sympathy or understanding stirred between us. And the fault was probably mine.

Dr. Howard, fattening, bald and in the vicinity of forty, is chief of TVA's research section. Armed with a letter of introduction, I waited in great expectation for him and while I waited read *New Poems* by D. H. Lawrence, which I found beside the thesaurus on the desk of his pretty young secretary. She had picked the book up, she hastened to explain, on the cut rate table at a book store down the street. And, speaking of books, she had been vastly disturbed to hear someone whose opinion she respected say that he did not consider Rhett Butler a veracious character. What did I think? But before I had time to pronounce my views on Margaret Mitchell's good wicked man Dr. Howard's door opened and I went inside.

In the pleasant sunlit room he showed me a whole shelf of unpublished researches made by his division on almost every aspect of TVA's work and activities which come close to approximating all human work and activities in the region.

"And what is your particular field, doctor?"

He lifted a shoulder. He had no field. He had completed one field and then turned to another. He had been eight or nine years in the graduate school at Wisconsin.

He probably said much more. Probably there was wisdom that I should have remembered. But I recall only that we talked about the value of the valley folk as human beings. I believe he said that statistics or studies or something of the sort indicated that they were able to meet the competition of workers further north when they left the valley. But I was oppressed by nine years of graduate work and a whole shelf of unpublished researches. As I remember it now I went like the unlearned out of his door in escape.

And I could not have fled farther than the office of R. H. Claggett, then and for a little while after, editor of the conservative and Republican *Knoxville Journal,* one of the papers which were battered and bartered about after the toppling of the speculative Tennessee empire which Luke Lea and Rogers Caldwell, politicians and financiers, built too quickly and too high. Mr. Claggett, a dry patriot, had fought the TVA in Knoxville, and had lost. Through a series of connecting buildings, up a stair, around a corner and down a corridor, I found him at an old-fashioned roller top desk.

"Oh, yes," he said. "I was half expecting you."

An acquaintance of mine, Edward Aswell, New York publisher, who had preceded me in a hunt not for the South but for books in it, had told him that I was riding the roads and might be expected to drop over the mountains into Knoxville. I am almost as glad that I found Mr. Claggett as that I found TVA. He is the patriot who dwells everywhere in Status Quo as well as in the South. He was born, he told me about it, in Hickman county, Tennessee, on the edge of the Dimple of the Universe. As the Dimple, where now they mine phosphate rock for sale, is rich, the Highland Rim about it upon which Mr. Claggett was born is poor to poverty. The birds and rabbits carry their provisions when they pass, he said. But Dimple and Rim have a bearing on Mr. Claggett's theory about the difficulties of the South. It comes to this:

1. The South was settled by people who have never liked to farm. The people who came from England were city and seaport people looking for gain or adventure, a few for religious liberty, not farmers looking for land. (See the results in the comparison of native farmers on poor Southern lands and the Germans at Lawrenceville, Tennessee, who have turned the Rim into a garden.)

2. To get away from farming the best men always went on farther and farther West, but fortunately in the old days the

women stayed at home and a good stock persisted. Now the women are also leaving the farm and Mr. Claggett expects a progressively more and more deteriorated race.

Not even TVA, or especially not TVA, can prevent the deterioration. But the South isn't so bad off, he said. It is slandered by the books about the South and the reason for the popularity of books about the South is the dirt in them. Not enough Southerners protest against the emphasis falsely put upon lechery and filth in the Southern scene. But Mr. Claggett does.

Once a Philadelphian came to Knoxville. He went to walk. From the bridge over the Tennessee River he looked down on the shacks built along the shore. He marched back to his hotel and wrote a letter to the editor. In it he said that in a long life of much travel he had never seen such horrible housing for human beings as he had seen from the bridge. Editor Claggett published the letter in *The Journal* but he put a little patriotic pot-and-kettle note at the bottom suggesting that the gentleman from the North must have failed to look out of the train windows as he rode through the cities of the North, including even the City of Brotherly Love. Mr. Claggett had looked out of the windows in that north country but he had written no letter to Yankee editors about the things he had seen.

The next day a former owner of *The Journal* came to call on Editor Claggett and bring his thanks. The property below the bridge was his, he said, but he had forgotten all about it until he saw the letter in *The Journal*. He had never collected any rents on it and he had no idea that it was occupied. That day he had visited it. He had found a strong old woman who was by no means glad to see him. On his land she had built three houses of old boxes, pieces of tin, and other scraps of material. One she occupied. Two she rented. Behind her house she had a pig pen. Around her chickens ran. She was withal one of the most content folk on the earth until the Philadelphian stuck his nose over the bridge above her. Mr. Claggett did not say so but I gathered that in this there is a parable about the South and the TVA.

As Mr. Claggett was far from Dr. Howard so Dr. John Neal and Mr. Camp, who lives in his shadow, are far away from Mr. Claggett. Dr. Neal would be a saint if Liberalism could be substituted for Christianity and the personal habits of the saints brought forward into this age. Dr. Neal is a man more concerned with ideas and events than with his appearance. Despite his marked individuality and his perennial candidacy for public office, he is undoubtedly one of the first Liberals and honest men of East Tennessee. Also he is one of its largest landowners. He was first lawyer for the defense in the famous Scopes trial at Dayton where Darrow and Mencken joined him and after which Bryan died. He went over the mountains into North Carolina to help defend the Communists charged with murder in Gastonia. Long before the creation of TVA he fought for the government development of its war-acquired power sites on the twisting Tennessee. But he is careless to idiosyncrasy about his dress. His dark suit is covered with dust never disturbed by whisk-broom. And beside him, Camp, the shadow, the unidentical unrelated twin, is neat and clean as pin and pan. In a strange world it is perhaps not strange that the poorer man is the neater man. In any world the doctor and his companion are like characters out of a new Dickens but they made good comrades in the crowded lobby of a hotel in a strange town.

The Farragut Hotel was crowded. A Scripps-Howard party occupied a banquet hall from which to shout to East Tennessee the news that the Federal Communications Commission had granted its radio station greater power. Here at its best was what newspapers call Promotion. The editors of little papers from all over that section of the State had been brought to Knoxville for the celebration. And, Tommy Tuckers of Tennessee, they talked for their suppers into the microphone: How happy, how very happy they were that Scripps-Howard's mountain voice would now sound stronger and clearer in their towns. Celebrities joined them. Among them Hugh Johnson, florid and oratorical. But, for Dr. Neal, more important was the presence of Martin H. Aylesworth, former president of the National Broadcasting Company and now United Press executive, who had once been a pupil of Dr. Neal's in the law school of the University of Denver. Dr. Neal wanted to ask Aylesworth back to speak at his law school in Knoxville. He would like to confer on him an LL.D. His whole school, Marshall McNeill told me, was no bigger than the editor's private office on a Scripps-Howard newspaper. "And there are such schools all over Tennessee."

I waited with them, Dr. Neal and Camp, for Aylesworth who never came. They had just come back from Nashville where the day before the Governor had named George Berry to the United States Senate to succeed the dead Nathan Bachman and already the two were talking of leaving and driving in the night to Louisville where the Kentucky Derby was to be run the day after. We walked across the street and I drank a beer. Dr. Neal was critical of TVA's sale of power to some of the very big companies which had fought it most. I noticed that he steadily used the pronoun "we," where another person might have used "I." It sounded royal in the beer parlor. And I wished I could have gone listening to the ideas and opinions of "we" across Tennessee and Kentucky. But I told them good-by. I thought of them next day at Norris when a policeman in the town office told me that War Admiral had won the Derby. I wondered when Dr. Neal was going to get some sleep. And perhaps a cleaning and pressing for his clothes.

6

EDEN: FRUIT AND SNAKES

UNDOUBTEDLY innumerable puns have been made about his name. A policeman could not wear it otherwise. And Captain Stanton Nail is a policeman for all that he is listed on the TVA payroll as a public safety aid and for all the distance between the new clean, persuasive officer that he is and the old slouching, generally courageous but often cantankerous deputy of the Tennessee hills. Captain Nail looks like the captain of a football team. He stands and moves like a member of the fabulous Canadian Mounted Police. Women in Norris smile in unerotic pleasure at the sight of him as at the sight of such a physical man as physical man should be. He knows enough about the construction of dams to tell a visitor how the vast one at Norris rose in great concrete teeth to make a lake covering land where once 3,000 families lived and where, in 5,000 graves, the dead waited for last doom. An officer has a great deal more to know these days than how to swing a stick or shoot a gun. Indeed, stick swinging and gun shooting are in the new dispensation evidences rather of failure than success. Only such officers as Captain Nail could deal with the problems of Norris, the Sunday thousands and such a perpetual problem as old man William H. Hawkins.

He told me about old man Hawkins as he drove me around the model town of Norris and out the Freeway to Norris Dam and the cabined woods above the blue lake where in one year CCC workers planted 1,446,700 shrubs and trees.

I sympathized with old man Hawkins who lived with his wife and daughter close to the lake. But not long ago he almost killed with an ax a whole crew of the forestry division who had dared to enter his land.

"Give me my $2,700 and you can come on here," he shouted at the crew. "Else run!"

They ran. His lands and the price he hopes for them are tied up in the courts between the Tennessee Power Company and the TVA. The years go by while TVA goes on with its program of navigation, national defense, flood control, erosion control and "production of incidental power." The years go by while the power companies fight that program and particularly the power policies which are always flown by TVA as the tail of the kite. The years go by and old man Hawkins, growing older and madder, waits for his money. And Captain Nail has to persuade him gently, very gently, not to kill anybody with the ax.

The story of old man Hawkins pleased me. I hate model towns and, for all that the landlord is the government, Norris is a model company town like Kohler, Wisconsin, Hershey, Pennsylvania, and Kannapolis, North Carolina. My observation has been that Edens are generally either pretentiously false or full of secret snakes. Of course, Norris may, as Tracy B. Augur, assistant director of land planning, said, "represent the town planner's basic thesis that the best foundation for a healthy community life is a community deliberately planned to provide it." I doubt the good sense of that thesis. I doubt its truth in Norris. Indeed, after my first seeing of Norris I hated it.

"The town of Norris," I wrote in my journal before going to bed in one of the completely electrified, model houses of the model town, "is a town without a cemetery, a town created without pain. As tourists come it may serve the American thesis that pretty house and lovely lawn may be acquired without pain. But this is not the planner's thesis; it belongs to the advertisers. In the end Norris, I think, may do more to make enemies for planned economy than all the Republican speeches and power company briefs in the world. Like a sign of the old Devil, I find in me and I expect to find in other Southerners a preference for cruel perhaps but good-natured Southern carelessness, and an increased faith in the ultimate malignancy of Yankee good intentions. Too many of us will prefer a sloppy South to a South planned in perfection by outlanders. We know out of our past that the worst carpetbaggers were the ones who came down here to improve us. The others merely stole and went their way, but the improvers have been nagging us forever."

I was wrong. There is a cemetery in Norris. And there is a boy buried in it. Despite the standards set up by the personnel division in the selection of the workmen who built Norris Dam (examining 200,000 men to hire 4,000), those standards provided no defense against religious fanaticism. And such a fanatic slipped through. He was no mountain man, as most of the workers were. And he was mentally as well as geographically alien. All day long he worked with his hands building the big dam. But his mind worked like sour wine in a maniacal fear of evil. In love of God and fear of the devil he beat his children unmercifully to drive the wickedness out of them and to keep them virtuous. So badly did he beat his biggest boy that the boy in dark terror killed himself. The man had committed no crime before the law, but through the army of workers who labored on the dam there spread an almost superstitious fear and anger. They would not work with the man. He went away, driven out, and what was left of his family, happier than before, remained. The boy provided the cemetery without which not all the planners in the world could make a town.

That is probably barbarism. It probably tells more about

57

me than it does about Norris. Still Norris is not blueprints but people. The surveyors of the original town in the woods are not half so important as the people who now fill the houses which were left empty by the completion of Norris Dam and the movement of many of the workers on down the Tennessee to the construction of the dams at Wheeler and Chickamauga. I am probably perverse but I was less interested in the fact that the big school building in Norris was electrically heated and had photo-electric cell lighting control than that in it the hill children of the big, poor families of Anderson county, Tennessee, sat at desks beside the children of engineers, children born on engineering jobs from Stalingrad to Patagonia, city children and world children, children born by choice. From that collision of children, it seemed to me, as much might be expected as from the meeting of farm and transmission line.

In other ways the electric quality of human living goes on beyond any planning of the planners. Norris may be (as says Mr. Augur, who believes Norris is "homey,") founded on a tradition that antedates the Constitution, the tradition of the early colonies, born of practical necessity and built to live in. The New England ancestry of the planned town, he says, is old and irreproachable. Also the Puritan tradition persists, old, too, but not necessarily irreproachable. I came to Norris only a few weeks after its most perfect demonstration. Both Chairman Arthur Morgan and his lady had strong views on the deleterious effect upon the human system and human happiness of alcohol and even tobacco. They have no place in Utopia. But in Tennessee the free people of Norris came to vote on whether or not beer should be sold among them. As far as stronger drink was concerned, at that time all Tennessee was dry despite the efforts of Boss Crump of Memphis. Though Norris is a "Company-owned" village in most respects its final law is promulgated by a town council of nine, elected by the residents on a proportional representative basis. Therefore Dr. Morgan did not lean down from the battlements of power (even if Lilienthal and Harcourt Morgan would have let him) to interfere with the ordinary details of village law like rules about beer and pretzels, cakes and ale. But, just prior to the beer election, Mrs. Morgan, who occupied as nearly as anyone could in the village the position of wife of the boss, circulated throughout the community a round robin or petition against the legalization of beer. One hundred and twenty-four persons wrote their signatures on her paper in a big round hand. But when the election was held—under Australian ballot rules—and the picked population of Norris expressed its views in the privacy of the voting booth only 104 persons in the whole town voted against beer. Certainly this incident proved neither the wisdom nor lack of it of the *Demos* or the desirability of the dictator—or his wife. But it seemed to me it did prove—and in proving pleased me and before me a good many people in Norris—that Norris is human and that not even a lady can pull it to perfection. (Perhaps also this incident more than some formal divisions over power policies pointed to the true crevice in the thinking of the Authority which widened to a crevasse of contention and which later resulted in the removal of Chairman Arthur Morgan by the President.)

Indeed, the evidence seemed to me to be pleasantly cumulative that Norris was by no means an uninterrupted Utopia or an Eden without a worm. True enough, in the drug store only medicines were sold which had the approval of the town doctor, but on the day I was there a sound truck came out from Knoxville roaring for a florist company sentimental advertising of Mother's Day up and down Dogwood, Dale and Orchard Roads. The sandwiches and coffee at the drug store were by drug store standards excellent, but the food in the community house was as inexpensive, healthy and as uninteresting as food always is when dietitians are in charge. The expert is nearly always a scientist, and food and living are among the arts. There was no room for me in the Guest House because an elderly friend of Dr. Arthur Morgan and of Antioch College was with his entourage in occupancy. But I was comfortably housed on Crescent Road in the very feminine house of Mrs. Chipman and her mother, Mrs. Crittenden. Mrs. Crittenden was director of the Tennessee Bureau for Promotion of the Welfare and Hygiene of Maternity and Infancy under Governor Alf Taylor whose campaign for the Governorship against his brother, Fiddling Bob, rises high and hilarious out of the most comic politics of the South. That is pretty high.

But at least one reason for the normal human quality of Norris seemed to me to be J. W. Bradner, thin, nervous, hard-headed town manager. One day he is going to write a book about his model town. It will be worth reading. While I waited for him in his office one of Captain Nail's fellow officers at the telephone switchboard had time between calls to discuss the world and the Tennessee Valley with me. It was he who told me that War Admiral had won the Derby and so set me thinking again of Dr. Neal and Mr. Camp. He also told me that at the moment there were 1,100 people living in Norris (281 new single houses, 10 duplex houses and apartments, a few remodeled farm houses: all designed to hold 350 families). Fifteen TVA policemen, plus three more in the summer, not only provided a big guard for their safety but also handled the vast Sunday crowds of tourists. On one Sunday there were 17,000 visitors, he said. Every State was represented and also Canada twice, "China onest, Russia onest, Sweden onest, and Greece onest." Lots of people. Three suicides so far, he said, have used Norris Lake.

During the 1937 flood on the Mississippi system (recurrence of which TVA engineers think might be prevented by more such dams and river systems as TVA provides) he and other officers had gone from Norris to Memphis: On the levees was Boss Crump, a man with long gray hair, who, in a red checked mackinaw, marched the threatened levees all day long.

"He encouraged the niggers, called them 'son,' but he sent out orders each day that he wanted so many thousand niggers. The police hired them or arrested them for vagrancy. Only difference was that those that were hired got $3.27 a day." The policeman shook his head. "You ought to have seen those refugees they brought in. I never saw such folks. We had to make them use the toilets and teach them how to sit down on 'em. It took two weeks to clean out some of the schoolhouses where they put 'em."

He looked up at the door. "Here's Mr. Bradner now," he said.

In his own one of the attractive model houses Bradner swung one leg over the arm of his chair in characteristic pose and told me how he came to Norris first to lay out roads and sewers and stayed to succeed the first man who had been brought there as manager. He did not state it exactly that way but I gathered that he had gotten his first experience as a town manager as railroad contractor and boss of a labor camp in Florida. There, every Saturday, he found his Negroes slipping away and on Monday he lacked the labor to go ahead at the pace he planned. There were no complaints about the wages, no complaints about the work. The Negroes, indeed, set to work with a will but on Saturdays with their wages in their breeches they disappeared—too often forever.

"Then one day the sheriff 'phoned me.

" 'I hear you have been having trouble with your labor.'

" 'Umhuh,' I said. 'I have.'

" 'Well, I'm sending you over a little brown nigger. You

pay him $25 a week and you won't have any more trouble.' "

Bradner hired the little brown man. And the fellow built a small shack near the camp. This, he told Bradner, was the Juke House. With two or three colored women who came with him, he opened it on every Saturday with music, liquor, dancing, and the game of skin. Bradner had no more trouble with his labor.

But the big Norris Dam and the town of Norris which housed its builders were both constructed without the aid of liquor or women or skin. Built at the low point of the depression, TVA could pick its workers carefully. The Authority seemed to put a handicap on itself in its determination so far as possible to use the labor of the region. But now Bradner, who has watched them work, swears by them. He has no faith in any suggestion that the mountain whites are a biologically inferior people. One or two generations of proper feeding and they would be as vigorous as any folk in the world. Already the children from the two old county high schools now consolidated with the school in Norris are developing leadership even among the children of the engineers though at first the meeting of the two groups was attended with difficulty. And some of that infantile difficulty, I gathered, was very sad indeed.

After all perhaps Norris was a mistake, I suggested. People had told me so. It had been, I gathered, the most expensive of the imperial plans made in the high, hasty days of 1933.

"I doubt it," Bradner said. "True enough it is not absolutely paying for itself on the basis of rents. But it is here and valuable here as a part of the show of Norris Dam. I think that's worth what it costs."

I was glad that he did not go into the longer, more involved arguments in defense: that a purely temporary labor camp would have cost $2,000,000 and left little salvage after the completion of the dam; that Norris is not camp for the building of Norris Dam alone but town for the long term TVA job. Therefore, true economy and good sense dictated the model town. That's the argument and it remains the argument despite the scornful laughter of critics of its construction. I was inclined to agree with those who laughed, but not ready to agree with the more disagreeable laughers that because Norris was a miscalculation, TVA was a mistake.

Of course, Bradner added, the difficulties in such a model town as Norris are multiplied. The town is not merely what other towns are. It is also butcher and baker, landlord and electric company, drug store and school. In such a town complaint all comes together at one point.

"And, perhaps," I said, "in such a planned town the Utopians are thicker than usual."

"Maybe. But I think the ratio of educated nuts—ineffectual intellectuals, I call them—is small. But," he added and grinned, "they can be very vocal."

He saw me home. The streets of model towns, as laid out in all loveliness in accordance with contour, are hardly designed for the quick way finding of strangers. Already I had been lost in daylight and once I wondered if town planners took design from maze and labyrinth. Norris streets swing in magnificent curves over lovely hills. They take full advantage of the rolling plain which runs from the steep hills beside the Clinch down wooded slopes to a second valley. But they are designed for seeing not seeking. In the darkness I was glad to have Bradner show me home, and if David Lilienthal had not come down the hill to find me I should never have found my way to the best breakfast and the best talk at his house in the morning.

7

BREAKFAST WITH A DEMOCRAT

THAT summer David Lilienthal was 38 years old, 17 years from graduation at DePauw, 14 from the Harvard Law School, but he was 32 years younger than Harcourt A. Morgan and 21 years younger than Arthur E. Morgan, his associates in the direction of the Tennessee Valley Authority. He was only four years old as a Southerner but already to South Carolina students he was using the pronoun "we" in contemplation of Southern problem and in discussion of action to solve it. He used it, too, when we talked in the green garden back of his pleasant house in Norris and drank the glasses of orange juice which pretty Nancy Alice had brought to us before breakfast. It was a good morning, full of sun. I had been up and waiting when he came to show me the way and to show himself to me: In a gray suit with a maroon slipover sweater for vest, a big man, a stout man in the root sense of the word, a pleasant, round-faced man, spectacled. He grins, wide and shrewd, and there is none of the wide-eyed staring of the Utopian in his eyes. He can laugh as well as talk. And Middle Western man in Tennessee, he can be serious without violating Tennessee's traditional Rule Number 5: "Don't take yourself too damned seriously."

"We must," he told me, "get down to legume roots, as Harcourt Morgan would say. Mere grass isn't definite enough for him."

Nor, I gathered, for the younger Lilienthal. And it was no secret in Norris that these two, the oldest and the youngest on the Tennessee Valley Authority, were often at odds with the Chairman Arthur Morgan who sat in age between them and in title (not power) above them. This Arthur Morgan, engineer, who became a college president without ever going to college, was born closer to the South than either of the other two members of the Authority—in Cincinnati, Ohio, from which, across a river, Mrs. Stowe observed the slavery she damned in *Uncle Tom's Cabin*. Lilienthal, the lawyer, was born in Illinois. Harcourt Morgan, entomologist and educator, had lived 44 years in the South when he was made one of the TVA triumvirate, but he was born in Canada.

It was in the South that Arthur Morgan, TVA's odd man, lost the wholeness of faith in the ultimate wisdom of the masses of men. Once he told his associates in Knoxville: "Years ago with my engineering associates at Memphis I planned and directed the reclamation of many hundred thousand acres of very fertile land. The philosophy of that development was that if you give people the means for creating wealth and comfort they will work out the situation without further help. Yet today that most fertile land in America is the locus of the most miserable share-cropper tenantry, where poverty and bitterness are general, and violence appears." Certainly that St. Francis River Valley country, where tenants struck and landlords flogged, which I was to see across the river from Memphis, has seen enough human troubles to discourage a man even in the Tennessee Valley. Coming in a lifetime from the one river to the other, Arthur Morgan may very naturally believe that "a certain amount of benevolent despotism" is a necessary addition to the best engineering plans.

But David Lilienthal talked undisturbed over his breakfast table and in his garden of the wisdom of the people when the people are given even half a chance to be wise. He talked with an almost folk-feeling of distrust for the experts in the

direction from above of the living of people. In the vernacular, he referred to "damn social workers." Of a man he was
quoting, he said, "He's not an economist, thank God." The
burden of all his talking—and apparently of his thinking—lay
along the way of faith that men in the Tennessee Valley and
in the world are capable, given the true chance, of providing
a decent world and living for themselves and their families.

This does not mean that he lacks faith in planning though
he does feel that about planning "much choice tripe was
uttered in the starry-eyed days of 1933." Once he said,
"There is something about planning that is attractive to that
type of person who has a yen to order the lives of other people. It has an attraction for persons of a vague and diffuse
kind of mind given to grandiose pictures not of this world.
Planning is a subject that attracts those who are in a hurry,
but are rather hazy as to where they want to go so rapidly, or
whether people want to scurry along with them. But planning and those charged with responsibility for the formula-
tion and execution of plans must, above all, be realistic and
pragmatic. Effective planners understand and believe in people, in the average man."

Far off from Norris I myself had almost believed that the
noise that came from TVA was a simple quarreling between
the power companies and the government over which should
sell power to the people. I had not quite believed that the
power attorneys were the only patriots and the TVA people
only wicked politicians. But I had listened to power company
officials make angry fun of the costs and rates of TVA power
in dollars and cents. I was then only vaguely aware of the
extravagance in the use of public resources for power and
profit alone. Only by multiple purpose river development
and control (for flood, navigation, erosion, national defense
and power) can the public safety and the public welfare be
best and most completely served. A proper division of those

costs in a proper development for all these purposes is possible only under some such system as is growing in the Tennessee Valley.

But I grow argumentative myself. That morning I was interested instead in David Lilienthal's statement that the noisy quarrel over power was only the surface division over the fundamental philosophic cleavage within TVA between those who hold the antagonistic faiths:

(1) that the good life, "the new civilization," must be imposed, upon people in general and the 2,500,000 people in the 42,000 square miles of the Tennessee Valley in particular, from above;

or (2) that the people themselves, freed from improper restraint and overwhelming handicap, are entirely capable of providing the good life for themselves.

Norris was not the last place I saw that conflict nor was David Lilienthal the last man I heard speak of it in the South. I think, indeed, that it is the central division in Southern thinking as perhaps in the world's. Not long afterward I was to pass the scene of similar conflict among Southerners on a mountain top at Chattanooga. I was to find it in the differences of Governors and in the quarrel of a chemist in Savannah with foresters over the protection of the pines from the pulp makers. Not rare, this division between faith in strength rising from the democracy and power descending from authority is fundamental and at the same time bewildering in the South where the toughest Bourbons are often the noisiest Jeffersonians and all slaveholder-thinkers vote the straight Democratic ticket.

"These Tennessee Valley people," Lilienthal declared, "are as capable of taking care of themselves as any people on earth. When we first began work at Norris the contractors did not want to use the mountain people. They were too light, they said; they were not used to working in crews. But it was the TVA policy to use the people of the region and after a year those who had opposed them said they were the best workers they had ever had. They were not only efficient on the job but they took advantage, too, of the opportunities for learning which were provided. I never saw people so full of pleasure in what they had learned.

"I remember a particular pair of men. They had come from a coal mine town called Wilder up in the hills, one of those worn out coal mine towns. I think the water had gotten into the mines. Making a living was almost impossible and living was a matter of perpetual fighting between the miners and the mine owners. There were thugs on one side and squirrel guns on the other. Well, not very long ago this pair came by my house to see me. They wanted me to know that they were pals though one of them had been a miner and the other a mine guard up in Wilder."

While he paused I looked at him uncertain whether he was Jew or Gentile. I meant to ask him and forgot. I had heard a power company president call him "Jew" as epithet. But I was less concerned with the stiffness of the bargain he might make with power executives, who before TVA had made almost whatever bargain they chose with the people, than with the idea that here might be a man flung centuries out from the dispersal who was aware that promised lands had to be made, not sought—something perhaps that the children of the first Americans have not learned. Indeed it may need 2,000 years in ghettos for its learning. The Jew might be back on the land, not in any plowing in Palestine, but as leader of the Under-ones on the earth. In a world that contained Hitler and a multitude of hard-skulled, empty-handed little Hitlers everywhere, the idea pleased me. I hope Lilienthal is a Jew. That would mean something in a queer modern world.

I asked him: "You don't think these Southern hill people are biologically exhausted?"

He smiled. "Of course not. They're good folk. All they ever needed was a chance. You couldn't blame them as long as they lacked even that."

"Can they be given a chance?"

"They must be given one. We don't live in a desert. The South is a land rich in resources and the South ought to be a market important to the nation, but the average spendable income for each person in the South was $315 a year in 1936 as against $546 in the nation—$250 in South Carolina against $843 in New York. And there are counties—a good many of them—in the South where that income is less than $100 and they are by no means all predominantly Negro counties. Is it any wonder that their standards don't meet the ideas of the social planners? Our people have been scandalously poor. And that poverty comes straight to the central problem of TVA. Naturally we are interested in it."

Mrs. Lilienthal—she was Helen Marian Lamb of Perry, Oklahoma—got up apologetically from the breakfast table. A pretty dark-haired woman, her eyes give the impression that she is wise enough to know that the world is as funny as it is sad.

"I'm sorry," she said, "but David Eli is concerned for my presence at a Mother's Day ceremony they're having at the schoolhouse. I'll have to go."

But David Eli's father, who was entitled to none of the day's honors and who had only recently recovered from a throat infection, stayed at home with me and sat in the sun in the garden. Perhaps I made him talk too much. Since he survived I'm glad that I did.

"I suppose—," he said as he settled into a chair under the pines, "I suppose that erosion is really the first element in our job here. It not only destroys the land and so calls for the wonderful work Harcourt Morgan is directing in the fertilizer program. It also may fill up our lakes, clog our nine-foot navigation channel, cut down the volume of the water we can hold back to prevent flood down the valley—last Spring we held back enough water here at Norris to keep the level at Chattanooga below flood—and, by cutting down the controllable volume of water, cut down, too, the possible hydro-electric power which we may produce."

He waved a hand at the people beyond Norris' well-kept green hills.

"Well, the poor man is behind all that."

"How?" I asked.

"Take a farmer and a little farm, and a steep slope on it denuded of trees by the farmer. He has to make a living. He needs this steep slope to grow the things that will keep his family alive, and so he cuts down the trees and plants his corn. The soil is washed off in a few years, and the nation has been robbed of just that much of its capital assets. That's a familiar story. What are we going to do about it? Well, one way of going about it is to say, 'We will pass a law that any farmer who cuts down the trees and cultivates a slope steeper than a certain grade is incapable of farming. He is injuring the community and the nation, and by this law we will take his land away from him and turn it back into forest or meadow.' That is one way of going about it."

"A pretty drastic way," I said.

"Yes. Fortunately, I think, there's another method—the method of giving the farmer a chance to make a choice. It is about time that we recognized that the farmer does not cut down those trees merely because he enjoys cutting down trees or because he likes to see the topsoil washed off and destroyed, but because he has a problem of feeding his family and making a living. He chooses only between washing hill and starving family. But give him a choice—a free choice—by making it possible for him to use his land in such a way that he will not only be able to support his family but at the same time protect his soil against depreciation. No need to fear how he'll choose."

"Yes," I agreed. "Farmers aren't fools for all the city folks that think so. But how are you going to make this free choice possible? That's not easy."

"No," he admitted. "But we're already beginning to do things here in the valley. I spoke about Dr. Harcourt Morgan's work with the cheap fertilizers. There has been too much draining away of the wealth of the South. We've been selling our soil along with our cotton. Sometimes even we've sold our people along with our products. We have added too little human skill to our raw materials. And, I think, we've been drained by systems of freight rates and tariffs that put the South at great disadvantage. There's plenty to be done and I believe the people will do it."

He repeated: "The people, these people here in the Tennessee Valley—in the South—they will do it."

The sun struck his eyes and he moved to escape it. He stopped blinking, smiling.

"I have no confidence in progress," he said, "that comes from plans concocted by supermen and imposed upon the rest of the community for its own good. I don't have much faith in 'uplift.' I deeply believe in the notion of progress and I have confidence in the general good sense of the average man and woman. I believe deeply in giving people freedom to make their own choice. It seems to me that the duty of leadership is to see that that choice is available."

"Why, that's democracy and faith in it," I protested. "I thought both were out of date."

He smiled with me.

"Yes. The people. I try to remember that always—that

71

while most of us are dealing with figures, with blueprints, with charts and budgets, with building things, that is not what TVA is all about. TVA is about people and for people. TVA is about men and women and children."

And that, I thought as I got up to go on looking for it, is what the South is about and what the South is. And supermen can't save them. Indeed, they've suffered enough already from the pretensions and the presumptions of masters. But the South can be helped—is being helped—by young men like this Lilienthal. He may be a carpetbagger. If so, he is one who comes neither to steal our money nor reform our manners and morals but in the best sense of leadership to share our destiny.

I rode down the Sunday road to the desert which men had made in the mountains about Copperhill delighted with the discovery of at least one democrat, ardent, intelligent and determined, in the Democratic South. He was not the last I was to see.

8

DESERT IN THE FORESTS

I RODE into Copperhill one hot, dusty Sunday just eighty years after Frederick Law Olmsted, who examined so particularly everything in the South, had examined the copper mining and miners of Tennessee. He saw no desert. Instead he came up the pretty valley of the Ocoee where hemlocks and laurels grew together in a perfection he had nowhere else seen. Beyond them he discovered several hundred Cornishmen ("London miners" the natives called them) who insisted upon having wheaten bread in this corn bread eating country and who longed in vain for ale instead of the ubiquitous whisky. He found, too, speculators in the woods which have since disappeared and was himself mistaken for a shrewd dealer in ores who was keeping his counsel when in fact he was telling the truth. In the dirty public house, where sheets on the beds were only rarely changed, "gentlemen of wealth" were ready to buy or sell or learn "the signs" of the copper lands. And all of them, Olmsted reported, stayed longer in the barroom than the virtuous Yankee Olmsted did.

Hemlock and laurel and every other tree and plant and shrub are gone now. Miles away from Copperhill, and its neighbor Ducktown, the trees begin to look sick and small. They become sparser and between them run deeper and wider ditches through the dry cracking earth. But where the true desert starts all is ditch or the color and consistency of dry ditch bottoms. The whole earth is washed down to clay, red, white, yellow, and the whole looks chancrous and diseased. Only 50 miles from the Great Smoky Mountains National Park and near neighbor to the Cherokee National Forest, this desert in the mountain forests is a terrifying picture of what man can swiftly do to his earth.

Those agricultural philosophers who would frighten us out of our carelessness with the far-away spectacle of the man-made deserts and the man-made hunger of China have not put enough stress on Copperhill. When the green skin of America is finally peeled back and the underlying desert is left bare beneath the feet of our grandchildren, the peeling process may very well have begun at Copperhill. Peeling has already begun there, but the trouble perhaps is that in the care of the land in the South and in America today, they are the farmers who need to be frightened, and they were not farmers but speculators from New York and London and miners from far away, who here began destroying every green and growing thing on the earth for the encircling miles around.

Perhaps Copperhill appeared to me to be uglier and more disturbing because I drove to it from the extravagantly green town of Norris and from the pleasant breakfast table of David Lilienthal, whose concern is as much flourishing earth as flowing stream. We drank orange juice between pine and grass and neither pine nor grass nor anything else grows, without nursing in soils brought in, at Copperhill. The road to the desert runs south of Knoxville pleasantly parallel to the last western spur of the Appalachians by green farm and hill and valley. It was decoration day along part of the way. Not the formal, official Decoration Day when flags fly and speeches are made over the graves of soldiers. This is different: A mountain boy to whom I gave a ride told me that in various communities different Sundays were chosen but that in all of them on some early summer Sunday everybody gathered to clean up the graveyards and, beyond cleaning up

74

the graveyards, to eat heartily, to frolic, to make love and have in general a high ole time. It is, of course, a solemn day for the old folks and all those who tenderly love the dead, but for the young it is a jolly day of picnicking in the mountains. This one toward which we rode was the second decoration day my companion had been to that spring. He was going, he said, to the church twenty miles from where he worked because there was a girl there whom he wanted to see. He grinned then and continued grinning until I put him down.

Not everyone was going to cut down the weeds and kill the snakes and kiss the girls in the country cemeteries. There were baseball games in progress at half a dozen places along the road. In one brown cotton mill town I saw a woman with white bare arms bending and rising over a washboard in a tub. In one hilly meadow all the trees had been cut down except in a little dark grove at the very top and all the cattle were gathered there, high above me, out of the sun. At Maryville a very solemn drunken man had come out when I stopped the car for a moment and begged a ride for an equally solemn and also aseptically and sabbatically clean little boy.

"His ma's waiting for him in Vonore."

The man waved after us, shedding his solemnity. The boy rode the twelve miles without speaking, then said, "Thank you," and ran like a baby cottontail scurrying for shelter. I was sorry I did not get a chance to see his mother. Somehow the gaiety of the father's waving hand made me expect a grim woman at this end of the journey with her child. But if I missed a woman worn down to grimness by a gaiety hard to bear, I found erosion before I got to Ducktown and Copperhill. It was in Etowah and it had nothing to do with sulphuric acid fumes or topsoil or copper.

There is a sudden economic erosion, like the abrupt slip-

75

ping away of earth, that can wipe out a whole town. And the old curly-haired man in dungarees told me about it in the filling station while I munched a sandwich I had bought in the community drug store at Norris. He had no duties in connection with the station. He was merely an elderly conversationalist and I suppose the filling station on the highway provided him with as many listeners as any other place in town. He told me the tragedy of Etowah. To him now it was a story with an end to it, an end if not happy at least unchangeable. He seemed to enjoy telling it as Lazarus probably enjoyed exhibiting his sores. His life had been in Etowah and until four years before Etowah had been a vigorous growing town.

"Why in those days," he said. He flung a fat hand across the street and the railroad which lie side by side to the dingy railroad shops beyond. "In those days when the shifts changed the men came out of the L & N shops by the hundreds. This street was thick with them. But four years ago the L & N decided to pull all its shops together up in Kentucky and it cut the men here from 700 to 75. All in one day. That's what happened to this town."

He shrugged. The story was entirely painless now, an item for the enlivenment of a conversation with an inquisitive stranger. As such he seemed glad to possess it and pleased to pass it on. As far as he was concerned nothing much could happen now. He was an old man and, if Etowah were dying, it would not be far ahead of him. But there was no such resignation in the boy filling the tank and checking the oil. He was irritated dully by the old man's talk. Obviously as far as he was concerned Etowah's story was not over. He thought aloud in terms of trade routes as men have always done.

"When they finish this road, it'll be the through road from Kentucky to Atlanta. People will come through on the way to Florida from Chicago. It'll be a good place to stop. We'll get the business then that's going to Athens and Sweetwater now. It won't be long."

The old man smiled at him benevolently, like one unwilling to disturb the illusions of the young, but also like one who had seen his town and his world go suddenly smash and had no faith in any recovery too late to include him. He listened critically while the boy told me the way to Copperhill.

"I'd hate to be caught up there after dark," the old man told me. "I got a friend who took a load of furniture up there by the back road you're not taking and he got caught up there. His car broke down. In the night he woke up. Some creature was scratching at his windshield. He never did know whether it was a big dog or a wolf. I wouldn't want to be caught up there after dark. They're bad lands to be sure."

The lands are ugly enough. A wolf living there would have to have his provisions shipped in. But every disturbing quality of ugliness is certainly to be found in the dry uninterrupted succession of gullies which cover the whole land. The earth everywhere looks like those relief maps, plaster and painted, to show in a little space mountain range and plain, river and basin. The big plant of the Tennessee Copper Company rises sooty and high and hideous against the town and above the desert. But beyond it the principal street running parallel to creek and railroad is an unimpressive thoroughfare and, shut off by its buildings from the desert, would be indistinguishable from similar streets in a thousand Southern towns. The two men I spoke to, loafing in the door of the drug store, might have been planters in the Delta or fish dealers in Louisiana. Actually they were young technical employees of the Tennessee Copper Company. And in exchange for a reading of my Olmsted on his trip here, one of them, using a much chewed cigar as a pointer and a picture postcard of the plant as chart, undertook to explain to me the processes involved in the extraction of acids and chemicals and copper from the ore. His chemistry was so much more advanced than mine that I lost the way after the first or second treatment of the ores. But I did understand what had happened before these processes began to make these mountains naked in all the country round.

The laurel and hemlock, which Olmsted saw growing in perfection, made good fuel. And as fuel the trees were cut down. Cutting down the trees in mountainous country is in itself enough to cause disastrous erosion. But in this bone-barren corner of Polk County, Tennessee, another rarer and more destructive event occurred. In the old days the ore was piled above the wood and roasted. And such a roasting of the ore generated sulphuric acid fumes which killed utterly all vegetable life wide and around. Now, the very fumes, which burned life off the hills and permitted the washing away of the topsoil which had been bound and held by roots, are the first profitable products of the mines and plants. Not in ingots but in tank cars, the Tennessee Copper Company sends its best money-making product away. And, according to the men in the drug store, so profitable is the business of catching and bottling the fumes that once destroyed the life on whole mountains that the operations went on through the depression. Now the mills and mines employ only native white labor who make as much as $9 a day. (Cornishmen, Olmsted reported in 1860, had their expenses paid out from England and forty dollars a month wages as compared with the four pounds a month they had received at home.)

It was interesting to ride across the Ocoee River into Georgia and watch the earth beside the road come slowly back to life, first the barren earth, then the sick green and finally the healthy growing plant and tree. But the ride back from green to desert is disturbing. Go back across the river and up the hill. Ugly and steep it runs to the school which sits like a first step in a hanging barren. Beyond the school is the graveyard and in it, as in flower beds before some houses and before the staff house at the plant, some enthusiasts have brought top soil from far away to nourish growing green. But there is little or no green anywhere along the last avenue of desolation which rises between drab worker houses almost perpendicularly to the pinnacle of the town. There, standing on the hilltop in his undershirt, I ran across the home-loving Southerner and home-loving man. He joined me where I stood looking off across the desert toward Ducktown.

"You'd be surprised," he volunteered, "how many folks come to look at it. Most of 'em say it looks like hell. I guess I'm used to it. I like it better than trees. There's nothin' unusual about trees. You can see them anywhere. But you ought to see what the sun can do to this."

There was before us a bad land loveliness. Even this hill, barren as a hill in hell, rose in its high hideousness close to beauty and wonder. Night and sun could give it every stirring quality of dramatic landscape. I looked at the man who lived in the midst of it and appreciated it. He was a small, wiry individual, dark, and darker still because of his celebration of Sunday by not shaving. His sharp blue eyes sat in lower lids puffed either by Saturday night dissipation, Sunday afternoon sleeping or—I wondered—by such fumes as had stripped these mountains.

"Were you born around here?"

He seemed suddenly proud: "Right down the hill."

"Did you ever hear the old folks talk about some Cornishmen who came here long ago?"

"Cornishmen?"

"Miners who came from England."

79

"No." He spat a brown juice onto the clay hilltop. "My sister might know about that. She knows about things like that. But she ain't here," he added thoughtfully. "Once I worked over in North Carolina at Spruce Pine. They brought some Eyetalians in there once and had a lot of trouble. I think they killed some of the poor little bastards. You have to feel sorry for them so far from home."

"Yes, it must be sad to die so far away from home."

"They don't like niggers there either. We don't here."

"Yes, a man down the hill told me that the workers here were all native white Americans and got as much as $9 a day."

"That's what he told you?"

"Yes."

"It's a free country. Man's got a right to say what he pleases."

He spat out the wet residue of his tobacco and took one of my cigarettes. With it he pointed where the sun and the shadow of a cloud striped the desert.

"Now ain't that pretty? You know it is. But I'll tell you one thing about this place, you can't always believe all you hear."

He lit his cigarette and mine with a skill against the wind.

"There are plenty of trees," he said. "I've seen 'em. There are trees nearly everywhere. But there are not many places like this one. Not near here. I think it's beautiful. And, damn, I was glad to get back home from Spruce Pine. To tell you the truth, I never could figure out what I went for, except maybe I was young and wanted to see the world. I'll take Copperhill every time for mine."

9

HISTORY OVER CHATTANOOGA

I RODE up Lookout Mountain to see where they had quarreled. I expected to see no signs of old violence on hotel
walls, but the more I had heard of the angry collision of
Allen Tate and William R. Amberson at the meeting of the
Southern Policy Committee at Chattanooga the more I realized that in the hotel rooms on the mountain, as directly as
on bloody Missionary Ridge below it, philosophies had been
fundamentally opposed. A man could not hope to understand the South who did not contemplate the conflict of these
two. It was as important as the quarrel at Norris. Here high
over non-union, hard-bitten Chattanooga, faith in the collective (but please not Communistic) use of new techniques
on the old land had been arrayed against the old pleasant,
poetic individualism of the free yeoman under his own vine
and fig tree within the sound of the cackling of his own hens
and the mooing of his own cows.

But here as I rode and considered the conflict I found, as
at Caesar's Head, that beauty is fenced about. Joe Reams,
aged 12, served as my guide and the more I learned of the
system by which Joe not only received pay from me but also
a kick-back from the owners of every fenced-in scenic wonder to which he conducted me, the more I wondered whether
the antagonism of philosophies is immediately important in
a South scratching desperately and sometimes shrewdly for
meal, meat and molasses and their equivalent in specie.
Again, the conflict may be more important for the scratch-

81

ing. At any rate, Joe rode with me to Rock Garden and got 40 cents of the dollar I paid for the privilege of trying unsuccessfully to see seven states from one spot. He went with me to Ruby Falls in the Lookout Caves and got 35 cents of the dollar and a half I paid. He could also, he said, conduct me to a cheap and clean tourist home.

"How much would you get for that, Joe?"

"A quarter. And I can tell you which souvenir stand is the cheapest and best and I get something back on everything you buy."

Joe and I were the last visitors that day at the caves. Only one cash customer hardly made it worth the while of the pimply-faced young man, who was playing catch with a Negro, to stop his exercise for us. But at last he turned from playing youth into recitative guide, geologist and aesthete; the Negro turned into elevator operator; and we sank deep into the earth: Confederate soldiers hid in these caves long ago when the mountain was besieged. Skeletons have been found up the dark corridors in the limestone. Around the close of the century seven adventurous men entered the cave at Lookout Mountain and disappeared up the twisting, dividing alleys in the earth. Many days later two half-crazed men emerged from a cave at Gadsden, Alabama, 80 miles away. The others were never heard from again. So he said.

Joe had a profitable and I had a pleasant afternoon on the mountain but there was no kick-back involved in showing me the hotel where Tate and Amberson quarreled. So I never found either the room or the hotel where they met with other Southerners and stated in angry words the conflict I was to see in white men and black men and the buckshot earth around Memphis. Perhaps this Southern Policy Committee, at the meeting of which they collided, is too little known. The original metaphor was that the State Committees, which make the Southern Committee which is a part of the National Policy Committee, were to be in a troubled time like Jefferson's committees of correspondence, little islands of lucidity in a chaotic South, nation and world. The committee, indeed, may be significant in the South as it contains—picked by the charming and zealous Francis Miller of Virginia—a good many of the Liberals of the South. Perhaps more than Liberals: They extend all the way from Amberson to Tate.

These two certainly made an interesting pair to discuss the fortunes of agriculture in the South. Tate, who wrote in 1937 from a rural address—Benfolly, R. F. D. 6, Clarksville, Tennessee—is poet and literary critic; Amberson, who wrote of Southern farmers and unions from the Marine Biological Laboratory, Woods Hole, Massachusetts, is physiologist. Both were—or had been—professors. Both had seen life from the vantage of the river bluffs of Memphis. And both with the best intentions would serve better living on the Southern land by saving it from the other. Each believes in angry sincerity that the other is an entirely misguided fanatic.

Tate—who was brilliant boy at Vanderbilt—*magna cum laude,* 1922—is the native. Indeed, he is more than native of the contemporary South. With a group of gentle writers and thinkers like himself in Nashville he is spiritually native of a Southern past honey-dripping with Southern virtues. This South, refuge from the soot of industrialism and the stink of collective loss of dignity, they have called Agrarian. But it is a brand of agrarianism nearer to the poetic sheep herding of Corydon and Amaryllis than to that agrarianism devoted to raising more hell and less corn which stirred the South along with the rest of America when these poets were inattentive babes. As such a one Tate precipitated the quarrel at Chattanooga where the Southerners had gathered at the invitation of George Fort Milton, editor of *The Chattanooga News.* In the chair at the meeting of the Committee on Agricultural Policy was Professor Pipkin of Louisiana State University.

83

Tate rose in native indignation to protest against the complication of the Southern agricultural situation by incoming Northerners. His voice sounded of carpetbaggers and Reconstruction. And once again in the South the fat-back was in the fire.

Amberson obviously was the incomer. Born in Harrisburg, Pennsylvania, in 1894, five years before Tate was born in Clarke County in the Kentucky Blue Grass country, he learned about farming as the son of a town man who owned an apple orchard in the Cumberland Valley and about tenancy as the landlord's son. The institution of tenancy there was not, as Amberson says, exactly similar to that which later disturbed him in the flat, rich cotton lands of the Delta. School and war and school teaching occupied him and it took hard times to interest him in problems outside the circle of the biologist's microscope. Indeed, he was 38 years old and solemn graduate student at the University of Kiel in Germany before he began to be actively interested in social and economic problems. But then he sowed his good oats late and furiously. On his return to America and to teaching at Tennessee, he did volunteer case work in Memphis for the Mayor's Unemployment Committee. And how dark must unemployment have been in that black river town. The Peabody Hotel and Saunder's Pink Palace are not Memphis. Neither is Beale Street the minstrel show crowning of a taffy queen and a chocolate king as comic relief for the white commerce of Memphis' Cotton Festival, nor swing music come straight down from Handy's Blues. Beale Street is not merely an avenue of high-stepping high browns; it is a street of little Jews with gaudy goods seeking a living on the trade of poor Negroes. Above all Beale Street is a street where much high-smelling food can be bought for little cash. And in 1932 when there was little cash in Memphis and when cotton around Memphis was selling for 5 cents a pound

84

unemployment in Memphis was a thing black and pitiful enough to make any pious Yankee feel that the Civil War left some things still to be done. Amberson joined the Socialist Party and helped organize the Memphis Unemployed Citizens League. Also he discovered things that went on in the world under Boss Crump, a knowledge which he thinks gave him a certain immunity in the years that followed. Better still, men thought that he knew more than he did. When later the Southern Tenant Farmers' Union was organized with the friendship and inspiration of Norman Thomas, Amberson gave it such advice and aid as he could. He did not, he insists, organize it, as many have believed. Certainly he has been one of its first friends through strike and violence and eviction, turmoil and distress. But "its strength has been," he declares now, "that it was indigenous."

He was not. And when Tate at Chattanooga spoke of Communists rushing into the Southern agricultural situation in an effort to get publicity and indicated that the Southern Tenant Farmers' Union was involved in aiding such practices, Amberson in natural self-preservation got solemnly to his feet. What followed I tried to piece together out of men's memories. But the pieces do not always fit precisely. Amberson's memory is not Tate's, nor Tate's Amberson's. But, when Amberson got up at the meeting, Tate, I was told, pressed his accusation directly to him.

"You," he said in effect, "refuse to entertain any solution of the tenant problem but collectivism. You want the tenants to become more degraded even than they are now and gathered on larger plantations even than at present so that in the end the set-up will favor Communism."

Amberson flushed but he spoke wearily. "The red herring of Communism."

Tate cracked at his weariness. "I'm only giving a name to what you are supporting." He relaxed and smiled, "Aren't you opposed to tenants raising their own vegetables and milking their own cows?"

Amberson retorted without smiling: "Your Agrarianism sounds fine, but under its pretty-poetry foolishness it is nothing but a plan to reduce the people to peasantry."

Tate snorted: "That's the stock retort of Communists to any argument in favor of small ownership."

"I told you there is no Communism involved in the Southern Tenant Farmers' Union," Amberson said. "And I'm no Communist. You may not know the difference between a Communist and a Socialist but there is one."

Those who heard the argument say that Tate spoke sharply. "I know the Southern Tenant Farmers' Union in the Arkansas country across from Memphis is Communistic. I went out there and I know."

In many respects Amberson is as solemn as the tradition of the Abolitionists, but he laughed suddenly. Then, as he informed me later, he told a story. As I heard it not only from him but also from others in Memphis, it had to do with a trip made into Arkansas by Tate and James Rorty in April, 1935. They drove out to the town of Marked Tree and interviewed various ones of those who upheld the landlord's side of the conflict between the landlords and the unionized tenants. That was all. But the interviews shaped by Rorty's direct inquisitiveness, a somewhat brash and impertinent inquisitiveness, Tate thought, stirred the land. The trip back to Memphis somehow wore the quality of flight. There was a sense of violence where no real violence occurred. Only angry voices followed them across the Mississippi bridge. Rorty was called in carelessness a Red and Communist. He was not one though he had supported the Communist candidates in 1932, a year which marked also his break with the Communists who have ridiculed him since as both Liberal and journalist. Tate, who is essentially the philosophic reactionary, was made in Arkansas anger to seem almost a radical himself. Obscurely he was, I think, embarrassed, though the President of Southwestern College, at which Tate was teaching on a grant from the General Education Board, stood loyally by him when a delegation of angry planters stamped into his office in protest against Tate's presence at Rorty's interrogations. I think that perhaps he remains embarrassed by the contact with the indignity of the hard emotional violence which followed him even across the river and with the sensational quality of Rorty's Liberalism. And Amberson told the story again at Chattanooga, told it so that it seemed that, if there had been radicalism on the Southern land, Tate had participated in it. He flung it like ice upon Tate's argument and somehow there for a moment Tate's surprise and embarrassment made him seem strangely and falsely comic.

Somebody laughed. Even Tate's friends grinned. Amberson scored on the anecdote. It was a body blow in that particular personal combat, irrelevant as it was to the philosophies beyond the personalities of the men. But the division in the thinking of the South, of those who think at all about what Tate speaks of as "the fascinating nightmare called the South," remains. It will not soon be healed. Indeed, I thought as I rode down the mountain having left the prosperous Joe behind, the probability is that Tate is as far from Amberson as Amberson is from Tate and both are as far apart as the sensible South is from the extremes of either of them. The highway twisted down steeply. Moccasin Bend turns grand and brown as ever around the mountain and in it the Tennessee goes on carrying, below Lookout Mountain on the way from Norris to Paducah, plan for a happier valley. At the hotel Hunt Clement, Julian Harris' first mate on *The Chattanooga Times*, met me. He is older than he was, more solemn than he was, when as young reporters together we covered the trial of a millionaire for murder. In dry Tennessee he brought a quart of Scotch. And we drank to Southern intellectuals, their Yankee adversaries and our own lost youth before we went downstairs and ate beefsteak for dinner.

10

PRICE AND POWER

IN CHATTANOOGA I did not see Cartter Lupton. And I am
sorry for it. After I had gone all the way around the whole
South I discovered what not even Chattanooga seemed to
know: That he is the best walking symbol of the New South
in it. The Pattens and the Luptons are the big folk of Chattanooga. And no wonder. Women all over the South, high
up the creek and close to Courthouse Square, scribble their
dates with stub pencils in the Cardui Almanac and at the
proper time of the moon buy that bottle of Cardui. It is, as
the benevolent Indian maiden on the label seems to be prom-
ising for the Pattens to the pained and pleading pale face female, excellent for Functional Dysmenorrhea from puberty
to menopause. In half of Dixie that whole period belongs to
the Pattens. Also, regardless of sex, from one end of the South
to the other, Southerners sustain themselves through the heat
of the day with bottles of Coca-Cola. It is sworn to be deli-
cious and refreshing. Cartter Lupton is grandson of that
Zeboim Cartter Patten, Yankee soldier who was wounded at
Chickamauga, settled at Chattanooga, and grew rich from the
purchase of the Cardui formula. He is son of that John T.
Lupton, Virginian born in the second year of that war in
which Zeboim was wounded, who married Zeboim's daughter
and bought control of Coca-Cola bottling throughout the
South and West.

Of course, I should have known the importance of Cartter

Lupton when I trespassed upon the loveliness of the Lupton place in Cashiers Valley. I should have recognized house and planting there as details of something more than the place of an ordinary millionaire. But sometimes millionaires are as apparently identical as are tow heads or pickaninnies. And not even Chattanooga seemed to know his significance as the tie that binds rich Luptons to the rich Pattens. One native newspaperman, indeed, even entertained me with legends of the feuds between generous Pattens and stingy Luptons. Certainly Chattanooga seemed not to appreciate the significance of Cartter Lupton as the link between pop and patent medicine which emphasizes that wealth in the South for those who sell in the South must come from a cheap luxury or a promise of cheap surcease from pain. The South could not pay for anything else. But no Southerner is ever too poor to pay a nickel for a luxury and any fearful Southern girl facing Functional Dysmenorrhea will somehow save enough dimes for the drug store. Patten-Lupton took the nickels and the dimes. They are rich in proportion. But it took TVA to teach the lesson of essential cheapness in a poor land to the power companies. And not yet in Chattanooga is the Tennessee Electric Power Company fond of teacher.

"Chattanooga," said my friend the newspaperman whose formal history was better than his family histories, "is central in the South but it is not a Southern town."

Both of us sat with our feet in the window and looked at the town through the V between our crossed shoes.

"Here the Union sentiment of the mountains met the Confederacy of the Deep South. The Yankees won. And after the war old Parson Brownlow and others like him made every effort to preserve the Union settlement here. They brought in people from the North. But the people who came in to develop the country and its resources were not rich. Most of them were poor men on-the-make. The only way they could accumulate capital was by taking it out of the backs of labor. So Chattanooga became a low wage town. It still is one."

The war that stirred about it made Chattanooga. There is no Old South anywhere behind it. It was Ross Landing until Grant's and Sherman's soldiers marched through. Its iron industry started in a rolling mill opened in order that the war-ruined railroads might be rebuilt. There were scarcely more than 5,000 people there when old Zeboim came to settle in 1865. There were only 29,000 people when young Lawyer Lupton married Zeboim's daughter, Elizabeth Olive, in 1889. Even when Cartter Lupton was born in 1901 there were only about 10,000 more. Now, even though Birmingham has run ahead of it as an even newer New South, Chattanooga claims 129,000 folk. So many are not enough alone to buy Patten's Cardui (and Black Draught—a GOOD laxative) or Lupton's Coca-Cola. But they can help. (Indeed, every man, woman and child in the town drinks 70 Coca-Colas a year. Not up to New Orleans' 120 or Atlanta's 100, neither down to New York's 6.)

"They're the biggest people in Chattanooga," said my friend concluding his legends. "I think Cartter has sold the cotton mills his father bought. I don't know what he does now. Like his father before him, he is always afraid somebody's going to pull his leg."

I am sure that is not an adequate description of Cartter Lupton. I should have sought him out and fixed his picture in my mind but instead I was misled into following the too obvious importance of the too obvious aspects of TVA. I believe now too late that Cartter Lupton is more important in the Southern picture than is the dramatic rising of the Chickamauga dam. And yet there I saw, more impressive to me than lock gates of vast tonnage which a man can swing with a finger, Negroes working in old time physical labor supplementing the power of the Diesel caterpillar bulldozer in the riprapping of the earth fill part of the dam. V. L. D. Robinson, TVA information chief at Chattanooga, must have thought me a little queer to be more interested in these big Negroes moving heavy rock under a hot Tennessee sun than in some of the more unusual engineering aspects of the dam. Queer or not, I watched out of preference the waterboys handing dainty individual paper cups to each hot and solemn Negro. I remembered this well later when at Delta Cooperative Plantation at Hillhouse, Mississippi, a Christian lady cooperator in lounging pajamas asked me would I share their common towel. I did. God, I am sure, will remember as He remembered the one good deed of the man who once in his life gave a starving man an onion. I am a hypochondriac who is afraid of germs.

But I run ahead of my story when I should be going back to George Fort Milton who may be as representative of an awakening South as Cartter Lupton is representative of that New South which may be only a prodigious somnambulist. Milton is not a pretty man. He is too fat and yet—amazingly —he plays tennis. His head looks small in comparison with the rest of him and his hands and feet are small, too. His eyes shine above his mobile mouth. Not seldom he looks like the cat that has eaten the canary. And surely sometimes he is properly subject to the good-natured fun making of his editorial competitor, the amiable Julian Harris, Uncle Remus' son. ("And George says, 'We must implement our action.' What implement, George, shovel or hoe?") But Milton, with his big words and his casual familiarity with the most abstruse ideas, holds his cigarette daintily. He puffs at it for the punctuation of significance. But he can talk and he can write. And Chattanooga and power companies have learned that this elegant fat man can fight.

I remember that first Sunday afternoon when I came to Chattanooga and sat a long time talking with him in his long library before dinner. It is a grand working-writing man's library filled with all the sources he has sought for his biographies of Andrew Johnson and Stephen A. Douglas and for understanding of the battles about Chattanooga. Closer to our times were books on lynchings and tenancy. There were too, I knew, the less dramatic charts and tables of power rates. We began far off from Tennessee with talk of that next war about which men speak in Chattanooga as in Geneva and Istanbul. Slowly we converged upon the South in longer talk of politics and demagogues. I remember, rejoicing in agreement, that he was not disturbed by the supposed Southern preference for demagogues or terrified by the word. It is a word applicable to anyone who stirs in the South. Milton himself had felt it flung by power company executives.

"All that the demagogues indicated," he said, "was that the people were sick of the old supposedly aristocratic crowd. The Bourbons and the Brigadiers. Those old fellows merely occupied the offices and drew their salaries. And the only question the lazy gentlemen offered to the voters was the slim one between the personality of one elegant ineffectual and another—a choice between stuffed shirts who often stood like screens between the people and skulduggery. And it was those engaged in skulduggery who screamed loudest of demagogues when the stuffed shirt screen was removed. The people turned in vast relief to the so-called demagogues. But they only gave them a chance. After election they had to deliver as Tillman did, as Long in some respects did. Otherwise they went out quickly, too."

He had nothing against a little political ranting. And yet there was no denying, he thought, that Bob and Alf Taylor introduced vaudeville into Tennessee politics, pulled it down from the platform and into the circus. And circus surely these two brothers must have made long ago moving across Tennessee, playing their fiddles, making everywhere the "melodious squeak of horse tail hair on sweetly sounding gut." Bob Taylor, the Democrat, specialized in the playing of "Rack Back Davy," while Alf, the Republican, reveled in the "Arkansas Traveler." Issues were beside the point. Bob and the Democrats wore the white rose of York while Alf and the Republicans wore the red rose of Lancaster. They must have made high entertainment for the people of Tennessee that hot summer of 1886 before Milton or Cartter Lupton or I was born. And, in case anyone at this late date should be interested in the outcome of that War of the Roses, Bob was elected, though Alf became Governor, too, long afterwards in 1920.

But people are not always to be circused, not even in Tennessee. Sometimes in the South they may be interested in bread and made to see that it may come in our times over a transmission line. That really is Milton's story and he talked too little about it. The fight still goes on and since it began another afternoon paper has entered the Chattanooga field in competition with Milton's *News*. And the Tennessee Electric Power Company has given to this Chattanooga *Free Press* at least their complete accord so far as its editorial policy on important power questions is concerned. But once again I'm ahead of the story.

The story began when the TVA was created on May 18, 1933. It came to first climax as long ago as March 12, 1935. Between those two dates Milton and his managing editor, Charles Poe, both of whom have felt and understood the promise in TVA and sought steadily its fulfillment, decided that Chattanooga ought to have the advantages of the cheaper TVA power. They began slowly the campaign for an $8,000,000 bond issue to build a municipal plant to take power from TVA and re-sell it to Chattanooga. An organization to campaign for the movement was founded with a young dairy executive at its head. But the organization made

94

the slowest progress in rounding up leading citizens on its side. Indeed, as the election approached the number of the Best People who took the TVA side against the fighting Tennessee Electric Power Company was so small as to be negligible. There was no enthusiasm for the change in the columns of *The Chattanooga Times* owned by the then living Adolph Ochs of *The New York Times*. Then when election day came it was cold and gray. It began to rain and the rain turned into sleet. It looked as if God were a stockholder in the utilities.

"I figured it was all over then," Charles Poe told me. "With the weather I didn't see how we could hope for a chance. And it looked like the weather got worse every minute. But about noon the boys began to come in with the strange report that in spite of the rain the people were standing in line to vote. People were voting who never had voted before. Old ladies afraid of a draft waited in the sleet. I knew that meant something but I wasn't sure. Oh, well, to make a long story short the unknown, ordinary folks stood in line in the rain to vote 2 to 1 for TVA power."

But Chattanooga had not begun to receive the power in 1937. The courts still held the complicated case. The Tennessee Electric Power Company was still running full page advertisements in protest against unfair governmental competition. The new Chattanooga *Free Press,* founded by a grocer in intellectual agreement with the utilities, was still publishing too. Yet if Chattanooga seemed a long way from TVA power, something had happened to power rates not only in Chattanooga but in all the country round. At the beginning of 1934 when TVA was just coming into being the rates of the Tennessee Electric Power Company in Chattanooga were slightly below the average of the rates in the country as a whole. The United States average was 5.49 cents; in Chattanooga it was 5.29 cents. In the three years following rates throughout the United States were reduced 14 per cent. In the Tennessee Valley they were reduced in the neighborhood of 35 per cent. In the area served by the Tennessee Electric Power Company they were reduced 46 per cent. And in Chattanooga, they were reduced 60 per cent. More important, perhaps, as the people are concerned, while average residential consumption in the same period increased from 604 to 725 kilowatt hours per year in the United States as a whole, in Chattanooga the average residential customer increased his consumption from 721 to 1338 kilowatt hours per year. (Friends of the power companies suggest that these figures fail to show that there was already a descent in power rates in progress before TVA began.)

Even these Chattanooga figures are still behind the reductions in rates and the increases in consumption in such towns as Athens and Tupelo where the so-called TVA rates are in effect and over which the TVA propagandists have beat the biggest drums and the utility propagandists have shouted in most anger. There is no disposition on my part to try to cry the ultimate truth above that clamor. But whatever may be the rate-making methods of TVA and Tupelo, the rates in Tupelo in the same period were reduced 75 per cent to a point at which they were 15 per cent below those of the Tennessee Electric Power Company in Chattanooga and 62 per cent below the average of the country. The consumption of the average residential consumer increased from 105 to 1704 kilowatt hours per year. Indeed, Tupelo has become more famous for its TVA power than it was even when Private John Allen, speaking in Congress in 1901 in favor of the creation of a fish hatchery there, declared that Tupelo was "the only place in the South where we have the same beautiful moons we had before the war." They still shine.

In Tupelo and in Chattanooga there is no doubt that the

96

rates have come down. The figures at least show that. But as one who hates naked statistics I considered that it might be interesting to know also how many pounds George Fort Milton, stripped after tennis, has added to his unperturbed figure since the fight began. Certainly he seems to have lost none. In Chattanooga or Philadelphia or Paris or Washington he holds his cigarette as daintily as ever in his plump hand. He is such an editor as is never chained to his desk, and the power fight has not chained him there. It need not. Cheap power for the South is, as even wise men say in the vernacular of our times, a natural. Not George Fort Milton but Cartter Lupton proves that, even though Mr. Lupton may not want to prove it. The possession of cheap power in the South lies implicit in the teachings of Coca-Cola and Cardui. The South will have and have cheaply some luxury and some escape from pain. It can have them only cheaply. But have them it will and must. And the South has been told eloquently to the creation of faith that cheap power means both. George Fort Milton and David Lilienthal can speed them; but the smartest lawyer seeking the biggest fee cannot delay them long. Mark it down in the Cardui Almanac: The South is tired of the dark.

11

CONVERSATION IN
CHATTANOOGA

IN THE newspaper office they were like twins who nad been separated. The years stood between them—wide and far. But they had not forgotten how to talk.

"Of course, my dear Julian, it may be a lie but I can't get it out of my head. I left the South a long time ago but now I'm getting older and this sort of thing pulls me back, sick and fearful, but it pulls me back. This man Caldwell wrote that he had seen two little white children on the floor of a Georgia cabin being suckled by a bitch. My doctor friends tell me that it is quite out of the question, that there is something in a dog's milk that is emetic to the human system. Maybe so. But I keep thinking about Romulus and Remus. And anyhow I know there are conditions bad enough among our tenant farmers and I want to help do something about it."

"Hump, you've been away too long and you've read too much. Certainly conditions are bad. They always have been. They need to be improved—need it like the devil. But Romulus and Remus! I suppose you think that those children will have to become Governors of Georgia. Hell, Ed, you can't wipe every nose in Dixie. There is nothing new about these people being poor. My God, weren't you a reporter on *The Constitution* back in 1900? Couldn't you see? The picture is not any darker. What you need is a drink."

"It's entirely possible that you're right. I may need a drink.

Sometimes, indeed, I feel as if I always need a drink nowadays whenever I'm south of the Potomac, but that doesn't answer my questions, it won't solve these problems, it won't cure this poverty."

"Ed, do you remember once when we were kids and I was city editor on *The Constitution* and Queen Victoria was sick and some paper out in Alabama asked me to protect them on the old lady but to please go light on telegraph tolls? So each night I'd wire them, 'Better,' 'Worse,' 'Same.' Then I was off the night she died and you sent 'em a telegram: 'Victoria, Queen of the United Kingdom of Great Britain and Ireland and Empress of India, died today.' I was back when that editor's letter came. He wanted to let us know in a nice way that he knew who Victoria was without having to pay tolls on her title. My, my! He talked worse about your telegram than you do about the status of tenant farmers. He had real feeling in the matter. There's nothing new about being poor."

"Bless my soul, Julian, I know that. Wasn't I poor? Weren't we all? But it's this spreading poverty that disturbs me. I knew there were poor whites but not people like these sharecroppers and more and more people in the South going down to sharecropping all the time. And there's a terrible spiritual sharecropping, too."

"Do you remember the story, Ed—an old story—about the fellow that went by a cabin in the evening and saw a lively dog chasing in a fine looking cow? He was hungry so he asked the old man on the porch for a glass of milk. The old man didn't move a muscle but he hollered to the old woman. She gave our friend a glass of milk. He came by the same house a year later and, remembering how good the milk was, asked for another glass. The old man sat exactly where he had left him twelve months before. 'No milk,' he said without stirring. 'The dog died.' "

99

"That's not very funny. You'll be telling me next about the tenant family so lazy they burned the porch railing, when there was wood to be had for the cutting thirty yards away."

"Porch railing, the devil! I've known 'em to burn up piece by piece the same house they were keeping warm in till they were all but sitting by the naked chimney in the field."

"Of course, there are people like that. There are people like that everywhere but they are bound to be exceptions among the hardy, native people of the South."

"I'm glad to hear you say that. I thought you might have got the idea that poor folks and degenerate folks were strictly limited to the South."

"What do you think I am? I'm a Southerner."

"Well, to be a Southerner you've got to be born here, but being born here isn't enough."

"Who could ask for more?"

"You see—you see! You've lost it. No true, uninterrupted Southerner could ask a facetious, sarcastic question like that over a serious matter like a Southern birth. I'm surprised at you, Ed. But come on, I'm going to give you that drink for therapeutic purposes. But I might as well be honest with you: You've been gone so long and you talk so scandalized that you sound almost like an abolitionist to me."

12

BY WAY OF SCOTTSBORO

I saw him standing in the dust of Governor Bibb Graves' road with a brown hand up for a ride. It was not a very commanding hand. In all his years I am sure there never has been any quality of command anywhere in Joe Poe. But in the Alabama dust, white as the jumpers and breeches of the convicts who under guns spread the crushed stone which made it, Joe looked too pitiful to be left standing. And he scampered like an old, lame chipmunk to catch up when I stopped for him. Altogether he looked a great deal like a chipmunk. His clothes were brown from a peaked hat to battered shoes. He carried a brown pasteboard box, bound up with twine, which held the obvious all that he had collected in his living. His skin was brown as old leaves and his eyes were dark like a small beast's eyes, bright and ready for fear. He climbed in smelling like the earth—he had been all night and the day before on the road from Chattanooga which I had already covered since breakfast that morning. He had gotten tired of staying in Chattanooga. The relief didn't give you anything but some flour and a few vegetables and this old age pension ain't nothing. So he was on his way to Birmingham and there he hoped he could get a job again in a cotton mill.

He was not clear about the pension. He was a Tennessee man but he had lived in Alabama and Georgia, in North Carolina and South Carolina, too, and there was not anybody to swear how old he was. They wanted the doctor to swear and all his friends. But they didn't know. All his folks were dead, mother and father, and sisters and brothers. He had never married: "I found out too much about women working with them there in the mill. Why, man, sometimes they'd go out with you like they was single and we'd come to their husbands in the street and they'd laugh and laugh. Lor', I wouldn't marry 'em. Not I. I found out too much about them."

Joe snickered over the scraps of pleasant memory. And out of his snickering laughter grew the whole picture of lusty women long ago in the dusty mill town street, flaunting their bodies to a little fellow too timid to take them. Probably the roundest and whitest and merriest of them are dead. Time and Death make some strange choices. But Joe now shook his head.

"Nobody wants old hands in the mills."

Of course, he was right. He knew as well as I did that there was not going to be any job for him in Birmingham. But I could feel without his telling how tired he was of the same scolding from the same social workers in Chattanooga. He had to be moving and seeking. And it was sad to be seeking so old because he had gotten into cotton mill work in the first place as a vocational adjustment made without pleasure for purposes of security. (The sociologists have us all talking their ugly language.)

"I was in the livery stable business." He did not suggest, nor did I take his phrase to mean, that he possessed many horses and carriages for rent to a numerous clientele. In some livery stable in Lindale, Georgia, Joe had had such an obscure job about horses as he had learned on his father's little lost Tennessee farm long ago. But 25 years ago even in Lindale, Georgia, Joe suggested the livery stable had begun to feel the pressure of the garage. The horse in the town was already doomed by the car.

"There was a fellow," said Joe, "a friend of mine who was the foreman in the cotton mill, and he kept telling me to come down—he'd give me a job. And then he came for me. But I was afraid of the noise of the machines. I didn't like it. And each time I went away. But at last one day he pulled me in and gave me a pair of brooms and I went to work. I worked, too, in Columbus, Georgia, and Gastonia, North Carolina, but I'm a Tennessee man. I worked up to be second hand in the mill, but I didn't like it."

"What's that?" I asked.

Joe looked mildly at my amazing ignorance. "I had to go over the cloth other folks made and find things wrong with it. But the other hands were always quarreling when I found anything wrong with their cloth. So I told the foreman I'd rather not have the money. Those hands were always fussin'. Some of 'em were real rough. I never did like it."

He looked suddenly and foolishly hopeful.

"Maybe I'll get a job in Birmingham. Nobody knows me where I was born. This relief ain't nothing and they want you to bring everybody in Alabama and Tennessee to swear for you about that pension and then it ain't nothin' when you git it. But it's funny: I can't prove I'm old enough and then they all say I'm too old."

I thought about Joe for a long time after I had left him with 50 cents which he took, pointing out with veracious insistence that he had not asked for it. I decided that Joe proved nothing. The only remarkable thing about him was his survival. He was in a predatory world, a little one born to be eaten by big ones. Perhaps he was not even worth the eating. But Joe is not important. Along some country road, up some Birmingham alley he is scampering like a lame chipmunk about the business of survival. Perhaps he has ceased to survive. Men may have buried him at the corner of some Alabama cotton field. Or he may be somewhere in a potter's field, if they have one in Birmingham. Wherever, the earth will take him like leaf mold. Maybe even medical students somewhere—but what a poor little old body Joe had to offer science. Only a God who watches sparrows could be interested in Joe. He knows where he is.

Old Joe had talked while we moved between the Tennessee River and the little green mountains on the way to Birmingham for him, on the way to Florence for me. He got out at Scottsboro where the road turns south. I got out there, too, to look at the little town that has grown so big in the world's vocabulary since March 25, 1931, when the arrest of nine young Negroes for the rape of two white women in a moving gondola car began making little Scottsboro a prodigious, ugly name. Scottsboro was an accident: Paint Rock where the Negroes were arrested is no more than a wide place in the road. It sits on the Southern Railroad at the tip of the Cumberland Plateau, just inside Jackson County of which Scottsboro is the county seat. Had that train, freighted with its famous crime, gone a few miles further the Negroes and the women in the moving gondola cars would have been taken in Madison County. And the whole world might have echoed to the cry against injustice threatening the Huntsville Boys. Scottsboro would have remained the little, quiet, sprawling country town that it is about a huge, ill-kept but not unpleasant Courthouse Square. And Scottsboro would prefer that. When I saw it a whole fleet of school buses was parked about the square. Stores surround it. For Coca-Cola and talk I went into the store of M. A. Brewster & Company, delicatessen and grocer. A pleasant man, such a man as might have been found in such a little grocery as his from Alabama to Maine, Mr. Brewster shook his head over the notoriety which had come to his town. Scottsboro sits in an agricultural country and farmers are not rich. The TVA has given work to many people and Scottsboro's merchants wonder what people will do when the dams are complete and the forestry and erosion work reduced to lower levels of employment.

A woman stuck her head in at the door.

"Excuse me, Mr. Brewster, have you got any cabbage plants?"

He looked carefully at his own stock.

"No ma'am, but I got some mighty nice tomato plants."

"I guess not today. I wanted cabbages."

Mr. Brewster turned back to me. "Yes, sir, we'll be mighty glad to hear the last of it. But it seems like every place was more stirred up about it than Scottsboro was. It just happened here by accident. And my, my! Cases like that cost money. And this ain't a rich country."

But if not rich, it is a pleasant river-divided countryside, growing more and more cotton but as far north as possible in the Deep South. As Alabama sometimes counts Negroes, as in Lowndes County, there are comparatively few in Jackson of which Scottsboro is the county seat. And maybe that helps prove that lynchings are rarer in the true black counties. Dr. Arthur F. Raper (*The Tragedy of Lynching*— Chapel Hill—1933) has shown statistically that Negroes are safer from mob deaths in the old Black Belt, where more than half of the population is Negro, than anywhere else in the South. They are in greatest danger per 10,000 Negro population from mobs in counties where the proportion of Negroes is less than one-fifth, in those counties where Negroes are not permitted "to stick their heads out of the train coaches." Such counties are often also the ones which stuck with the Union in the Civil War. Jackson County has 7.3 per cent Negroes in its population. (New York County, New York, has 12 per cent.) Sprawled on their porches in Scottsboro they seemed entirely unafraid.

But unless we count Joe Poe—and I for one refuse to

count him—I failed to find in the Scottsboro country any white folk who would meet the specification for Southerner in this country presented by Samuel Liebowitz, chief counsel for the Scottsboro Boys on his return to New York from the trial in the spring of 1933. Mr. Liebowitz described the Southerners whose verdict was against his clients as follows: "If you ever saw those creatures, those bigots whose mouths are slits in their faces, whose eyes pop out at you like a frog's, whose chins drip tobacco juice, bewhiskered and filthy, you would not ask how they could do it (convict the Scottsboro Boys). When I got home I felt that I needed a moral, mental and physical bath."

Undoubtedly as well as unfortunately there are some such in the South, and not only in the South. Certainly there are foolish folk in Scottsboro and round about it. They made Alabama's long discomfiture in this case when, despite the National Guard, they forced the court in effect to become the instrument of their anger. I rode on to Paint Rock where that anger began. In the shimmering sunlight over the road and the railroad station it was hard to conjure up the excitement which must have attended the taking of the nine Negro boys and the two slightly soiled representatives of Southern womanhood from the train. I found nobody in Paint Rock who would admit remembering that exciting afternoon in 1931. Instead I found that like rings which run from a rock flung into a pond the water grows slick calm again at the center while the rings go on forever.

In the perfect quietness at Paint Rock Mr. Freeman was sleeping on a bench before a filling station where I stopped with my curiosity. He woke up to ask a ride and got it. I suspect that Mr. Freeman and Joe Poe are about the same age. But only their ages would be alike. This Tennessee Valley was a road to Joe; it was a happy land to Mr. Freeman. He talked like a bird steadily singing.

"I see you got a North Carolina license. Well, I was born in South Carolina myself. Right near Greenville. But I was a restless kind of boy and in spite of all my old mother could say I went off. Why, I've been in 30 states and worked in 10. I was a cowboy in Wyoming and I liked it fine. But my brother wrote me my mother was sick so I came on back home. I went up in the mountains and worked at a big saw-mill with my brother. The man that owned it had a daughter that worked in his commissary. I went to board with them and by boarding in a good place I married myself a good home. She's been dead fifteen years. And I lost money when the banks shut down in Huntsville. But me and my children live with my mother-in-law. She's got two fine farms. This is a grand section to live in. You can get a good living here without having to work too hard. My girl's smart and my boy's doing fine. He's on the basketball team at the Huntsville High School."

"Won't he want to go off to 30 states?"

He looked suddenly bereft.

"No! No!" he said insistently. "Boys aren't like that nowadays. He's interested in basketball and things like that. And I don't talk about wandering around him."

We drove on in silence for a little and then he spoke again as if he were convincing his boy.

"This is a fine place to live. You can make a good living without working too hard."

We rode past an Alabama chain gang laboring in a gravel pit beside the road. All the workers were big Negroes in white, white shirt, white breeches, string suspenders. The white dust of the pit rose around them as they swung with a right good will the picks in their hands. There must have been guns but I failed to see any in the hands of the white men.

"Oh, yes," said Mr. Freeman. "They got guns. But the

niggers don't run. They don't treat 'em bad." He looked at them in the half hiding dust benevolently. "Les' they do run."

We rode on through the fertile valley through young cotton and fruit trees and green grass for cattle to Huntsville, where Mr. Freeman on the completion of his journey insisted on showing me in hospitality the really remarkable "big spring" which bubbles out of the hill below the center of this old and thriving valley town. We parted fixed friends and I went on alone, by Athens and Rogersville to TVA's big Wheeler Dam and the construction village beyond where, contrary to Norris, class distinctions are as sharply emphasized as by brick houses and board and paper ones. I turned back across the wide top of Wheeler and then crossed the Tennessee again on Wilson Dam where, in wartime and for purposes of munitions for destruction, this creative valley movement began. Now plants turn out fertilizers and the workers stand by ready to turn again to nitrates and explosives when that next war comes.

Beyond this Wilson Dam lies the town of Muscle Shoals. So close to the planned economy of the Tennessee Valley Authority it sits in a beautiful demonstration of the motives of private profit and the extent of private hope. Here in long unoccupied streets and avenues, which run back between elaborate light standards from the highway, the real estate developer has left his mark. A great city mapped and labeled extends for miles on both side of that water tower bearing the name and address: Howell & Graves, 350 Lexington Avenue, New York City, and on both sides of the Howell and Graves Junior High School. But the streets are empty. Grass grows in undisturbed pasturage in both the business districts and the residential sections. Here is building boom ten years after and it may be building boom a few years before. The road into Florence led through more available real estate (as much even as T. S. Stribling described in *Unfinished Cathedral*) and also over a most precarious wooden bridge across the Tennessee. But on the other side of that bridge, far away from city planning of boomers, as also from that of the social planners, is a pleasant town along a good street which runs wide and straight to the door of a columned mansion.

"Isn't this the town T. S. Stribling wrote about in *The Store* and *The Forge?*" I asked the young filling station keeper.

I had noticed that he put down a book before he came to attend to my car. He was distinctly pleased. "Why, yes," he said, "it is."

"How'd the people like them?" I asked, remembering how the Asheville library had banned the books of its Thomas Wolfe from its shelves.

"Oh, fine. My grandmother says she can remember things just like he writes about in *The Store*."

"Are there any Vaidens in Florence? Are any of the people in the book real people here?"

"No. He used street names and place names. He spoke about Intelligence Row where the lawyers had their offices. But nobody particular is in the book." He brought the book I had seen him put down. "People don't like this one, though."

From the place of the road map which he had in it to mark his reading, he himself liked it well enough to be moving through it. The condition of the book indicated that it had been read many times before. It was Carl Carmer's *Stars Fell on Alabama*.

"Why don't people like that?"

He seemed suddenly puzzled as if he had never faced that question before. Then he turned the pages to the famous anecdote about the ante-bellum Negro stud who expressed the opinion that a hundred mile trip to a plantation where there were a hundred Negresses was a long way to go for a couple of days' work.

All of us, the filling station keeper, a friend of his who had been sharing the sound of his radio, and I, read the story again in the much-thumbed book.

"Why don't they like that?"

"I don't know," he said. He grinned. "They don't like it."

"I think it's funny," said his friend without showing any sign of amusement. "Reminds me of another story I heard. There was a planter down near Butler. That's down in the southern part of the State. And this planter was saving a little nigra girl for himself so he made her wear a belt with a lock on it to keep the other niggers off. The old man kept the key in his pocket. Did you ever hear anything like that?"

"Yes," I said. But I thought long ago and far away, not in the twentieth century but the fourteenth, not in Alabama but Navarre. Butler was south but my road ran north to Nashville where Agrarian gentlemen, with perhaps no less difficulty, would keep the South faithful to a very precious past.

13

NIGHT IN NASHVILLE

SOMEWHERE in some one of his essays John Crowe Ransom has called attention to the coincidence that in the same Nashville in which the Agrarians shyly grew in cloister to a legend of nostalgia for the past, the South's biggest and most high-geared promoters, Senator Luke Lea, the politician-publisher, and Rogers Clarke Caldwell, the banker-promoter, also roared to power and tumbled to prostration. One thing I like about my South is this very pregnancy with paradoxes. There was another paradox even in the way I came. Between wide meadow and white fence the Nashville Road ran across the Dimple of the Universe. In Knoxville old man Claggett, then of *The Knoxville Journal,* had told me about that Dimple, rich blue grass land above phosphate rock within a circle of barren hills. He had been born there, but on the Rim. He had left the land for the journalism that had carried him through Lea-Caldwell deflation to the moment when he talked before his piled roll top desk. There he had told me that the trouble with the South was that Southern people hated the land. And across the very earth which he had left in demonstration of that lack of affinity, I rode to meet Donald Davidson who knows passionately that the only hope of the South is to seek and hold to old patterns of man and earth together.

It is hard to see how a man could fail to love the earth in this green Tennessee country. Certainly I felt an injury myself in the manner in which the land has been opened to take out the phosphate rock for sale and in the diggings left like uncovered empty wounds. That is probably sentimentality and the sale of the phosphate rock for fertilizer is as much the proper mining of mineral of this country as gold is of California. People need money here as elsewhere. Even in the Dimple a few years ago they had a hard time. "A mighty hard time we had," said the two boys, lively twelve year olders and sons of a commissary manager and a junk dealer. They rode with me from Mt. Pleasant to Columbia which is prepared to admit that it is home of the mule as Lexington, Kentucky, with the same kind of grass is home of the race horse. Beside the road men were drying the newly dug phosphate rock. The boys knew all about it and undertook to explain to me the intricate processes of digging, drying, grading and packing. One got out of the car and ran to a smoking pile. He came racing back with an especially fine piece given him by the man in charge.

"He thought maybe you were a buyer," he said. "I didn't tell him any better."

We rode on together and I learned that even so far inland the junk business had greatly improved since rearming nations began the search for scrap iron. But for a while the junk business had been worse than the phosphate business. There was an immediate difference of opinion about that. Well, both had been bad, very bad, and both were better, some better. They knew their world and its troubles and they were undisturbed. I left them like old friends and I wished later that Donald Davidson and I could have felt just a little more of the same certainty in the understanding of our world in the long talk we had that night.

I came to Nashville at a bad time. The iris gardens were blooming and ladies of Tennessee had gathered to see them. The Legislature was in session and the legislative emissaries of Boss Crump of Memphis were fighting to make Tennessee wet against the stern, religious hill folk who wanted to keep it dry. The bankers of Tennessee, or some of them, had picked that time, too, to meet in Nashville and compete with legislators, lobbyists and ladies for hotel accommodations. Finally, Donald Davidson was engaged with other professors at Vanderbilt in giving oral examinations for graduate degrees. After it had all worked itself out, as it did, and Davidson and I sat talking together, I wondered if all the difficulty were not proper and symbolic. I had come to the poet-voice of the Southern Agrarian through a South noisy with people and their demands, crowded with problem and packed with bankers, who did not understand ladies, and ladies, who did not understand bankers, and legislators, with a few drinks aboard, who did not give much of a damn about any of them. All were far away from the coughing Jewish salesman whose room connected also with the bath room where the clerk let me wash before he found me a place to sleep. The salesman was so profusely polite in leaving the bath room to me. And I suspect he was dying slowly and secretly while he traveled. Certainly his coughing in the quietness of his room seemed to make the hotel lobby louder than ever.

The distance from the lobby of the Andrew Jackson Hotel to Davidson's book-lined study at Vanderbilt is all the way from one world to another. And the slim, soft-spoken Vanderbilt professor seemed miles away from the understanding of the noisy Tennesseans in the hotel. There is a gap there deep and wide. Since he and Ransom and the others first began to put their thoughts and their poems together in the little magazine, *The Fugitive,* they have more often seemed to me to be cut off by lack of understanding than injured by opposition.

"I have always been powerfully amused," said Davidson, "at the picture of the typical 'Agrarian' as a kind of lily-fingered aristocrat or secluded academician yearning romantically for some sort of moonlight-and-roses old plantation life."

But he seemed that night not so much amused as disturbed and puzzled.

"The Nashville Agrarians," he went on, "are not that sort. They are a hard people, who have or have had calloused palms and soles, and who in their voracity after true gospel have ranged from Homer to Sophocles, in college days, to sociology, political science, economics, physiography, and history of all schools in later times."

He was, of course, right. But I could not escape the feeling that Davidson and the others felt a sense of personal defeat not in their failure to impose an agrarian way of living on the South but in the failure to make even contact with the imponderable mass of Southern thinking and acting. I wondered if the very ones, who recognized in wisdom the necessity of renewed Southern contact with the earth in terms of older Southern patterns of living on the land, had not themselves somehow in the schools lost contact with the folk of the Southern earth. People who range from Sophocles to sociology sometimes lose their way in the brush on the farm.

That seemed improbable. Davidson is fairly typical of the group. His people are mostly country folks, who go back to pioneer times in Tennessee and have fought in most of the wars from Andrew Jackson's time on down. Plain people, too, not possessing great mansion or wide pasture but part of the true tradition of the South.

"I believe," he told me, "that I know about as well as anybody—and first hand too—both the spare poverty and the eternal good-natured hopefulness of the rural South; and since I went to war in Europe and then went into college teaching I have learned a good deal about cities and towns and people in the United States east of the Mississippi. I went away to a boy's boarding school when I was twelve years old. I had my first job shortly after. I began to teach at the age of 17. I have done all kinds of work, manual and mental. I do not have a Ph.D. degree and never will have."

But he has written poem and book which is more than most of the manufactured Ph.D.'s have done. Perhaps the verse was too dazzling for literal minds. The South thought, even other intellectuals thought—or pretended to think— that the poetic-professorial gentlemen of Vanderbilt urged a retreat in force to the Old South. Some saw in it the spinning wheel but not the nakedness of Gandhi—rather more clothes —velvet and laces, roses and the sword. Some even suggested, undoubtedly facetiously, that the Agrarians proposed the denial of bathtubs to the Southern rural population (academic surely that!); and, though John Crowe Ransom in equally facetious answer has formally conceded bathtubs, such misunderstandings or statements in satire remain. For the Agrarians were easy to satirize. They did seem a little like a quaint and quixotic group of gentlemen singing down from the ivory tower when in pre-1929 days they began to question the noisy virtues of a surging South. Lea and Caldwell's empire seemed eternal by their little essays, their gentle verses. Furthermore, they not only antagonized protagonists of industrialism in the South, which in its grimier aspects they rejected entire; they also antagonized important "Liberal" Southern writers by declaring that their work was "palpably tinged with latter-day abolitionism" and that they had become spiritual companions of Harriet Beecher Stowe.

So a good deal of laughter has been expended on the Agrarians. More I think than was ever deserved. Because surely sensible Southerners know that, if the South could not go bodily back beyond the Sixties, neither did the South need, in the alteration from the old plantation system to the new factory system, to swallow without smelling all of the aspects of industrialism. Possibly the high holding of the

Southern way of life against the prevailing American way did warn and perhaps did half halt the South as it moved before the pressure of the promoters toward the more violent aspects of ways of living alien to the patterns of the Southern past and, in truth, to the deepest preferences of the Southern present.

But, of course, the Agrarians never proposed any bodily return of this South to the Sixties. Such a proposal, however, would have sounded a good deal more fantastic than in fact it would have been. This present South of a few rich and many poor white people beside a vast black poverty is no remarkable alteration from the South which went to war because Lincoln was elected. In that pre-Civil War South, out of 8,000,000 white folks, a liberal estimate would give to the slave-owning white families a membership of about 1,600,000. Wade Hampton of old South Carolina may have owned 3,000 slaves; if so he was as rare as Cartter Lupton of modern Tennessee.

But my mind runs after the ghosts of the rabbits of the past. As we sat in Davidson's spare living room to which we had driven from his crowded little office-library in the classroom building on the campus, he seemed as he talked to be a very sad man. Indeed, despite the infusion of new bubbling intellectual blood and the transfer of emphasis from a Southern way of life shaped after a satisfactory past to a new faith in the virtuousness of Littleness in industry as in agriculture in this mass production present, I felt on that Nashville night that the Agrarian group was one overcome with a sense of lostness. Perhaps that was not strange in a South turning back to the seeking of more and more industry, any kind of industry. Even little towns not far from Nashville were bonding themselves to build little factories for foreign promoters who would pay sweaty wages. The eagerness for industry had been

heightened certainly, despite the Agrarians. Or maybe the
Agrarians had never been heard.

How should the Southern people listen? By the thousand
they are careless between the Southern way of the Agrarians
and the American way—so-called—of the industrialists. They
move only instinctively to eat. And too often do not. Perhaps
it all goes back to cotton picking but, whatever the cause, the
South has produced large families for larger population
though the land was scarcely able to support those already on
it. The children continue to come: the youths continue to
press on the towns from the often impossible land and beyond the towns upon the North and West. In 1930 the South
had sent 3,500,000 people to other regions. And now in other
regions the unemployed are still being counted and fed. No
Southerners are needed. And, as Robin Hood has shown
(*Industrial Social Security in the South*—Chapel Hill—1936),
if the entire cotton textile industry of the nation, on the basis
of 1929 employment, were concentrated in the South, only
some 200,000 additional jobs would be opened in a section
from which more than this number have annually departed
in the past in order to find work and food. For most of the
Southerners there is no such free choice, as David Lilienthal
demands, between Southern way and alien way—earth and
industry. They must take what they can get.

Below industrialists and professors, the man or the woman
in the South is eager for any work along any way. And not
only is eagerness for industry growing like the roar of a train
above the well-modulated Agrarian voice. I did not know
that night. Davidson did not speak of it. But I learned later
that the Agrarians, who—even if mistaken—seem to me to
have done more to give Nashville place in the thinking South
than any others there, are no longer in good odor at Vanderbilt. A row over issues of academic reform was probably stir-

ring behind the faces of the professors even when I was there. John Crowe Ransom then stood with some of the younger members of the faculty in the difference of opinion with the administration. And so, later, when Ransom got an offer, in some respects appealing, from Kenyon College in Ohio, nothing was done to retain his services at Vanderbilt. His departure left on that campus only a few of those twelve who wrote the thesis of their revolt against the increasing, careless industrialism of the South and the growing Yankeefication of the Southern life and mind in *I'll Take My Stand* (1930—Harper's). So far as Nashville and Vanderbilt are concerned the Agrarians are gone. Perhaps neither cares. Nashville continues to contain a copy of the Parthenon as testimony to its culture. But the dispersal of the Agrarians is complete though some eighteen Americans (some the same) succeeded the twelve Southerners in complaint against the mass production industrialism of our times. (*Who Owns America?*—Edited by Herbert Agar and Allen Tate—Houghton, Mifflin—1936.) They speak a little more loudly but I am not at all sure that they will be heard any better in the South.

Davidson and I talked a long time not only about the Agrarians but also about the complex present South around their traditional thinking. While we talked it rained a little, sharp against the window panes. The noise called me back to time. Between rains he drove me to the hotel. I remember I spoke of Colonel Luke Lea whose great charm I had felt when he was at the bottom of his fall.

"I always think of Colonel Lea with appreciation," Davidson said. "I don't know anything about his business methods but he got me to edit a book page for his papers and he paid me generously—very generously." He paused looking far beyond his wheel. "That was a long time ago."

The lights shone on the late streets. We crossed an iron bridge. Then we came faster than I expected through the brighter section of town to the incandescent island of bright light about the door of the crowded hotel. I stood in that light a little while, watching Davidson's red tail light disappear down the street, before I turned into the hotel. Then I went up to sleep in a bed set up in great loneliness in an enormous sample room. Outside the window across the open square was the capitol and while I looked on it the rain fell between it and me. Poets and policemen were getting wet outside I thought, philosophers and industrialists. The just and the unjust alike. And the people had no more chance than the rain to choose between them.

14

FESTIVAL IN MEMPHIS

THE way I found to the East Arkansas tenant problem was
up an ill-lit stair out at the straggling end of Broad Avenue
in Memphis to a dark hall where galvanized iron washtubs
were catching the drip of rain creeping through a leaky roof.
Dayton Moore, United Press correspondent whose home was
out in Arkansas near the plantations where organized sharecroppers had struck at cotton picking time, showed me the
way. Without him I should never have found the people I
wanted to see. We moved in his car and by his watch through
a rainy Memphis at Cotton Festival time. Certainly I should
never have discovered the way alone in that gray rain. But
even he was lost in the dark hall under the leaky roof. A
dirty child on the shadowed stair was solemnly ignorant and
a slatternly young woman peered from a doorway as if she
thought we might be seeking her instead of J. R. Butler,
president of the Southern Tenant Farmers' Union. She had
never heard of him, she said when we asked, nor any union.
So down the stairs Moore and I went. But in both the Easy
Way Grocery and the M & C Market they were sure that the
office was upstairs. The young woman coming down laughed
at us. And this time beyond the second tub on the damp
floor we found on a door crudely scrawled: OFFICE OF
S.T.F.U. While we looked at the sign Butler himself opened
the door and let light into the dark hall.

In the doorway with a single unshaded globe dangling
from the ceiling behind him he looked even taller than he is.

His wiry blond hair—true hill billy hair—stuck out in every uncombed direction. As he moved back into the room shaking hands and giving us chairs he was steadily talkative. He sat down beyond another tub into which water from another leak fell. Plup-plup, it dripped. But he disregarded it. Gradually as he talked he gave me the impression not only of having read Marxian books full of impressive words and phrases but also that he might have seen something of a wider world than the river bottoms and half-hearted hills of Arkansas and Tennessee—perhaps as a soldier or sailor. I think I got that feeling from both his cleanliness and his eyes. President of the organized tenant farmers, he said he had never been a tenant himself. Later in the Delta I was to hear landlords say, laughing, that he was a filling station helper in the same little town of Tyronza where H. L. Mitchell, his associate and secretary and treasurer of the union, was "a pants presser." Actually Mitchell ran a small dry cleaning establishment and Butler said of himself, "I was a teacher by profession." He was born on a farm in the Ozarks as the son of a hill billy father who was not a sharecropper but a renter (a decided step higher in the social and economic scale. A renter is what the term implies but most of those involved in the East Arkansas hunger, organization and conflict were sharecroppers of the lowest grade who contribute little more than their own and their families' labor to the growing of the cotton). In 1907 Butler became a Socialist in a local near a now lost community named Davenport in White county, which is nearer the Ozarks than the river. Norman Thomas was a theological student then. He had never heard of Butler, nor Butler of him. But Butler's Socialism was entirely philosophical and conversational till they met. The hill billy had risen from sawmill helper to "teacher by profession" when in 1934 with Mitchell and the blessing of Mr. Thomas, he formed the Southern Tenant Farmers' Union. He told me about it as if he had told it many times before, never wearying.

"I don't know how much psychology you've studied," he said suddenly. He looked doubtfully at Moore and even more doubtfully, I thought, at me. "But psychology teaches that people begin to feel that they own what they've been permitted to use. Arkansas planters, permitted to use tenants like they pleased, began to think they belonged to them. They did for a fact."

Beyond Butler sat a plump and phlegmatic young girl of the same coloring as himself. Afterwards he introduced her as his niece. She had stared at us when we first came in but now she went on typing while Butler talked as if she had heard everything he said many times before.

"You go out there," Butler went on, "and you'll see men and women living in homes that ain't fit for cattle. They are cheated by the planters, forced to pay high interest for credit, made to buy at the commissary, and the government shows that the average family out there, even with all the children working, makes only from $70 to $213 a year. Matter of fact that's more than most of 'em get. Why, the sharecroppers had no way out but to organize."

Plup-plup-plup: the water fell into the tub. And another woman in the next room made other little noises as if she wanted to enter the conversation but only dared punctuate it with the tap of her heels, the shutting of cupboard doors and the putting down of piles of books on tables. Butler paid no more attention to the noises than to the dropping water before him or the typing behind him. Dayton Moore looked at his watch.

"About a year after some dozen or so of us organized the union over in Arkansas, the plantation owners began a campaign against us. Right in the middle of the winter about 200 families were given eviction notices. Some of them were put right out on the road. And it gets cold in Arkansas, wet and cold. They passed around blacklists and folks were driven off government farms on account of union membership. The planters and their riding bosses raided our meetings and beat up our members. Some of our people were thrown in jail. Masked men killed some. Ole Governor Futrell wouldn't protect our meetings but he sent in both State Rangers and National Guardsmen when the planters asked for them. Oh, that's not half. The sharecroppers and those who befriend him are the victims of the lowest forms of brutality."

He sat back solemnly then in his chair and regarded me across the drip tub. It was my turn to say anything I had to say or ask anything I wanted to know. He was waiting.

I asked him: "And what have you accomplished?"

The girl from the next room came to stand in the door and hear his answer. I was surprised. She seemed to belong to a different race from Butler and his niece. She looked like the girls I had expected to find in the court of the Cotton Festival. Butler drew himself up for an utterance.

"We've accomplished this at least." He paused for dramatic effect. "Tenants are able to hold their heads a little higher and look you in the eye a little straighter."

I answered as solemnly as he spoke, "That's a great deal." But I considered that they were probably slowly starving still. Organization had not interrupted that.

Dayton frowned at his watch again. "It's time for us to go," he said.

The girl in the doorway smiled her approval of Butler's declaration. And Butler, observing her, introduced us to both her and his niece. She was Evelyn Smith, young New Orleans Socialist who had come up the river as a volunteer stenographer for the union. She looked less like the conventional intervening idealist than anyone I ever saw. And Smith seemed a poor name for one so little, dark and gay-eyed from New Orleans. She deserved to wear one of the lovely old names from the Vieux Carré. And certainly she seemed younger and gayer than most of those girls who that day in Memphis were having fun despite the rain in the river town's annual Cotton Festival.

I asked Evelyn Smith, "And do you think there's any chance for these tenants?"

"I know," she cried against my questioning. "Of course. I've just been down to the cooperative farm at Hillhouse in Mississippi. You must go there. It's the way. I know it is."

"If we're going to see the Beale Street show—" Dayton began.

"I'm ready."

Evelyn Smith began to pile pamphlets on us. Butler gave me a copy of a speech. His niece presented me with other printed and mimeographed papers. I promised to read them all. On the way down the dark stair and the late afternoon streets Dayton and I agreed that Evelyn Smith was as pretty as she was enthusiastic. A few more such Socialists and no one could tell what might not happen to the always susceptible South.

We rode the long way across town to meet big, merry George Carmack, city editor of *The News-Scimitar* (later editor of *The Knoxville News-Sentinel*), on Beale Street, where the colored half of Memphis and of carnival was to crown its king, a chocolate undertaker, and its queen, a taffy virgin. The rain cleared up soon enough to let them broadcast their coronation before a crowd in Handy Square that included every type of Negro from slim, erect brown men to black and long armed, gangling earth apes. The last seemed lost, staring and uncomprehending on the paved city streets.

The Beale Street Negroes, however, were not any more various in shape or color than the white people in the huge high lobby of the Peabody Hotel. Of course, the South has changed. No more "floating palaces" move on the river past this river town high on the old Chickasaw bluffs. But the people, changed, are still the same. The slim brown planter in his linens, the erect colonel and his erect lady, the soft-handed gambler, the soft-breasted prostitute and the almost indistinguishable young matron, the bony little girls like bright identical beads and each a belle come to carnival, speculators and salesmen, the square-headed overseer (farm manager now), modern counterparts of old-time perfumed dandies and rag-money racketeers, politicians, lumbermen. The whole Delta comes for pleasure from remote plantation and little town. The Peabody has room for them all. There is no sign of revolver or bowie knife, both of which Memphis has known, but swaggering rowdies, quiet in passage, move through the lobby just the same. This world still stirs by the old-time conviction of the Deep South that a gentleman should eat when he is hungry, drink when he is thirsty, dance when he is merry, vote for the candidate he likes best and be ready to knock down anyone who questions his right to any of these privileges. Memphis, corrupt and content, hard-boiled and romantic, sits above a gambling land, the Cotton Kingdom. It is the Paris of the plantation country. Good cotton pickers go to Beale Street when they die. Planters hope to come to the Peabody while still living. Its lobby is the white man's Beale Street. And both have seen strutting and hunger and sometimes both together in the same man. The lobby was crowded at dinner time. But though Dayton had made an engagement for us with Dr. William R. Amberson, of the University of Tennessee, for some time later in the evening, he looked at his watch as if we had plenty of time. We had lost Carmack who had another engagement, but we had come upon two other merry Southerners who had emerged from Mississippi for the festival. The grill room was crowded but the waitress who brought us menus and water was so lovely that when I looked up suddenly and saw her I stared like a man first seeing the moon.

"She's pretty, isn't she?" Van Court, the Mississippi lawyer, smiled. He looked around the low-ceilinged room. "They all are."

"I'm only starting," I said, "but these must be the prettiest girls in the South. If they are not, no wonder the Deep South is romantic. I'll be afraid to go further. I can't see the Tenant Farmers' Union for looking at the pretty girls. They must be a long way apart."

"I'm not so sure that they are," Van Court declared. "I want some of this cold beef. And beer. Now Leonard—" He turned to his companion. "You ought to have a good thick soup."

"To hell with it," said Leonard, who I gathered owned a plantation of impressive dimensions down below Greenville. "Beer and beef is all right. Of course, these girls are a part of the cotton problem. I've seen 'em before. I know. The pretty ones get hungry just as quick as the ugly ones. But I prefer nigger tenants myself."

I looked around the room at the waitresses again. They were as well groomed as the Delta belles in the Cotton Festival. "These aren't country girls?"

"Maybe not," Van Court admitted. "Maybe these came on from the little towns which in turn were filled up by the country girls."

Our waitress came back with the beer.

"Mr. Daniels thinks you're pretty," Leonard told her.

"That's nice. And who ordered beer?"

"Are you a country girl or a town girl?"

"Heber Springs," she said. "I'm not sure which that is."

She was off about her business.

126

"Of course, you know," Leonard explained to me, "that cotton and large families go together. The growers have to have more labor in the spring and the fall and it's fine if it's all in the family. Landlords have preferred that and given better places to bigger families. So, anyhow until recently—you know now they're using more and more tractors, gang plows and multirow planters and cultivators and they're talking about mechanical pickers—the Rust brothers have one here—anyhow until recently big families have seemed an asset to both the tenant and the landlord. But the cotton-picking, cotton-chopping children grew up to be great big hungry, restless boys and girls. And they not only increase the population on the land where they aren't needed—less than ever now—but push on through the little towns to the big towns and to the North."

"Like lemmings," Van Court said, grimacing.

"Exactly," Leonard agreed. "God knows what's going to happen to 'em. Of course the boys have always been leaving the farms. Now the girls have begun. That's what shirt factories are for. And that's why wages are low."

At the next table a big man with rolls of fat at the back of his neck was grumbling loudly over the slowness of a slim, sensitive looking girl with pale gold hair.

"It's a quarter of nine," said Moore.

"I saw a sign out in Lepanto the other day," Leonard continued, unconcerned with time, " 'Permanent wave, $2.00.' My sister tells me such a price is improbable, but it's there. I saw it. And two dollars there is a lot more money than two dollars in my sister's pocketbook in Memphis. They all want to be pretty. And I'm for it. God Almighty, how ugly it can be for a girl—or a man either—out there. I don't want to spoil anybody's dinner. But not half the tenant houses have privies. You have to go to the woods.

"Pluh!" He blew out his disgust. "I'd leave, too, even if I

wasn't pushed. Certainly if I was a girl and pretty I'd leave. Some of them go North. The weakest and the dumbest go into the whore houses. That's better than sharecropping in East Arkansas. But the pretty and smart ones get jobs like these. That's fine counting the tips. Only, of course, they're pushing out the colored waiters that used to have all these jobs. God knows what they're doing. Probably walking Beale Street."

"No," Van Court announced, "they're dead. They died even before the Negro people knew it—or the white girls came."

I know I looked puzzled. So did Leonard. "How's that?" I asked.

"The Negro servant we've all heard so much about—you know the kind. You'll find him more often in the whisky advertisements than in the South. Long ago he was a superior member of his race—the house servant class before the War—there wasn't a cornfield nigger in the crowd—and when his sons had a chance to rise they pushed them up from waiters to doctors, from bellboys to dentists. And their places were taken by thicker-skulled and heavier-handed creatures from the fields. And except in rare and sometimes beautiful cases, like our Alonzo, the head waiter upstairs, the old excellent, gracious and intuitively helpful Negro had disappeared from the hotels before the girls began to put on aprons."

Leonard said, "I think Alonzo is kept as an antique. Certainly he is a beautiful example. Maybe he is the reason the change is less here than in some other Southern towns."

"It's almost nine o'clock."

"Well, the little girls came," Van Court added. "And no wonder. But the best waiters were already dying or disappearing when these girls were little tow-heads on a thousand farms, some from the hill country and some from the Delta, even from Crittenden and Mississippi Counties in Arkansas.

And they are dispossessing the increasingly simian waiters."

Leonard passed me the mustard. He gulped his beer.

"I don't like waitresses," he announced, "and particularly I don't like pretty waitresses. I want my attention on my food and my companions, not on the servants. But I accept them. Van Court's right. The Negro is gone forever."

Van Court who had talked the most was devoting himself to his dinner, catching up. Leonard finished the last of his beef and his beer. Once again Dayton Moore was looking at his watch.

"I understand," I told them, "that Tuskegee has gotten the head waiter at the John Marshall Hotel in Richmond to teach the Negroes the almost lost art of waiter."

Leonard leaned back in his chair. "It is lost. And the best thing to teach Negroes now is not the old service trades but philosophy. They've lost the trades and the philosophy may help them while they starve. Go look at them staring through the windows of those stinking eat houses on Beale Street. You can get half a horse there for a nickel. But they're hungry. And God knows how they'll feed." He sucked at his teeth. "I wish our pretty, pretty miss would bring us a menu. I want some dessert. I'm hungry, too."

"My God," Van Court interjected. "Sometimes I think you're the cause of half the Southern malnutrition. You consume the food supply."

"My share," Leonard admitted. "I used to worry about the underfed. But I got to thinking about how much of unoffending beast and pleasant green growing thing even an ordinary eater like myself consumes. Somehow that's more disgusting to me, more terrifying than pellagra."

"Don't be a fool," Van Court begged.

"I'm a philosopher."

"If we're going to see Amberson—" Dayton said.

It was a long, still wet way we went, uncertain where to

turn off the main street in what seemed like a whole city of similar streets, from Van Court and Leonard to Dr. Amberson. When we left them they were going up to dress for the Cotton Festival ball. When we found Amberson, who had argued with Allen Tate on top of Lookout Mountain, he was busy reading some new technical paper in his field of physiology. I had seen his type before in the colleges of the South. He gave me the impression some others I have known have given me: of going native in the South not in moral relaxation but in an overindulgence of moral activity in connection with the vast amount of social uplift that needs to be done. There is so much darkness to light, such a vast hunger to fill. As they ought not to be, the best natives are hardened. The man of energy and good heart can play God. I think that had much to do with the old popularity of the mission field. But the flowering of appreciation softens a man, too, like drink. I think a good physiologist was saved when Dr. Amberson, soon after I was in Memphis, escaped from activity in Socialism back to physiology by way of Woods Hole and the University of Maryland. He laughed when I asked him about the quarrel with Tate in Chattanooga.

"But the New Deal and the Southern Policy Committee are adopting the Agrarian philosophy about the farmers," he said. "Exhibit A so far as the government is concerned is the Dyess Colony out in Mississippi county, Arkansas. The government is following individualism along the lines of 40 acres and a mule. You go look at it. They're afraid of being collective even though the plantation system has always been collective. It's the only system for this wide flat land. But no: out there every farmer has everything on his own little place. They've got bathrooms though the water isn't running and electric wiring but no electricity. That's all right. But they've used enough lumber in giving every colony member his own individual barn to build a barn big enough to take care of half of Arkansas."

He laughed. "You go look at it. And then go down to Hillhouse and see the Delta Cooperative Farm we started there in the winter of 1934–35. Some of us picked up the project and tried to get aid from Rural Resettlement. We didn't get it and in the meantime as a relief measure we pushed ahead with the plans the next year. I am responsible for inviting Sam Franklin to undertake to run it, and he interested Sherwood Eddy who raised the money and publicized the project. They are getting along rather well, with a second farm already under serious consideration. But they need money for that and for equipment. We've got to have it."

He frowned over the problem.

"We can't demonstrate a successful new pattern of life for the agrarian South unless we can get the very latest and best equipment. In the long run we believe that technological efficiency plus cooperative organization will lift the level of farm life far above that possible on one of the primitive homesteads idealized by the Agrarians."

The last sign of rain was gone when Moore and I drove back toward the Peabody.

"It isn't simple," I said. "The tenants are organizing. But plantation and landlord are changing, too. And machine farming and tariffs and subsidies and lost markets and rayon out of pine trees. Pretty little girls coming to town. And the old-fashioned plantation, a profit enterprise. Now the cooperative plantation. And still in the plantation South the free yeoman on the little farm. It isn't simple at all."

Moore demanded, "Who the hell said it was simple?"

I had no answer to that. But, though the rains had hardly dried, the young people of Memphis were dancing in the streets. And all night long it seemed to me the blaring bands of carnival pushed their music to my room. The Cotton Kingdom went on celebrating in its city, louder and merrier. But I wondered if on Beale Street Negroes lost from the Delta were still staring through the glass at the hamburgers.

15

ARKANSAS GENTLEMAN

You ride across the big bridge over the Mississippi to the suburb of West Memphis which is compounded in almost equal parts of roses climbing on roadside fences, liquor stores and filling stations. Then you turn north in the direction of Missouri. Within an easy hour from Memphis you are in that land which Dr. Arthur Morgan helped drain to make a fertile paradise and which Norman Thomas discovered as a hungry hell. I rode in Arkansas thinking about Mr. Thomas who passes through the same country almost every year and every year preaches a sermon about its sadness. Maybe many such are needed. No Socialist, I am one who heartily respects the good intentions of Mr. Thomas. Also in my discovering I generally found the men behind him to be men of good will, too. My quarrel has been that they have sometimes been men who think with their hearts instead of their heads. But often the choice has been between them and men who think with nothing, neither head nor heart, who see without stirring to either an emotion or a thought. The Northeast Arkansas country (and much of the other plantation South) is entitled to both.

Certainly Crittenden and Mississippi Counties, where Mr. Thomas urged the Southern Tenant Farmers' Union into being, are with their 15,638 tenants out of their total of 17,817 farmers fairly representative of the worst tenant farm areas of the South. And in them the oppressed tenant is also the oppressed Negro since 10,000 of these tenants are black men.

But as I rode out, so conveniently after pleasant breakfast in the Peabody, I considered that it was at least a comfortable coincidence that these two counties lie just across the river from Memphis. In Memphis was one (now two) of the crusading Scripps-Howard newspapers, the mid-South bureaus of the United Press and the Associated Press. There, too, were intellectuals who shared Mr. Thomas' sympathies for both the tenants and the Socialist program. Indeed, with only a bridge between them were sad Southern scene and all the machinery for its projection to America.

Unintentionally, perhaps, but effectively nevertheless, the planters cooperated with Mr. Thomas in that projection as in the famous Birdsong incident during his visit of March, 1935. Then, according to the union's chroniclers, thirty to forty armed and drunken planters forced their way into the Negro church at Birdsong where he was to speak.

"Ladies and gentlemen," the Rev. Howard Kester began in introduction of Mr. Thomas.

In chorus the planters interrupted: "There ain't no ladies in the audience and there ain't no gentlemen on the platform."

Mr. Thomas waved a copy of the excellent Bill of Rights of Arkansas at the advancing planters. They disregarded it.

"There ain't goin' to be no speakin' here. We are citizens of this county and we run it to suit ourselves. We don't need no Gawd-damn Yankee Bastard to tell us what to do with our niggers and we want you to know that this is the best Gawd-damn county on earth."

There was no speaking at Birdsong. This version of the incident comes from the book of Mr. Kester, clergyman gently educated to a fury of indignation. To him also belongs this anecdote of the cabins in the cotton: When a New England woman, who had just purchased a plantation, began to furnish her tenants with out-houses, she raised a flood of pro-

tests from her planter neighbors: "You are making our tenants dissatisfied. If you build out-houses, we will have to
build them, too. After all, Miss, all that a sharecropper needs
is a cotton patch and a corn cob."

It is not necessary to believe all the atrocity tales. But certain it is that here so conservative a Southerner as Allen
Tate was made to seem a sansculotte merely for being there
looking as I was looking. Indeed, anyone who as a stranger
has been in one of these small Arkansas-Mississippi towns will
feel the possible crime of his presence. I was put in no jail
but when I rode in the back country I was forever aware of
the arresting eyes. The smaller the town the more searching
the eyes, for no town is so small that it does not muster the
group of white men sitting in idleness as if there were nothing creative to be done. Moving before them is a strange
sensation. You are not exactly stared at. The eyes are seldom
met but your skin seems sensitive to the focus of the eyes
of white men and—more secretly—of Negroes. A woman told
me that in such little towns she always felt naked and hot as
if she were stripped in the sun.

Marked Tree was crowded. It had rained hard the day before and in this low country it is impossible to work after it
rains when the water is high as it then was in spring rise.
Indeed, this land made rich by the river often lies under the
sprawling Mississippi. And in Marked Tree, along the one-
sided business street which parallels the railroad, men stood
about in high boots and a few went so shod with their women
into stores, the windows of which were piled with cheap
merchandise. So cheap. Wealth has been taken out of this
land in both timber and cotton but it has been completely
taken out and away. There are few, if any, big houses and no
evidence of planter grandeur beside the tenant poverty. The
unscreened cabin is everywhere but I saw not one house before which the familiar white columns rose in even the pre-

tense of classic responsibility. I walked by Marked Tree's stores and Marked Tree's eyes. Of course, I thought, if there were rich men living on this land, they would buy in Memphis. But it was impressive how directly the town's merchants made their appeal to poverty with the heavy necessities of living—the three M's, meat, meal and molasses—and, in luxuries, with the rawer, cheaper brands of liquor, the more florid rayons (not all women make their shifts out of flour sacks) and the most sweetly stinking soaps.

The man I wanted to see was not in. So I drove on to Lepanto. Over the railroad, past a sign: "We buy mussels, pearls and slugs," and already I was off the main road in the plantation country. The Delta country is beautiful. Whatever may happen upon it now to human beings the land runs in flat loveliness to the lines of trees left standing for windbreak or for fuel. Such an earth, 40 to 100 feet deep in topsoil left by the river, may, as some men contend, be perfectly suited to machine farming that will dispossess even the tenants unhappy now. Certainly it ought to give men plenty: but it betrays. Everywhere in the South, the poorest men are on the richest land. Without entirely distrusting union propaganda I wondered where on this land would be Brother George Wells who was reported by the Workers Defense League to have eaten the spoiled pig which he found and the dead turtle which he took from a big water snake. The Negroes on the land seemed as same as the unchanging surface of the earth. I did not stir the stupid ignorance or the cackling laughter one of which I knew would be lifted to meet a strange man's prying into their union or their lives. And yet I knew that if I did, the stupidest seeming clod, black as the buckshot earth, would send word about me by the grapevine telegraph that would run ahead of my car to Lepanto, back to Marked Tree, even to Memphis.

Before Lepanto, water was on the road. There was in this

country, reported to belong to the terror, the same sentimental plea to the motorist which I had seen in TVA's town
at the Wheeler Dam: "Drive slowly—We love our children."
And sure enough in the main street beyond was the sign
Leonard had reported, "Permanent Wave—$2.00." I stopped
by the big gin of the Portis family to ask, "Can I drive on
this way to the Dyess Colony?"

A young smiling man in the washed-out khaki which is
almost the white man's uniform in the Mississippi cotton
country shook his head. "Not even with mules. You'll have
to go back by Tyronza. There's a rock road from there."

So I drove back and this time found in Marked Tree the
man I was looking for. The way to the office of C. T. Carpenter, the country lawyer who defended the sharecroppers
in the courthouse, is almost as dark and difficult as that to
the union headquarters in Memphis. I went up the narrow
stair to the unlighted hall that ran the length of the second
floor over a grocery and the street level office of Lawyer J.
G. Waskom. I knocked at the wrong door first and got rum-
bling directions from inside that the door I wanted was half
way up the hall. I found it directly under a bare place in the
ceiling where the plaster had fallen down. But the door
opened pleasantly to light and neatness and beyond his anteroom to Mr. Carpenter, a surprising individual.

I had heard that Carpenter had defended some strikers at
the Singer Sewing Machine plant in Truman and that twenty
years ago when he fought a peonage case he had faced a
planter's gun. And so while respecting his courage in such a
country I had expected to find a somewhat brash rural radical. I was entitled therefore to be surprised. The man I found
was a pleasant country gentleman, an old-fashioned Southern
Democrat but a Franklin Roosevelt Democrat, too, though a
little disturbed over Roosevelt's attitude toward the courts.
He looked like a kindly family physician, not as briskly

scientific as the new graduates but gently wise. He regarded me and my questioning through fairly thick rimless spectacles.

He considered the union and the violence that attended its organization as past. It did not offer cure for the tenant problem. That was a problem too difficult for solution in simple antagonism.

I asked him about his own defense of the sharecroppers. He threw up his hands but I thought without any sign of real regret.

"Oh, it almost ruined me, but now my old clients are coming back."

But he snorted at the suggestion that members of the planter-lawyer-merchant-doctor class of the country who had undertaken to punish him by dropping him as a lawyer, might also have undertaken to ostracize his family socially. Without saying so he suggested that so far as most of the local folk were concerned the idea of the social ostracism of his family by them was a vast foolishness. Mr. Carpenter is a Virginia man whose father was a student of Robert E. Lee at old Washington College in Lexington. Against such a background the planters and lumbermen of East Arkansas are an upstart race on an entirely new land. Of course, it was not pleasant after he had undertaken to defend without fee the civil rights of the sharecroppers and their organizers to see his law practice drop away. But no one can talk to Mr. Carpenter without feeling that his appearance for the tenants, which drove the timid landowners and other property-class-conscious folk away from his office for a while, gave him a chance for bigness and accomplishment which he otherwise could not have had in a life devoted to drawing the wills and deeds of Marked Tree and the country round about.

"There are no aristocrats in East Arkansas," he said. Before I came I had had something of the old patterned idea of the oppressive patrician master and the blameless brutalized slave about this country. Mr. Carpenter erased it. This has been lumber country and cotton growing is a late by-product of the big companies on their cut-over land. The landlords are often absentees or corporations or both. They may be men who came down from the hill country to the new land and became landlords while men like themselves became tenants by the same journey.

"There are no aristocrats in East Arkansas."

I think there is one. Perhaps the German family, which owns most of the land about the town, is only one generation old in wealth and perhaps the founding father came from Iowa as a laborer. Perhaps the big lumber magnet, whose corporation cut the timber from the land round about and now with sharecroppers plants it in cotton, has a daughter who has been queen of the Memphis Cotton Festival. She lives in Memphis and her grandfather was a Yankee who came down after the war. But Mr. Carpenter who came to Arkansas as a school teacher and has remained as a lawyer possesses as few men do in the modern South—or the modern world—the patrician ideal.

He is a country lawyer, not without vanity. Rather his vanity is less shrewdly clothed than would be that of the city corporation lawyer in a five name firm who has never turned his law to anything but profit. Mr. Carpenter is not surrounded by retainers whose service is less to protect him from public intrusion than to impress the public with the god-like quality of the city lawyer's inaccessibility. Mr. Carpenter is frankly proud of his efforts in defense of the civil rights of men in East Arkansas and also of his efforts to find some way to light in the agricultural darkness of the plantation South. He has written about that, studied about it; he plans to study and write more. The drawers of his desk are packed with scrap books and loose clippings about his defense of the unionized tenants and with articles he wrote for the Scripps-Howard papers about tenancy.

Beside him in his office his book case contains not only law books but books also on tenancy and other Southern problems, many of them from the University of North Carolina Press at Chapel Hill.

"Do you know Odum?"

"Yes."

"And Vance?"

"Yes."

"Have you read Raper's *Preface to Peasantry?*"

I nodded.

He turned to his case of books.

"I've got 'em all. That's a great University at Chapel Hill."

Out there in that little half lost Arkansas country town he spoke a little wistfully, I thought. The University of North Carolina to him represents an intellectual ideal. He never saw Lee but the line of his aspiration to integrity goes straight back to his father's teacher. He has never been to Chapel Hill but he finds its Liberal intelligence stimulating to his own.

What a place to find him, I thought, as I looked at the wide one-sided street of Marked Tree again. He is supposed to be in Charleston or Savannah or New Orleans. He might even live in the big house of a plantation between Greenville and Natchez. But who would expect to find the Southern aristocrat up a dark stair and down a dark hall in Marked Tree? But here he was. I know his marks. Not stiff neck and wide acres, but tradition and intelligence and responsibility. My friend, Judge George W. Connor in Raleigh, quoting Maurois on the virtues of English civilization, called them "continuity and flexibility." There the man of the virtues was in East Arkansas, the defender of Negro tenants against rapacious white landlords. And said I to me, "Anyone who is surprised to find the Southern gentleman here about such business does not understand either South or gentleman."

Too little of either remain.

16

REFUGE AND REALITY

FROM Tyronza, where H. L. Mitchell brooded over the fate
of the sharecroppers while he cleaned the clothes of the
planters, a road crosses the railroad and turns toward Dyess
Colony and the big river beyond. Across a land as flat as a
floor, I followed it to Whitton which is no more than a store
and a school and, when I arrived, a road full of children. I
stopped and watched them pass. Frankly, in this tenant
farmer country I looked at the pupils of the country school
for signs of rickets and hookworm and all the other marks
of hunger and disease. But the children with the rickets
must have been kept in. Perhaps the children with hookworm had been too weary to come to school. Those who
trooped past me, boys and girls, were sturdy-looking children, red-cheeked and round-legged. They appeared very
much like the conventional image Longfellow made long
ago of the school children who looked in at the blacksmith's
shop, and like the modern children who go home from
school in Brookline and Bronxville. They were not so well-
dressed. The boys wore blue denim overalls and brogans.
The girls wore well-washed cotton dresses. Indeed, I was as
much impressed by their cleanliness as by their health. I
watched until the last was gone. Then I wondered what could
be wrong with this seeing. Many of these must have been
tenant children since Whitton lies away from any substan-
tial towns in Mississippi County in which 4,612 of the 5,911
white farm operators are tenants. Their apparent well-being

surprised me as no languid poverty could have done. And I rode on to Dyess puzzled about them. I still am puzzled.

Where do they live? Beside the road the houses are those which every year tear Norman Thomas' heart. One and two rooms, they sit on the earth, the color of the earth. Half-naked and pot-bellied pickaninnies play in the dirt before them, careful as if from birth not to trample the little cotton plants which come almost to the door. Occasionally beside a cabin a decrepit automobile sits. I remember one that had three flat tires. But there is hardly ever a tree beside a house. I asked a big boy with an imposing armful of books about the absence of trees around cabins.

He contemplated my outland ignorance. "They'd stunt the cotton," he said.

And so no shade. But the pretty, painted houses of the Dyess Colony beyond the cabins seemed almost designed to emphasize their sunburnt littleness and dusty squalor. Indeed, the last unpainted and unregimented "shotgun" cabins before the colony began were exceptionally tiny and drab as if the government had set them there as measure for its benevolence. Benevolence is there: the houses of Dyess in the Arkansas Delta look like debutantes in the slums.

I crossed the colony line like a man moving across a frontier. Here, says H. C. Baker, secretary and treasurer of the governmental corporation which owns the colony, is to be "a new order of things for those who through no fault of their own found it almost impossible to make their way." Here certainly for them a garden has been cut out of the wilderness. The roads and the drainage ditches run straight and clean through this land which old owners abandoned for its taxes and allowed to grow thick in jungle. Now back from the road in their bright colors sit the pretty houses, designed for the late W. R. Dyess, the Arkansas contractor, mule dealer and dreamer who was Emergency Relief Administrator in this State, by Howard Eichenbaum, young Jewish architect of Little Rock. Behind each house is each house's own barn and chicken house. Each house, indeed, whether it be one of three rooms or five or be surrounded by 20 acres or 40, is an independent seat patterned for that old, almost lost figure on the American land, the independent American farmer. Certainly, as Dr. Amberson had told me in Memphis, they seemed models for the Agrarian ideal. But I doubt whether, all facts considered, the Agrarians would accept them as such.

As we, the well-off in America (a company which includes all those who are accustomed to plumbing, electricity and a little house paint), judge housing for ourselves, these are by no means extravagant dwellings. Certainly the American farmer should be entitled to one bath; to none at Dyess has Mr. Eichenbaum given more. Both the Roosevelt administration and the Agrarians have approved of such rural electrification as is praised and produced by TVA. The wires are in the Dyess houses. And sewerage. There is nothing city folk would call fancy at Dyess. But the 500 houses on the 500 farms come to an average cost per house of $1,885, while the average farm house in Arkansas, owner house and tenant house, has been recently valued at an average of only $391. (And the relief clients who have become the colonists at Dyess were not able even to make a living at the standard of that Arkansas house.)

Between such houses I drove on to the community center, which sits, like the neighborhood business district of a modern real estate development, on "Park Lane Avenue" which runs between trees to the park-plotted banks of the Tyronza River. Before the door of the Community Building the same sort of rubber-booted men as those I had seen on the streets of Marked Tree stood about talking in an idleness enforced by rain and high water. Their eyes followed me through the door of the building. I could feel them on the back of my neck.

Inside of the building, the secretary of the colony-manager was a city type, pretty and young. But she was not entirely helpful. Mr. Dudley had just departed. And, "No," there were none of the farm supervisors about to show me the colony or any of the houses in it. But I could look about. She made it clear that she did not encourage that or forbid. And beginning with the pretty stenographer herself and circling outward beyond the company of the colonists gathered at the door were houses for 40 members of the staff of the colony, experts and officials, doctor and nurse, teacher and engineer. Close about, too, were the community store, library, café, barber shop, hospital, service station, cotton gin, garage, canning factory, ice house, sawmill, seed house, four warehouses, feed mill and—mark undoubtedly of final freedom for the farm woman—a laundry. Beyond them all the pretty houses again. And already when I was there cotton and corn were growing. Cows were being milked and while I wandered about I heard both a hen cackle and a rooster crow.

I stopped beside an old woman walking the colony's road with a tow-headed child. I asked the way which I already knew, and in exchange she asked me the time which probably did not press her.

"You all are fixed up fine here," I observed.

"Oh, yes, sir," she agreed. But she seemed not very enthusiastic about it.

"Don't you like it?"

She smiled half ashamed and showed a wide gap in her upper front teeth.

"It's grand," she said, "and the folks are clever. My son— he's going to make money. But—" She cackled. "I don't count anyhow. I'm just an old woman. But we got a saying here in Arkansas that a hill man won't stay in the bottom and a bottom man won't stay in the hills. I'm a hill man. All my folks have been. And this land's so flat. It's rich all right, I guess, but God knows it's flat. Sometimes I think I'll die lest I see a hill."

She was no longer grinning.

"I was born up by Mountain Home in Baxter County. Have you ever been there? I lived there all my life. It's a long way from here. And I guess I'll never see it again till I die. There are hills there."

She stooped and wiped the nose of the tow-headed child with a fierceness that left it red as a berry.

"Oh, it's grand here," she cried. "And the government's going to give us these places and we're going to grow a lot of cotton besides. It's a heap better to be fed here than hungry in the hills. Even an old fool like me knows that."

She went on up the road then and I watched her until she turned, fiercely pulling the child after her, into the yard of a pretty little house with a diminutive barn behind it and the land beyond it stretching flat and forever. The old lady disturbed me. It was undoubtedly possible, as the colony's Mr. Baker said, that "history is being made within this colony." But Norman Thomas may be nearer right in describing the experiment as "subsidized peasantry." To use simpler language than either of them, it appeared to me as if the late Mr. Dyess (he was killed in an airplane accident in January, 1936), Harry Hopkins, Col. Lawrence Westbrook and others had been merely playing doll house there. As long ago as December, 1936, the Emergency Relief Administration had invested more than three million dollars at Dyess, a sum which included $315,484.40 advanced to the colonists as subsistence. Since the "first thirteen colonists" did not arrive until October, 1934, it seems hardly probable that the full 500 were present for the full two years from then until November, 1936. But, counting all 500 as present all the

146

time, each received subsistence (not including housing and some other important things and services) on the basis of $315.48 a year. That, sadly enough, is more than T. J. Woofter, Jr., in his *Landlord and Tenant on the Cotton Plantation*, published by Harry Hopkins' Works Progress Administration, found was the per family average annual net income of similar folk on the private plantation in the cotton South. Also on the basis of the Dyess investment, the Dyess colonist either stood under a $6,000 debt or has been the recipient of at least a part of that $6,000 as gift.

Certainly I would not have Mr. Hopkins use my taxes or J. P. Morgan's taxes or Oscar Johnston's taxes to keep down the pitifully low annual income of the sharecropper. That is a scandal that does not belong wholly to the South or to the landlord in the South. Certainly that tenant ought to have better housing than he does. But unless we are concerned only with the 500 relief clients who are now colonists, it is hard to see how Dyess contributes anything to the welfare of Arkansas or the South. In Arkansas the Federal Government gave a few families (little more deserving than sweepstake winners) a standard of living which they could not earn money to maintain. Yet certainly the product and scene of that giving makes a pretty show even if its relation to the problem of the cotton land and the cotton cropper is tenuous in the extreme. On the flat earth it reminded me of model town in the rolling hills at Norris. Only Dyess seemed to me both sadder and sillier.

The colony might not have seemed so wonderful to Mrs. Roosevelt, it might not have given the play to Mr. Eichenbaum's imagination, it might not have provided the monument to Mr. Dyess' memory, but if the ERA had been a little less pretentious, a trifle less Utopian, it could have done important things at Dyess. Model things, I fear, but they might have set up a model plantation in the plantation country

147

where uncheated tenants under wise direction might seek a living in relation to the realities of the cotton South. That might have helped all tenants—and landlords, too. It might have proved the possibility or the hopelessness of decent living standards from cotton culture. Or, choosing colonists carefully and lifting their standards slowly, the New Deal might have made at Dyess a body of independent yeomen. But no small Southern farmer is independent under a $6,000 debt, and, if the government should free him from the debt made for him, his security would be a product of benefaction and not of farming. But Dyess—I say it sadly and with the expectation that I shall be answered swiftly and sharply —Dyess seemed to me to be a toytown cut out of the jungle.

More than a little depressed, I rode away from it, away from its erect painted houses to bulging shacks under tottering chimneys. I had to look further, I knew, even for the possibilities of solution of the dark problem of the little man on the land. So far as I could see Dyess means nothing to the South.

II

A bridge had washed out above the spring rise of the river on that other day when I rode south from Memphis over Mississippi's dusty roads. So I was pushed into the back country for a little while before I came back on the main highway and down into the rich Yazoo-Mississippi Delta past Tunica and Clarksdale and Sherard and Greengrove to Hillhouse. I found it a good deal less impressive in appearance than I had expected it to be. Perhaps I had expected another Dyess. Certainly I had seen even sawmill camps more elaborate than the Delta Cooperative Plantation appeared to be. Obviously, it was not designed to contribute to the view. It sits close to the river and close to the line between Bolivar and Coahoma Counties, tied only to the world by dusty road and telephone. No architect laid out its streets or designed its houses. Indeed, at first glance it appears to be as poor as it is hopeful. And I had the feeling that I had come upon a conference of Europeans on a desert island in the South Seas that morning when I came into Sam Franklin's office and found him and A. E. Cox and A. James McDonald in conference over a new type of fence, a single strand of barbed-wire carrying a cattle-disturbing but not cattle-killing charge of electricity. I do not know whether they bought the wire or not. But I do know that all the staff of the cooperative seemed to me like Robinson Crusoes washed up by good will on the Delta of Mississippi where they were applying their city brains and missionary Christian enthusiasm energetically and ingeniously to the hard problems of the isolated land.

Sam Franklin—I suppose it should be the Rev. Sam H. Franklin, Jr.,—is the motive power that has taken some of the most difficult land ever farmed in the Delta and some of the tenants evicted from Arkansas plantations because of union membership and come further than anyone had any right to think toward successful farming. There is undoubtedly a fire in the man. Born in Tennessee at Maryville, he entered the Presbyterian ministry and thence went into the mission field. In Japan he touched the powerful spirit of Toyohiko Kagawa whose Christianity has been concerned with a Japanese worker and peasant whose social and economic insecurity is not greater nor less than that of Franklin's folk at Hillhouse. These white men and black men, I felt after seeing them and him, remain his children while he, by the greatest individual labor, shows the world that they are men who can by their own cooperative efforts create the security and the well-being of all. No wonder his eyes are tired. Slim and booted, he moves about the plantation with jumpy step, patient and persistent, but he has to stay close behind each "member," watching and pushing that the work be done. I remember that we came back from the sawmill by the poultry house where he found that the chickens had not been properly watered. We stopped long enough on the way to see that the water was provided. He had a suggestion, too, to make at the sawmill and at the very sparsely furnished consumer's cooperative.

There are no tenant farmers at Hillhouse. All who might be such are "members," members of both the farm cooperative and the consumer's cooperative which exists across the road in lieu of the ordinary commissary. Out of starvation, or the borders of it, they were set up as such. Each member gets an unceiled two-room house with an unscreened porch and behind it a "modern" fly-proof privy. That is standard equipment. There is no electricity and no plumbing. The water comes from shallow wells. But each member can add to his dwelling as he will at his own expense and with his own time.

The cabins sit in two rows, one on each side of the community building, which contains the library and clinic, nursery and a big room for religious and social gatherings. Here, too, the colony gives to Negro children four months' schooling in addition to the four niggardly months the public schools provide. In one row of cabins live the white members and in the other row the Negro members. On the bank of the Mississippi the directors of the cooperative are almost as sensitive about Jim Crow as it is possible for human to be. Whichever way they move they may bump into their own Christian consciences or the community's dangerous prejudices. They want to take the Christian attitude toward race, but they do not want to complicate the cooperative experiment unduly by unnecessarily alarming Mississippi. The result is a queer compromise. There must always be at least two Negroes on the plantation council of five. The "Mr." and "Mrs." and "Miss" which the South denies to Negroes are studiously applied here. The Negroes and the whites gather together in the community house for the cooperative meeting, but the whites have their social meeting one night and the Negroes theirs the next. The separation of the cabins, Sam Franklin says, was done at the suggestion of the Negroes.

"We are upholding the true Christian attitude toward the races," says Franklin, "but not doing anything foolish."

The economic set-up at Delta seemed to me to be excellent. The cotton plantation has always been a collective and its transfer from cotton capitalism to cotton cooperative is far simpler than a transfer from the collective plantation to the collection of little independent farms as at Dyess. And Hillhouse is besieged by no Agrarian fears as to mass production on the land. John Rust, one of the inventors of the Rust mechanical cotton picker, is a trustee of the farm, and the machine itself has been tried in picking the plantation's cotton. Tractors have been used in clearing the bottom lands. Nothing less would break the buckshot earth. Furthermore, Delta Cooperative Farm offered to its member refugees from Arkansas terrorism no vastly higher standard of living. The standards the members have are within the possibility of men working in cotton fields whether the landlord be a preacher or a profit-seeker.

Franklin left me for luncheon with his associates in the direction of the plantation. After I had washed and wiped on the common towel we sat about a table loaded with a variety of food. The wife of a member cooked well and served it with calm country informality. And over it we talked but nothing we said seemed to me so interesting as the company.

Blaine Treadway, associate director, appeared to have his feet flatter on the buckshot earth than anyone else on the plantation. A delightful person, he is a former Memphis printer. Now he directs men plowing the earth.

A. E. Cox is a Texan and graduate of a theological seminary. A quiet individual, he is more interested in good works than preaching. He heard Sherwood Eddy talk on the Delta Plantation and asked to be allowed to come. I think he keeps the books.

Alice Rex, the plantation's director of religious activities, is a loan to the cooperative by the Episcopal Church League for Industrial Democracy. She is a trifle buxom but young and pretty. She seemed a little startling, nevertheless, as I first saw her coming down the duckboards over the muddy land between the cabins of the members, wearing lounging pajamas of a golden olive color.

It was she who poured the water by the dipperfuls into the basin for me before lunch.

"Will you share our towel?"

I shared, remembering that the Negro laborers at Chickamauga had had individual paper cups in an aseptic age.

Dr. L. Etta Vaughan is a very nice and religious old lady who from California offered her services as physician. Accepted, when she arrived she turned out to be a homeopath. She is nevertheless in charge of the cooperative's clinic in the community building and talks very frankly of the problems.

"Christianity is the whole basis of the cooperative," she says. "Sam Franklin's Christianity, and without him the whole thing would go to pieces."

Mr. McDonald, a Canadian by birth and a wanderer since, is in deep disagreement. Before he became stenographer for the plantation, he was stenographer for the radical, inventive Rust brothers, but before that he was a member of the cooperative plantation at Llanos in Louisiana.

"The one basis of cooperative effort must be economic soundness, and nothing worse can happen to a cooperative than the dominance of one man. I saw that at Llanos down in Louisiana."

Lindsay Hail, the nurse, was not at luncheon. She was born in Japan of missionary parents and her father was killed soon after her birth, during a volcanic eruption. She received her nurse's training at the Massachusetts General Hospital, thorough training, but when she first came to the plantation her nerves almost cracked under attendance upon a member's wife in 14-hour labor. When I was at the plantation, she had gone up to Memphis with two members, Negro man and Negro woman, to whom she was giving special nursing in a Negro hospital under a Negro intern.

Another person, absent from the luncheon but important in the cooperative, is Wilmer Young. A Pennsylvania Quaker and mathematics teacher, he decided at 50 or thereabouts to become a Southern tenant farmer. And he did it. Now a smiling, intelligent city man, he is in charge of the plantation's cooperative vegetable garden and when I saw him he was disturbed by a yellow marking which might have been a disease on a cabbage. His new relationships are not quite made and his old relationships are not quite cut. The people of the lower depths of the Delta who are his fellow members are not quite at ease with him, and his family and their needs (he is accustomed to giving his children special and costly medical treatment if they need it) are not to be quickly reduced to the tenant-member level. Even in Mississippi his daughter wants a bicycle, and the time may come when his boy may want to go to a good Quaker college. Meantime the return to the land and the adoption of the land's poverty is still to some degree subsidized in his case by well-to-do Quakers back in Pennsylvania. Of course, he is no ordinary tenant; he hoes in the cooperative garden with a right good will, but he also thinks as he hoes: How the plantation might have movies, if some philanthropist would give it a projection machine, by hitching it up to the engine of a tractor which would provide the necessary light and power. Franklin and I left him squatting over the disturbing yellow marking on the cabbage leaf. And his intellectual ignorance over that leaf seemed to me then, as it does now, to be the tragic flaw in the Delta Cooperative Plantation.

None of those in the immediate direction of the Delta Cooperative are farmers. Planters who wish the cooperative no good say that the very beginning of the plantation marked it for failure, since the land which Franklin still regards as a bargain, 2,133 acres at $6 an acre, is in fact land so difficult to farm that at least two planters have gone bankrupt trying to cultivate it. That may be planter hope-talking. But it is true that the staff of the plantation is better grounded in social and religious doctrine than in agricultural science. Franklin has a cousin, a professor of agronomy in Georgia, who gives them general advice and helps lay out general policy. The first year a neighboring dirt farmer came three times a week to oversee and advise; the second year his coming was reduced to once a week. That may be all that is necessary. If it is, farming is a good deal easier than it has seemed to me, or Delta Cooperative is luckier than even it has a right to expect.

So far, however, Delta Cooperative claims success on a straight profit basis. From cotton grown and timber cut it already fixes profits for the members, after all costs and a proper payment in interest and amortization of the purchase price, at a figure higher than the average sharecropper was found by Sociologist Woofter to receive. But plantation bookkeeping, as tenants found under grasping landlords, may be a mysterious thing; it may be as mysterious when benevolence is the motive, as when robbery is. It is interesting to observe that one writer (Jonathan Mitchell in *The New Republic*—September 22, 1937) who announced the financial results of the year 1936 at the Delta Cooperative as demonstration of the success of the experiment pointed out that the cooperative paid nothing for the direction of

Sam Franklin, the assistance of Dr. Sherwood Eddy, or the advice of Dr. Amberson. But Franklin's services alone he estimated as worth $25,000. If so, the profit of the cooperative's members is a present from Mr. Franklin, which proves only his Christian benevolence and not the members' cooperative success.

Indeed, it seemed to me, as I rode up the dusty road along the river, so far Delta Cooperative, while a good deal nearer to reality than Dyess Colony, has not even begun to test the cooperative plan. It still hangs dependent upon capitalistic philanthropy and, so long as it does, it does not rest upon the cooperation in brotherhood of the common man. The Southern sharecropper is apt to be the common man at his most ignorant. And worse than ignorant, at his most willingly dependent. Cotton is not the big crop at Delta Cooperative. Cypress timber is not the big crop. The one dependable cash crop is rich Yankees of soft heart most of whom would be outraged at the connotations of Communism but stir in sympathy to the churchly sound of Christian Cooperation.

I shall never forget Mr. Young's perturbation over the cabbages which included not only real worry but also amusement at his ignorance. And something of the same thing hung in the cooperative's memory of the rich and enthusiastic lady who came to visit and observe at Hillhouse. The cooperative had high hopes of her cooperation. Then she slipped and fell on her behind in the mud. And she contracted poison ivy. But when I was at Hillhouse word had come back that her enthusiasm remained and Hillhouse hoped that she would at least give a motion picture machine, if not a tractor. No better crop than such enthusiasm grows anywhere in the South and so long as such middle-aged Christians still bloom the members of the Delta can count on cooperative success. The boll weevil doesn't bite them.

17

MISSISSIPPI SHORE

UP THE hot and dusty road I stopped for gasoline for the Plymouth and Coca-Cola for myself under the high-and-wide porte-cochère before the big commissary at Sherard. A middle-aged white man, sitting in the afternoon shade, shouted for a Negro to come fill my tank. I went into the store and got my own drink. The man who had shouted greeted me with increased interest when I came back. He had seen my North Carolina license plate. And his wife, all the years since she had come with him to Mississippi, had been talking about some mantelpieces left behind in the house of her family near Goldsboro. That somehow seemed to make us nearer kin. So I pointed with my bottle at the grass-covered mound which ran parallel to both road and river half a mile before the store.

"Isn't that levee pretty high?"

A younger man, who had sat on the porch so still as not to be seen, stirred.

"It's the highest in the world."

I turned and looked at him. He was such a young Southerner as must have roused himself from the sunny lethargy of the eighteen sixties to go riding like the devil with J. E. B. Stuart. Blond, almost pretty, with a Southern voice as soft as a girl's, Jack Sherard wore the conventional well-washed khaki clothes of the white master class on the Southern land. An open collar showed a white throat. He wore congress boots with elastic sides. Sprawled on the piazza of the commissary, he seemed soft. But before he moved I sensed a young iron in his indolence. His was the physical economy in the sun of the Southerner who had the hardness and vigor, sometimes the violence and the cruelty to master a whole race of slaves, of the white gentry which kept to the shade in stillness except when it moved, as it could move, in dramatic fierceness in the summer hot between the sun and the river.

"If you'd like," he said, "I'll show you."

He took the wheel of my car and drove it across the flat Delta toward the huge mound flung up against the river. He had been born on this flat land. In the winter just behind us he had assumed the responsibility as the chief of those who rode the levees in that section watching for the first sign of break in this big dyke which stood huge enough but fragile enough, too, between the flood and the plantations. He drove my car as I would never have dared to do up and down the steep and narrow lanes to the car-wide track at the top of the levee. We stopped and he pointed on a marker where the flood waters had stood. The waters were high in "spring rise" when we rode. The river—the true river—was nearly 15 miles of submerged earth away. But water stood what might have been a full river's depth below the high point of the 1937 flood which had sent the timid scurrying out of Coahoma County.

Slowly this levee had risen. It had begun "back in the time of Grandfather and Colonel Dabney." First the Negroes had piled up dirt. Then Irishmen with wheelbarrows. Then Irishmen and mules and slip scoops. Then newer and better methods each lifted the levee higher. Each time men on the plantations back of the huge protective mound had expressed confidence that the levee was as high as it would ever need to be. And each time afterwards, it had been lifted higher against new water and new fear.

Sherard pointed out in the muddy lake—sea rather—before us where trees stood in water.

"They call that the eighth wonder of the world."

I looked at the trees. There seemed to be nothing strange about them except the water.

"The weight of the levee lifted those trees," he said, "like a load on one end of a lever."

We rode down the top of the levee to a point where Sherard had stopped during the flood soundly frightened. Far down below us at the foot of the levee a circle of sandbags surrounded one of those sandboils which unless promptly and skillfully dealt with may cut a crevasse through the stoutest wall of earth. This one was still working a little: If the boil bubbles clear water, there is no danger; but, if muddy, the water may be taking earth and strength out of the mound.

"As soon as this water goes down," Sherard declared, looking back at the waters which had spread back miles from the channel of the river to this man-made hill, "I'm going to plant corn out there. The flood waters are like a spread of nitrate of soda over the whole land. You can plant the ridges before the bottoms are dry."

As we rode back toward the Sherard plantation and the Sherard acres of big green pecan trees I considered that all the lost earth beyond the levee looked like unproductive muck to me, the bottom of a muddy sea. But Sherard had his teams and his Negroes ready for the planting in that fertile mud.

He drove me back to the commissary and to the uncle whose wife still missed the mantelpieces. I spoke about my trip to the Delta Cooperative Plantation.

"How about Hillhouse?"

The older man showed a clear hostility.

"First place," he said, "they bought the worst farm in Mississippi. It's broke two men."

"That buckshot land there," young Sherard explained, "gets saturated when the water's high like this. When it's wet, it rots the seed; when it's dry, it falls open in such cracks it isn't safe to ride a horse over it."

"There's plenty of good land in Mississippi they could have got, if they'd known what they were doing," the older man said. "They need a farmer down there, too."

"They think they got a bargain," I said. "They only paid five or six dollars an acre."

"It ain't worth that."

"Three of the niggers down there," young Sherard reported, "came up here and asked Daddy to let them have places here. You know how niggers'll talk to their own kind of white people. They said, 'Yes, sir, they do call you "Mister" down there. Yes, sir, they call us, "Mr. Brown—Mr. Jones." But when there's any work to do, they holler quick, "Mr. Brown—Mr. Jones!"' You ought to have heard those niggers laugh."

"It's crazy," said the middle-aged man who was not amused. "Crazy. Mistering niggers in Mississippi. They don't know good land from bad."

He shook his head in angry and helpless exasperation. But I looked up at the sky. The afternoons are long in Mississippi but the sun was well on its way down.

"Where can I get across the river?"

"I think the ferry's running at Friar Point."

"And how do I get there?"

The angry elder man lost his anger in direction. I was to keep right on as I was going. He even smiled over the road. "It messes around a little like everything else in Mississippi but I don't think you'll lose it."

159

He was right. The road follows the levee and I remember the picture of a man and woman on horseback on the levee between me and the sky. But the ferry was not running at Friar Point and the day was not getting any longer. I drove on as they told me there to a ferry which they thought was still running opposite Helena, Arkansas. Twisting and turning beside the bending river and that Moon Lake, which is one of the bends the river left permanently behind, the road ran up and over the levee on a path too narrow for any turning back to an end on a tiny tongue of land where a ferry float was anchored.

There, too, was a tiny house on wheels from which came the smell of fish frying in hog grease. At its door was the bright red and white promise of Coca-Cola. But when I went to the door the weazened proprietor of the store on wheels and a buxom woman were sharing a bunk in the rear of the house-wagon while their supper cooked in stinking fat. The man in some perturbation came forward to sell me a drink and to say that the ferry ought to be there soon. As I drank on that last land in the swollen Mississippi, I considered that there might be places in the South never penetrated by civilization. As it grew darker I was half prepared to believe that this might be one. But Coca-Cola has reached them all.

Two children, a pretty, tongue-tied boy of ten or so and a girl a little younger, were playing in the dirt of the narrow ferry road. The boy regarded me seriously and with considerable self-assurance asked me if I was coming back that way again. It was possible, I told him. Then, he suggested that I lend him two bits until I returned. I gave him a nickel instead. He took it and paid me promptly by pointing to the ferry, then a struggling dot on the yellow water. It came slowly puffing and pushing up from Helena against the stiff current of the flooded river.

Going down to Helena was easy. And also going down as the dusk deepened somehow seemed to me like escape. It seemed to me as I stood on the deck of that insubstantial ferryboat that no writer or painter had ever done justice to the sinister quality of a forest running back from a river in flood. Anything, it seemed to me, might lie in those flooded shadows. Here certainly was Mark Twain's river but he had been too full of dark brooding to express himself directly in dark brooding. But how much violence there had been in that floating of Huckleberry Finn. Yet people remember Huck as a comedy for juveniles. I wondered as I watched the darker and darker shore if Huck's river had not been Mark Twain's sense of the swollen aimlessness of an earlier American and Southern living. It was the same river and the man and woman in the house on wheels and the tongue-tied child before it were people Huck might have met. The stinking grease of their supper cooking would have been familiar to his nose. It was such a river as still might float a corpse. And the night seemed to run to the river from under the trees. Before we reached Helena, it was dark.

18

PIAZZA IN HOT SPRINGS

KINSHIP is notoriously long in the South. I doubt whether either Gilbert Leigh, of Little Rock, or I could count the exact degree of our relationship but we know that the blood kinship is there. The rest is a good deal less certain. Economically and politically he leans to the Right, I to the Left. Physically, he is a man who carries a set of golf clubs everywhere; I am one who seeks a chair and conversation. But I think Gilbert is the flowering of the practical American. Big and handsome, very intelligent but never academic, he is vigorous and active insurance man, building and loan man, banker, former director of the Chamber of Commerce of the United States, and friend of Harvey Couch, the utility executive. He sent his son from Arkansas to Culver, then Lawrenceville, then Princeton. And he told young Gilbert as he went off to Princeton that he was careless about what he learned in the class rooms, but that he did want him to learn three things: to play a fair game of golf, to play a fair game of bridge, and to dance well. Young Gilbert learned only the dancing, but he wrote an impressive thesis on the South and the New Deal. Then he brought the six feet, three inches of himself home to Arkansas to go roving over the State in his father's insurance business. He also took the money an aunt had left him for a trip to Europe, plus some supplement from his father, and bought an airplane. Every Sunday he is in the air.

"All week long," Effie Leigh, his mother, told me, "I hear

planes going over and I'm happy that it can't be Gilbert.
But on Sundays I fly—I fly—all the time. Right here under
my heart."

But she would never really wish to stop him. Women and
men live in a modern, western tempo at Little Rock. They
look back across the flat country from the beginning of the
hills. They can consider the past without ever wishing to
halt or alter the movement of the present. Young men fly.
A mother may be frightened. But a modern accepts the new
shining mechanism in the lives and manner of men. Some
have suggested that Arkansas was the ultimate in mediocrity.
I think it was rather the middle between original American
coastal complacency and ultimate restlessness, between the
South of the piazza and the West of the pony. The elder
Gilbert told me:

"It was too easy to make some kind of a living in Arkansas. The less ambitious and the less venturesome stopped
here in the grand trek west. And today on one side of the
Missouri-Pacific Railroad they are a different people from
those who live on the other: Bottom folks and hill billies.
Bottom people are broad, expansive, liberal, extravagant,
free spenders themselves and for large State appropriations.
Hill people are narrow, hard, tight and conservative. Between these people I think is perhaps the line between
Yankee and Southerner. The South ends where the hill billy
begins."

He told me, too, a revealing story about one of the combination farmer-merchant-bankers of Southeast Arkansas. A
book agent came to sell him a set of books on scientific agriculture. The old man thumbed through them.

"No. I don't want 'em."

"You ought to buy these books, sir. If you had these
books you could farm twice as good as you do."

The old fellow settled himself more comfortably in his chair.

"Hell, son," he said, "I don't farm half as good as I know how now."

I laughed. "That story doesn't apply to Arkansas alone— not to the South alone. Its merit is its universal truth."

"I suppose so," Gilbert admitted grinning, "but it fits some Southerners all right. It takes all kinds of people to make the South."

And to make Arkansas. I know. I met there the very picture of Southern girl. She wore one of those stiff and much-pressed dresses which girls in the South wear without ever wilting them in the heat. Her home was a little town in South Arkansas, but she had gone recently as young wife to live in Florida. When I saw her she was home on a visit. She said:

"The niggers are getting unbearable in Florida. I got a girl and I told her to dust the living room.

"She said, 'OK, Sister.'

"I said, 'Nigger, you get out of my house, and if you ever see me again you start running the minute you see me.' "

She finished cool and placid as ever. There was not a wrinkle in her precisely ironed summer dress, not a displaced strand in her smooth dark hair. But as Southerner I was as shocked as if she had smashed a mirror with an ax.

But all of them, cousins and acquaintances, men and women at the country club high over Little Rock, and the men and women, black and white, whom I had seen on the earth low and close to the Mississippi, brought me a little better understanding of Arkansas before I talked with the Governor of Arkansas about his State on the long porch of the Arlington Hotel in Hot Springs. The Governor was in the famous bath resort to address a State Federation of

Labor meeting. I was attending the convention of the Southern Newspaper Publishers Association.

(Perhaps I ought to write something about the S.N.P.A. In many respects it is more revealing as to flaws in Southern life than the Southern Tenant Farmers' Union. If I did not belong to the lodge, I could point out the confusion which exists in many of the members' minds as to the ancestry of journalism in America. They seem to be under the impression that the American newspaper is descended from the Constitution and that the "freedom of the press" is a defense against labor unions, government regulations and the child labor laws. And like many others who have arrived at opulence, they are entirely forgetful that the advertising industry of which they are a part had an ancestor in America in the guitar player whose twanging accompanied the sale of a sovereign remedy for all the ills of man. Some of the traits of that ancestor are still discernible. Also it was interesting to observe that many of the publishers whose papers in the solid South had been and remained solid for Roosevelt were themselves solid against him. "He's a demagogue," they said. And they could not bear that. But, as a member of the lodge, I say nothing except that while salesmen who are now defenders of the free press and free profit golfed, Governor Bailey and I talked on the piazza.)

Unattended, the Governor strode into the lobby of the Arlington looking for me. I had missed him in Little Rock and young Thomas Fitzhugh, who is devoted to advancing both Carl Bailey and Arkansas, had arranged the meeting in the resort. Bailey needs no outriders for his dignity. It is part of the man. He was born 43 years before I saw him in a little town named Bernie 30 miles out of Arkansas in Stoddard County, Missouri. Today he is a thick man, not handsome; his hair is yellow and his skin looks weather-toughened. But I could understand how women might mistake his strength for handsomeness. He speaks easily and directly. But I remember that when he talked sometimes he stuck his tongue out in a slight nervous affectation, wetting his lips for more talking.

His people are of old American stock and, even on the lively frontier in Arkansas and Missouri, his Grandfather Bailey must have been a character: He was a scamp and school teacher at the same time. As result the teacher's children had as little education as the proverbial shoemaker's children had shoes. Governor Bailey's father grew up without schooling to work as laborer and later as a little salesman of hardware and farm implements.

"I doubt if he ever made more than a hundred dollars a month in his life," the Governor said. But from these earnings his father raised his family, and made it possible for his sons to secure some education. When he died he left a home paid for and a little life insurance policy. Also he left an indelible impression on the life and philosophy of his son. He put into his son an indestructible but never sentimental faith in the simple man.

I told him I had been in the counties where the sharecroppers had organized. Was there any escape for them? Or hope?

"Of course," he said. "I'm not committed to any such fallacy as that farm tenancy is a relationship which should be entirely abolished. Not every tenant is capable of farm ownership and management. But we must improve the condition of all. That isn't going to be easy. The problem is big and complex."

He shook his head.

"I don't know what the mechanical cotton pickers are going to do. But they have already been built. They function now, it is true, with indifferent efficiency. But that they function at all is warning that they will be perfected.

And when that is done, they will displace thousands of individuals in the cotton belt, thus creating suddenly the most perplexing social and economic problem. I'm afraid of the meaning of the picker; but we might as well face it. Ultimately, I think, not only cotton, but wheat, sugar cane, all the basic crops, are going to be raised by mass production methods. And I'm scared of the human consequences."

Then he paid what seemed to me to be a real and unconscious tribute to the results of the efforts of the organizers and intellectuals behind the Southern Tenant Farmers' Union in Memphis and East Arkansas. They had screamed and they had been heard.

"A few years—even a few months—ago it would have been politically suicidal for a State official to talk out loud about the tenant problem. He would have been played into the attitude of a demagogue stirring racial prejudice and stirring class against class. State officials were supposed to be devoted to proving that everything was beautiful and everybody was happy. We were supposed to meet every effort to identify bad conditions and to inaugurate plans to correct them with a blast of demagoguery."

"Was that Southern oratory?"

"What passed for it."

"And the Southern demagogue."

"Remember this. Not every man who is called a demagogue is one. Some were statesmen and some were stooges. Many of the Southern demagogues of the past were not the political rulers they pretended to be. They stood between the people and the real powers. The demagogues were not always real rabble rousers. Sometimes they were like criminal lawyers making a violently oratorical display before a jury that was already fixed. They got credit for great powers of persuasiveness; actually they were just making a show. So often in the old days the gang declared the nominee no matter how the actual votes were cast. And the sound and the fury of the nominee was just play acting."

He smiled. "The noise had no more to do with the re-sult—" He looked across the street where a magnolia tree was in full bloom. "It had no more to do with the result than that magnolia tree has to do with the height of that mountain behind it."

I looked at his mountain behind his magnolia tree and recognized it for a very precipitate hill, but no mountain in the North Carolina sense. The Governor went on, un-aware of my North Carolina contempt for this Arkansas mountain.

"I think we're changing and moving. I doubt if we could have done it if the national administration were not pro-viding the leadership. There's resistance still. But Arkansas is looking at its problems and looking at them realistically. I believe that in the development of a State the function of a State is to make and disclose opportunities. Protect the forests: we're just beginning to realize the resources there. Develop the parks: this hotel is the center of an industry we want to grow. Aid in the development of the State's waterpower resources and in the protection of fertile land from floods; that increasingly means dams and reservoirs and the protection of forests rather than levees."

He punctuated a pause with a restless tongue.

"The way to get industry is to provide and disclose oppor-tunity. Industry worth having can't be moved by promotion and subsidy. The right kind of industries don't want sub-sidies; they want an opportunity to make money. And they ought not to be tax exempt. As a matter of fact, industrial development creates need for greater governmental services. It's bound to. But if there is a real chance, industry will take it; if there isn't a chance, there isn't subsidy enough to do anything but enrich promoters."

His proposal to make that chance in Arkansas in order that men might seize the chance offered by Arkansas reminded me of David Lilienthal's insistence that men have a chance to make a free choice. With Lilienthal, Bailey had the faith that men would choose wisely if men could choose freely. I was to remember what he said when I went back across the Mississippi and talked to Mississippi's Governor White whose plan for the development of Mississippi is based on naked subsidy. I spoke of it to Bailey on the long hotel porch in Hot Springs.

"They are making a tragic mistake," he declared.

"Suppose your plan is right," I said. "Suppose you've got the resources in land and forest, minerals and parks. What about the people? Can they make a decency for themselves? Are they slaves? And if they are, can they escape from slavery? Why, some Arkansans tell me that a bottom man can't live in the hills and a hill man can't live in the bottoms—"

He was quickly impatient. "Oh, that isn't true. Why, one reason for the tenant problem is the descent of the hill people, who give up scratching hard, eroded hills and go down to the bottoms as to the Promised Land. And as in some other promised lands, they find the land all taken before them. Then at last they are caught in all the difficulties of Southern agriculture and Southern tenure relationships. But they're not caught alone. Often the landlords are caught, too. Oh, there are hard landlords and shiftless tenants, but both are often the products of the system that enslaves them rather than the makers of it."

"Well, what chance is there for the people at the bottom of the system?"

He shook his head in a solemnness just short of despair.

"Some tenants are terrible people and some are pitiful people. In America there are 40,000 more of them every

169

year. No plan I know can work fast enough to save them. And some of them couldn't be saved in a million years. But much can be done. Not so much for the present tenants as for their children. This business isn't new. It's been growing for a hundred years and more and it is not going to be ended quickly. But we're aware of it, we're facing it and I think the States and the nation together can do something to lift the pitifully low levels of living on our land."

He smiled slowly. "I'm an optimist. And you know the present interest of the country in the South is encouraging. Part of it, of course, is due to lurid tales printed in the Northern papers. I'm not denying the stories so much as pointing out that poverty isn't peculiarly Southern. And beyond those stories there is an instinctive sense in the North and East that development is taking place in the South now as it once was in the West. When the West grew we heard about cowboys and Indians; now the South grows and the books and papers are full of Negroes and wild white men. That's encouraging."

The Governor encouraged me. He seemed both aware of difficulty and undisturbed by it. But that night I talked to other men, some of the few editors who had somehow come to the newspaper convention. I think they knew the Deep South.

"Slavery is still in force," one said, "but not generally profitable."

"That lack of profit," another declared, "is, I think, largely responsible for the noise about tenancy. Before the war some Southerners were opposed to slavery but they didn't know what would become of the land with the niggers loose on it. Now the planters can't afford to keep the niggers and they don't know what might happen if nobody keeps them. Neither do I."

"The niggers will take care of themselves," said the first

man, pouring himself a drink of a printing machinery manufacturer's Scotch. "I stand by my training. I was raised on
an Alabama farm. And I was taught—or at least I learned—
to love the nigger and to despise the poor white. The niggers
will take care of themselves. I don't know what the poor
whites will do. I never could find that they were good for
anything. Not even the girls. Their bones hurt you."

And we laughed.

19

HOTSPUR'S HOUSE

IF, AS David Cohn once wrote, the Mississippi Delta begins in the lobby of the Peabody Hotel in Memphis and ends on Catfish Row in Vicksburg, it also has its middle and its meaning in Greenville which sits, close behind the levee, on one of the long, narrow loops of the writhing river. On the night I came to it on a crowded ferryboat from a dusty Arkansas, it contained Will Percy, David Cohn and Roark Bradford. Down the river Harris Dickson, who knows Mississippi better than most men know their own yards, told me that Percy is the true last of the great family of Hotspurs. David Cohn is a strangely romantic but illusionless Jew, who came back from New Orleans to find the essence of the life on the earth in which his parents lie. And Bradford, born in the Tennessee Bottoms, has shaped his art out of the black men who make most of the people and nearly all of the cotton in the hot, flat land. If I had searched Mississippi I should not have been able to find three men better able to give me the basis for understanding of the Delta. What looks to me like the truth seems to me very sad. It is: In the cotton countries along the river in Mississippi, where there are three black skins for every white one, the gentlemen are afraid. But not of the Negroes. Indeed, the gentlemen and the Negroes are afraid together. They are fearful of the rednecks, the peckerwoods, who in politics and in person are pressing down upon the rich, flat Delta

from the hard, eroded hills. They may lynch a Negro; they
may destroy the last of a civilization which has great vices
and great virtues, beauty and strength, responsibility beside
arrogance, and a preserving honesty beside a destructive
self-indulgence.

"They call me a Negrophile," Will Percy said of himself. He is a diminutive man, frail, ascetic. But he was the
man I remembered when a tiny, hard-headed, famous woman
said to me in Atlanta that little people are far more dangerous than big ones. "They have to be hard," she said, "or
worms." Certainly there was nothing of the worm about
William Alexander Percy. Nor anything hard either. But
the strength was there with the sensitiveness. He was the
poet, but the soldier, too, who could not only win the *Croix
de Guerre* but be aware in war of wild canaries singing suddenly and strangely above the roar of guns. And planter
and lawyer. And gentleman.

If Will Percy is Negrophile, his is a love entirely different
from that of, say, Sam Franklin at Hillhouse. Percy's is the
feudal lord's love for his serfs, and as such is not only love
of his own but responsibility for his own. He is not concerned for the black man's morals. Indeed, he holds that the
Negro is to be judged by entirely different ethical standards than those supposedly applicable to white men. I had
the feeling that Percy loved Negroes as another gentleman
might love dogs and that somehow the fiercer the beast the
more he might prefer it. I remember his tale of a "charming fellow," a gangling Negro, who came pounding on his
door deep in the night. Percy opened the door and the fellow fell into the house. Down the river the day before he
had been in a fight with another black man. He had fled up
the river to Mr. Will.

"You fool," shouted Percy, "don't you know these fights
will get you into trouble?"

"Yassah, I reckon so but I knowed you'd tell me what to do."

Suddenly a drop of blood fell on the polished floor.

Percy stared at it.

"Yassah, Mr. Will, he shot me a little."

That night the "charming fellow" got his hide mended and somehow he found the money to disappear. And he stayed away until he got arrested for bigamy. Then he came back for Percy's help again. He got it as others have and others will.

Nobody knows how many hungry Negroes Will Percy has fed. Nobody knows how many Negroes in trouble have had the benefit of his counsel and his pocket book. The South may be full of white men oppressing black men but such men are not the whole South. For instance, in Greenville, Mississippi, there is Will Percy. Without the least solemnity he understands that privilege entails responsibility and he is never so angry as when he finds a white man who does not. He laughs at himself, waving an eloquent hand, declaring that in every mob that lynches there may be men who are taking care of whole families of Negroes as they would take care of children. But he did not laugh when he heard that a sheriff, having commandeered the labor of a black boy waiting trial, denied responsibility for the boy's injury when a beam being lifted into a gallows fell upon him. At the request of the boy's old father Percy, the lawyer, sued the sheriff and pushed the suit. For himself he disregarded whispered reports that the sheriff's sympathizers might attack him. But he took the colored boy into his home as house servant for the boy's safety. The sheriff paid the black boy. And the black boy ran off with personal possessions of Percy and David Cohn and was arrested with them in Memphis.

"Lawd, Mr. David," he said, "I foun' 'em on de flo'. I thought you th'owed 'em away."

174

David Cohn told me that story. Harris Dickson told me another.

"Rednecks," he said, "are raised on hate. Here's an example. When Will Percy was chairman of flood relief he found an old starving peckerwood in Greenville and he set him up in a little stand to sell papers and apples. He told the police not to bother the old fellow. And every day Will would buy an apple and a paper from him. But one day as he was crossing the street the colored boy who had caddied for him at the club ran out with papers. Will bought one and went on to get an apple. The old fellow was glaring at him. 'I hate a nigger-lover,' he said."

The night I came Will Percy went to bed early, leaving me with Hodding Carter, who fought Huey Long and his heirs and assigns in Hammond, Louisiana, before he started *The Delta Star* in Greenville, to wait for Cohn and Bradford. I had a feeling that Percy's weariness was deeper than the physical. I felt—I wondered if he felt it—that he was not merely the last of the Percys in Mississippi but more important perhaps one of the last of those in Mississippi who are aristocrats less because of what they have than because of what they are. It has been a long time since that retired British naval officer landed at Natchez to establish the Mississippi house of the Percys. It has been a quarter of a century since big Leroy Percy, Will's father, fought Vardaman for the United States Senatorship in the Legislature and won, and soon afterwards before all the people, rednecks and aristocrats, fought again and lost. The rednecks hate the Delta and Leroy Percy was all that the Delta meant to them. And then even in the Delta, even in Washington County there rose the revised version of the Ku Klux Klan, designed this time for rednecks. But old man Leroy, Mississippi Episcopalian who married a Catholic Creole, lived to see the Klan licked at the polls in Washington County and to participate in such a celebration at his house as is still lively in the minds of all who remember it. But that one victory did not stop the influx of such folk as the old planters would have regarded as poor whites. And not long after such a victory Senator Leroy was laid low in the Baptist Hospital at Greenville. Harris Dickson told me he went to see him.

"I never expected to find you among the Baptists," Dickson said to the Colonel. And to me he said years later, "I think that was the last time he ever smiled."

So he died and Will Percy had erected over his father the marble figure of a knight in full armor. There are not many such in Mississippi. Nor anywhere else. And I suspect that Will Percy felt that not only was his father dead but that also a great defender of the aristocratic ideal was gone. But Will Percy remains. And fragile in body but stout in spirit, he walks the Delta every day and he has walked the threatened levees before the town as his big father, cursing men and the elements, had marched before him. (John Hudson of *The Times-Picayune* once in his paper quoted the Colonel when he cursed an army engineer. Next day Hudson received an imperious summons; he answered it in perturbation. The Senator boomed: "Young man, that was the God-damned most accurate piece of reporting I ever saw.")

Will Percy will be the aristocrat till he follows his father over the last levee. But I am afraid he has gone the way of other gentlemen out of action into intellectuality. The avocation of the Senator was politics. The avocation of Will Percy is poetry, excellent poetry. But Cohn and Bradford who came in, wandering slowly out of the warm night, are writers and intellectuals. They look alike. Both are growing plump and getting bald. But Cohn is far the more voluble. Bradford is dark in the saturnine tradition of the Mississippi humorist which Mark Twain began. They are informal and bitter and contemptuous. Of a Negro Bradford says, "The poor bastard," and of a poor white Cohn murmurs, "The simple son-of-a-bitch." At the Cotton Festival in Memphis Cohn remembers that somebody was speaking of some individual as a fine man.

"He's not a fine man. I know. In the store we used to get the checks of the wages he paid his girls. Such pitiful little checks for work with the heavy denims he makes. He's not a fine man. I know what he is."

Nowhere had I seen men who seemed so certain of the quality of the earth beneath them, but upon it they appeared like twins lighting with anger and humor a darkness like despair. Cohn talked most but he seemed not only to talk for himself; he and Bradford apparently shared an unloving knowledge of the people on the land which they loved.

Bradford told the story of the Negro farm foreman who ran the white man's farm. The white man let the Negro do everything without even consulting him. And he did it so well that white men decided to help him become a landowner. Then he went all to pieces. Weeds choked his cotton. He let his mule starve. Moral: He needed the white man even though he never consulted him. He took strength out of the fact that the white man was there.

Too much now the planters of the Delta, Cohn declared, have no real love of the land. They are migratory birds. All their land is for sale. When the price of cotton goes up and they have money to spend they don't spend it on their plantation houses. They go to Memphis. Planters in money spend money showily on showy women. The people have been weakened as white men always are by proximity to a dark race. White people learned to rob the Negroes.

"Planters in the Delta did that?"

"Of course, they did it. Less now than before 1920 when a million Negroes picked up and went north. But they still do it."

He spoke as if it were unpleasant but unquestioned.

"The land and the Negroes do something to people always. Often it is hidden. Nowadays in the Delta you never hear of a shooting over adultery as you did twenty years ago. The people are no worse now, but there is more adultery due to the automobile and the removal of fear which knowledge of contraceptives means."

The land and the presence of a white race beside a black race patterns the people. In two generations, they agreed, rednecks sometimes turn into the planter pattern.

"Hell," Cohn added, "in this country even Chinamen lose their thrift and become like Delta people."

I laughed. But I pressed my questions about tenant farming, in which Mississippi leads America. The Delta leads Mississippi.

"It's not hard to get land in the South," Cohn declared. "It is foolish to talk of the difficulty of a farmer acquiring land in America. Almost anybody can get it on almost any terms. Credit has been too easy in the South. People were insulted if you asked them to pay an account 90 days old. There's plenty of land for sale. Right up near the Dyess Colony in Arkansas, Governor Lowden of Illinois had some land which he sold. The buyers were to pay nothing for the first three years, but were to clear half the land the first year and three-fourths in three years. But a lot of the people went ahead and did the whole clearing job the first year so they could get in a crop the second year. They built themselves cabins, too. And right beside them Dyess was setting up in houses with electricity and plumbing people from relief rolls. They're getting from the government probably for a good deal less a good deal more than what the people

next door labored like the devil to get. But when I was at
Dyess some of the colonists were grumbling and complaining. Some told me they'd be glad to go elsewhere as tenants."

He shook his head. "It's not land; it's the people."

"I can't understand," I said, "such people as those who
lynched a Negro up at Duck Hill with a blow torch."

"That's only a hundred miles from here," Cohn said.
"There are plenty of people who could do it. You don't
know how they hate the Negro. They feel vastly superior
but they have to compete on the same economic level. That's
basis for a stinking bitterness—the killing kind. I remember
once I went back in the hill country when they were trying
to catch a Negro to lynch him. All the people were sitting
around talking about what they were going to do if they
caught him. One of them suggested that they get the women
to pick the Negro's eye-balls out with needles."

"They wouldn't do that?" I said incredulous.

"You're damn right, they would. They're terrible people.
Landlords are scared to death of them. Most landlords much
prefer Negro tenants to white ones. Negroes aren't revenge-
ful but if a white man thinks he's got some grievance against
you, he might stick a knife in your back. I know landlords
who are getting rid of white tenants as fast as they dare because they're afraid of being shot."

"I don't blame 'em," Bradford said.

In the Mississippi darkness beyond the circle of Will
Percy's light any sinister quality of white hate might be possible, but when we went out into that darkness itself it was
so sweet and warm that it seemed improbable that any men
anywhere in it could stir in the cold-bloodedness Cohn had
reported. We walked up the wide street under the thick
night shade of the trees. Bradford and Cohn went to meet
the Carters and Mary Rose Bradford. As we walked Bradford remembered that he went as a reporter for Hearst's

Atlanta paper about Georgia with the redoubtable Tom Watson.

"He said so many damn fool things," Bradford reported, "that finally I asked him about them. And he said—he always talked in a high, piping voice—he said, 'Young man, I'm going to tell you something to remember forever. It is impossible to overestimate the stupidity of the American people.' "

We laughed in the Mississippi darkness. They went on their way and I turned to the hotel. I walked with my back to the river facing the hills. I felt suddenly that I was glad that I would be gone from the Delta before at last the barbarians came down. With blow torches or needles or ballots. They would rise about the stone knight in the cemetery like the waters of the flood.

20

MEN AND MULES AND MACHINES

"I CAME back from Lexington, Kentucky," Oscar Johnston told me. "My wife had been sick up there. And I found out that some of the planters round about had been having night meetings. They didn't like the Hillhouse cooperative experiment. And some of 'em said they were going to push it in the river."

He grinned. This most successful cotton planter on the biggest American cotton plantation at Scott, Mississippi, ten miles above Greenville, is a merry man. And though near-sighted, he sees the cotton South clearly in every detail. His charm lies in his conversation, wise, lively and lucid. He went on.

"I heard about it and called some of my friends up. 'Look here,' I said, 'once long ago, some Jews lynched a fellow and they made a religion. Let's not make any martyrs out of these folks.' Then I went up to see Sam Franklin and I invited him down here. He's a nice young fellow. I think he was a little surprised. He said the other planters hadn't been so hospitable."

Johnston laughed when he told me and said, "I laughed then. I told him, 'I want you near where people can see your failure and not far off where missionaries can make it sound like a success.' "

Mr. Johnston candidly does not expect either the share-cropper or the South in which he lives too often in a sprawled squalor on the land to be saved by governmental experiment at Dyess or Christian socialistic experiment at Hillhouse. With a pardonable pride, based upon his own excellent and profitable record as the resident president of the English-owned Delta and Pine Land Company at Scott, he believes that the better chance for the sharecropper and the cotton South lies in such big corporate cotton enterprises as Delta and Pine which can give the little farmers of the South the agricultural direction as well as the management and marketing which little fellows cannot provide for themselves. Neither the Agrarians nor the Socialists would agree with such an idea. And, though neither Socialist nor Agrarian, I also disagree. Delta and Pine under Oscar Johnston proved only, it seemed to me, that Oscar Johnston is in charge at Delta and Pine. But he is a man and not a system. I suspect that he would be quite as successful as the director of a cooperative or as papa in paternalistic colony. Indeed, the capitalism over which he presides from his far from monumental clapboard house at Scott partakes of the qualities of both. Once Mr. Johnston described the terms of his management of a plantation occupied by a thousand Negro families as "in loco parentis," and in an interesting number of aspects the life and lot of the Delta and Pine tenant is improved by cooperative activities.

While he was finishing the dictation of a speech, he had sent a young subordinate to show me over the physical layout of this biggest single section of the Cotton Kingdom which spreads in 38,000 flat acres of deep alluvial soil around the plantation's practically private town of Scott. (Dyess Colony has 16,000 acres; Delta Cooperative has 2,133.) Delta and Pine's acres are divided into eleven farm units over each of which a unit manager presides in lonely residence among so many Negroes. As we rode over the exquisitely tended earth I was interested in uncovering the opinion that a good unit manager must have in him the stout, earthy qualities of the redneck. But such a redneck is by no means to be confused with po' whites though the confusion is ancient. Poor white men in the South are by no means all po' white even in the hills. Lincoln and Jackson, to name but two, came from a Southern folk the back of whose necks were ridged and red from labor in the sun.

We passed by gin and lake and church and cabins, the last far less impressive than the dwellings of Dyess but seeming stouter than the cabins in the white row and the black row at Hillhouse. We moved on past the big central barns at which on each unit a black hostler under the unit manager presides over all the stock and tools. A mule-loving Scotsman directs the care and management of all the stock; each year the poorer mules are sold and new ones bought to keep at highest level the animal efficiency of the plantation. Once some tenants at Delta and Pine had their own mules stabled behind their own cabins. But since Johnston came, all tenants on the plantation have been half tenants who contribute only their labor and the labor of their families to the farming and get half the cotton they raise on the landlord's land with the landlord's seed and tools and stock. But such half tenants since the advent of Johnston have often made more than the old three-quarters tenant who furnished not only labor but also rusty tools and scrawny, night-ridden mules.

When we drove back to the big brick commissary at Scott Mr. Johnston, like any normal thirsty Southerner, joined us at the soda fountain. The speech was being typed.

"Did you see enough?"

"More than I can quite get into my head. I never saw such rows of cotton nor so many Negroes. All your tenants are Negroes?"

"All of them."

"Do you agree that white tenants are dangerous?" I asked and told him what I had heard.

He shook his head. "Where you can pick your tenants yourself, I prefer white ones. When I was farming my own land and could pick the tenants individually, I had all white tenants. I saw to it that they not only were satisfactory to me but to each other. And fine folks they were. But here the number is far too large for individual selection. When that's so, the Negro is better—and safer—as having neither gratitude nor resentment." He drank from his glass. "The Negro is more amenable to discipline."

I asked the questions that were becoming my stock in trade. "Is there any way to security for either the white or the Negro sharecropper? Are little farmers in the South going to keep on losing their land till they are all share-croppers on big farms like this one?"

Mr. Johnston considered. "I'm not sure the tenant, as tenant, is so bad off. He might not be any better off if he owned the land—maybe not as well off. The workers don't own the factories." He paused. "We Americans get ideas fixed in our heads. We see the increase in tenancy, but I doubt very much whether the percentage of farmers who fail as independent operators is any greater than the failures to hang on to independence in the towns. As a matter of fact, once I tested this doubt of mine in my home town of Friar Point up the river. And there at least more people had disappeared from independent business than had dis-appeared as land owners in the country round about. The change was much greater in the town. The farmer hasn't suffered in independence any more than the city man."

I doubted whether the sociologists would admit that Mr. Johnston's test was entirely scientific. But I asked:

"But isn't the farmer's insecurity growing? Especially in

184

the South? What will happen to the cotton farmer in this country when the cotton picker is perfected?"

Mr. Johnston took off his pince-nez glasses and rubbed them clean with the handkerchief—both the lenses that help his squinting near-sightedness and the tinted glasses above them in defense against the Mississippi sun. Deliberately he put them back on. He regarded me through them.

"Well, I've witnessed in operation every picker which to date has been publicly discussed, including the much heralded and advertised Rust Brothers Picker."

"Up at Hillhouse, they say it is already working."

"Yes," he said, a little wearily, it seemed to me. "Yes, I know."

He gazed past a cow-eyed colored girl, who looked as if she were extracting ecstasy from a pop bottle through a straw, toward the big galvanized iron gin house across the road. Then in the almost empty store he seemed to take up the whole cotton problem for my instruction.

"As you know," he began, "most cotton is grown by family units, producing from about three to five bales per family. But there are two exceptions. First, there are a relatively small number of operators, farming large tracts of land, who are using in the main power-drive agricultural implements. They hire day labor or wage hands who are paid by the day to do the work that cannot be done mechanically, like chopping and picking. And second, there are farmers operating in parts of the West, particularly in irrigated sections, where a single family works as much as 100 to 125 acres." He looked at me questioningly. "You follow me?"

"Yes."

"All right. Now cotton opens irregularly, that is to say, the bolls near the bottom of the stalk mature in the late summer or early fall, while the plant is still growing and

185

putting on additional fruit. The last bolls to develop near the top frequently do not open until after frost. To get the best qualities it is important that the cotton be picked as rapidly as possible following the opening of the boll. And to delay picking exposes the open cotton to damage from rain and from the grass seeds, particles of foliage and other foreign matter shed by the plant in the fall and caught by the lint fiber. That would lower the grade. But a single family, cultivating from eight to fifteen acres of cotton, can pick from day to day as their cotton opens and so get the best qualities by avoiding exposure of the lint to damaging elements. And anyhow these folks haven't any other market for their labor. They might as well be picking cotton as it comes. We never bring any pickers out here except in rare cases. It's unnecessary and it's unfair to the tenant."

But I clung to the possible danger. "But suppose a picker should be perfected?"

He shrugged his round shoulders. "The present method of farming would shortly become obsolete. The small family operators could not afford to own a picking machine. Nor could they afford the luxury of paying the owner of such a machine to pick their cotton since to do so would require either a cash outlay or a payment in kind. Land owners who now rent considerable tracts of land to millions of farm families, who rent either for cash or a share of the crop, would discontinue the renting system and proceed to farm large areas themselves using mechanized equipment including the picker. I should estimate that within five years after a successful picker was developed at least a million farmers, now engaged in the production of cotton, would be out of employment, their buying power would be destroyed with consequent economic disturbance not only to the South but throughout the nation."

And that, I thought, would be freedom, freedom again

for black men in the Delta, where sharecropping succeeded slavery when freedom turned out only to be another name for hunger. The Yankee was ready to end slavery; but he was not ready to make freedom. And he was afraid of the only plan which might have fulfilled the purpose of his fighting: Forty acres and a mule. All my life I had heard those acres and mules referred to in derisive disdain and in all my life it was the only proposal I had ever heard which might have solved the agricultural sickness of the South. It seemed too late when I talked to Oscar Johnston. Already a new freedom threatened and men shivered at the thought of it.

"My judgment," he declared, "is that the cotton picker is not an economic necessity. In our operations here at Scott, we have planted approximately 11,000 acres of cotton. The production of this crop gives employment to about 900 families consisting of around 4,000 human beings. With a successful cotton picker and by the use of tractors and other equipment designed for labor saving, we could operate this property with probably 75 or 100 laborers. That would mean the discharge of 90 per cent of the people now making a living here. The necessity for human labor to pick the crop prompts the employment of human laborers through the year for planting and cultivating instead of the substitution of tractors and other labor saving machinery. That prompting will go with the development of a picker."

He smiled suddenly out of solemnity.

"But I've seen all the said-to-be cotton pickers. All of them. And I have seen no picker yet which in my judgment constitutes even a vague threat to labor, particularly to the Mississippi Valley. Indeed, there has been no fundamental mechanical principle suggested by any of the pickers now being talked about which can succeed in the face of conditions as they exist in the Mississippi Valley. Some can do

187

a fairly good job in the irrigated areas of the West."

"Cotton is still human, then?"

"And the most important things we've done here are human. Let's go look."

First, we went to see men engaged in the installation of a big community refrigeration unit, the final step in the plantation's effort to encourage the tenants to improve their diet. This is an effort which has advanced from the encouragement of gardens and the distribution of free yeast to this new provision of refrigeration to preserve the meat of the tenants' own slaughtering of their own animals. I was interested to see that the electrical work was being done by such a skilled Negro as is supposed to have been so common on the pre-war plantations. But such workers are less and less numerous in the free South where white men seek a monopoly of the more skilled and better paid work— and generally secure it.

Such a community cold storage unit is only an item in the cooperative activities of the plantation from which the plantation expects to profit directly as in the boll weevil dusting or indirectly as from the health program. The large scale farming at Delta and Pine makes it economically possible to use airplanes in dusting with calcium arsenate against the boll weevil. Only the infested fields are dusted by the low-flying, hedge-hopping planes, but since the boll weevils move (they advanced from the Rio Grande to Scott in 19 years), all tenants pay a share of the cost of the dusting whether their fields are infested or not. In other ways, too, the tenants as a group receive benefits not possible to individuals. But Mr. Johnston is prouder of the cooperative health plan (to which the plantation makes a large contribution) than almost anything else he has done at Delta and Pine.

In the wooden hospital on the other side of the trestle

across the bayou, black faces peered at us above white sheets. In the wards of both the men and the women a silence preceded us. Both the sick and the visitors solemnly watched us pass. Only when Mr. Johnston stopped beside a boy did he speak.

"What's been the matter with you, son?"

"Malaya fever. Yassah."

He translated. "Malaria."

Certainly there was nothing metropolitan about the hospital. It did not sparkle white and clean. Indeed, it seemed of another world from the tiny gleaming hospital set up at TVA's construction camp where the Chickamauga dam was rising. But it seemed comfortable and it smelled antiseptic. And it was a great deal nearer TVA's hospital than to the medical and obstetrical practices which too generally prevail among the rural black folk of Mississippi. Each tenant pays 75 cents an acre, an average of $9 a year, for all medical, obstetrical and surgical care. Mr. Johnston and the unit managers have reduced almost to non-existence the diet disease of pellagra. Mr. Johnston and Dr. I. I. Pogue, plantation physician, have almost eliminated typhoid fever. But Mr. Johnston is entitled to almost all the credit for the first large private campaign in the United States to eliminate syphilis from a group.

The Negro, whom some Southern white men sometimes treat as if he were entirely insensitive, may be, as sensible Southern men know, a suddenly strange and sensitive creature. The mule may bolt like the stallion. General Manager Jesse W. Fox and a unanimous body of unit managers opposed Mr. Johnston's plan to undertake the elimination of syphilis among Delta and Pine's 4,000 Negroes. It was useless, they said. You couldn't keep out the lean and yellow wenches from Greenville. And, most important, it would stir up all the Negroes on the place. They might move off in groups in one of those inexplicable migrations which sometimes occur among tenants even on the best plantations. But Mr. Johnston took the responsibility. He demanded only that each unit manager have all his tenants and their wives in the churches on their units on particular days. Mr. Johnston would do all the talking. He did.

First he made clear their relationship, the people and the plantation, Johnston and tenant. It was a partnership.

"When you make money, I make money. When you don't, I don't; and when I don't, you don't."

Negroes nodded. "Yassah." "Dat's so." "It's de truf." "Ain't no doubt about dat."

"Now we've got the best veterinarians to look after the stock. They keep the mules well-fed and lively. I mean to see to it that the people are well too."

". . . Hmmmmmmm. . . ?"

"I don't intend," he announced, "on this plantation to have a $250 mule at one end of a plow and a syphilitic nigra at the other."

Later he told me. "They got it. One laughed and then others and I knew I was headed right. I told them that there wasn't any sense in trying to hide syphilis. Once, I said, they called syphilis the King's Disease because all the kings and queens had it; and that it was a good deal more pleasant to contract than typhoid fever which could only be gotten by the taking of human excreta into the mouth. Finally I ended up by saying that we weren't going to force anybody to be examined or take treatment. But we would have the doctors and the nurses at each unit on a certain day. Then I said that if three-fourths of the people did take advantage of the examinations and the treatments, I was going to protect them. I told them, 'I'm going to insist that the other fourth not endanger the rest.' " He laughed. "We had one hundred per cent cooperation."

With the smell of carbolic still in our noses we walked back across the trestle and up the stairs to Johnston's office.

"Negroes are a remarkable people," he said. "I think every sensible Southerner realizes that. I'm not any Unreconstructed Rebel but I always have thought that one of the cruelest and most diabolical acts ever taken by an American President was when Lincoln issued the Emancipation Proclamation. All the white men except the old ones were gone from the plantation country. It was already black enough; their going left it blacker. Only the children and the old men and the women remained. And the Emancipation Proclamation was issued as an act of war. It was in its effect if not in its terms an invitation to the Negroes to rise up in the South."

He looked out of his windows at his all-black tenant plantation where less than a hundred whites clustered around Scott worked in the midst of 4,000 Negroes, and at Bolivar County around it in which there are three Negroes for every white man.

"As far as I know," he went on, "there was not a single instance in which the Negroes took advantage of the absence of the white men to avenge themselves for their slavery upon the women and children who remained. I think that is a great tribute to the Negro race—to any race."

I nodded in agreement.

"It isn't to be quickly forgotten," he said.

I got up to go and he walked to the stair with me.

"You're going to Margaret Wynn's for cocktails, aren't you?"

"Yes."

"We'll see you there then."

Across the forever flat land of the miles-long fields between the narrow bands of trees and the green margins of the drainage ditches I rode back to Greenville. As I drove

I wondered what Johnston and Delta and Pine together meant. Of course, they meant conventional material success. But I wondered if that success was the end or merely the most obvious evidence of what was going on on the big plantation. Beyond the counting of profits, it seemed to me that Johnston had a sense of the integration of man and animal and earth. Definitely he had shown that cotton growing could be made profitable without squeezing the profits out of Negroes or removing it from the fertility of the earth. And he held a faith that cotton growing could be kept profitable without dispossessing the people who had grown dependent—too dependent—on it for a sorry sustenance.

Here on the Mississippi Delta Johnston seemed to me to be leading not so much a resistance against the machine as a demonstration that mules and men, well-cared-for and well-fed, under wise direction, even in the old plantation pattern, might still together live well and happily on the rich earth of the warm South. For a little while at least.

I said out loud to myself, "Under wise direction." And I thought then: How many Oscar Johnstons are there between Charleston and the levees? The sad answer is—the tragic thing is—that wisdom is not only rare among tenants. It is also rare on the piazzas.

21

FERRYBOAT RIDE

WE HAD waited so long on the dusty shore that when the ferryboat at last came so slowly across the wide, muddy waters there was hardly room for all of us on the boat. And what a company we were moving south by automobile over a swollen river down which no more boats carried the motley companies of Southerners! Except ferryboats. We were all aboard this one. I think almost every aspect of the South, lacking possibly dignity, rode on the way from Greenville in Mississippi to Lake Village in Arkansas, where better roads led south and back into Mississippi again. There was a man in his car who might almost have been the white-haired colonel of the Southern legend. But his colored chauffeur wore a blue shirt, a white hat and was chewing gum. On the seat beside the gentleman was a woman who at her best could have been only a Southern charmer of the school given to pink rayons and heavy, cheap perfumes. This one was at the age when both the rayons and the perfume are more apparent. Her scent stirred in the breeze above the river like the smoke of the engines. And she got out to join the increasing company which diverted itself during the trans-Mississippi voyage by playing the slot machines of the side-lever (one-armed bandit) type.

The coatless Negro driver of the car in which she rode played the machine next to her. A group of Delta Chinamen played a third. But more interesting than all the others to me were the men of the two dirty couples, each with a dirty baby, who occupied a huge, obviously secondhand Lincoln car with a Louisiana license. I never saw anywhere any couples who seemed to me probably more like the pioneer Americans actually were and less like the pioneer Americans, praying in their covered wagons, were supposed to look. The men wore dingy cloth breeches and the women were dressed in green and purple slacks with silk stockings showing through the toes of their sandals. In them all was a continuity of American restless youngness all the way from the natural young, whom Horatio Colony rediscovered and made alive in *Free Forester* about old colonizing Daniel Boone, to almost as forgotten John Dillinger. One of those on the ferryboat held his baby in his arms while he played the slot machine. I noticed that their women were young and pretty though they had dirty heads.

While I watched, a fat and effeminate man got out of the sedan in which he rode with four Chinamen and stuck his head through the window of my car.

"Good morning," he said in a melting soprano.

"Good morning."

"Have an apple."

"No thanks."

"I saw your license plates. I used to live in North Carolina, but I've been out here a nice long while. I like it. It's very pleasant."

I looked at him with careful distaste but I asked, "Tell me, what do the Chinese do for a living in Mississippi? Do they farm?"

He looked back at his companions. "Oh, no, they're business men. And that one yonder is a preacher, a Presbyterian preacher. Oh, they're fine gentlemen." His eyes filled with pleasant dream. "You ought to see a Chinese boy I know. He's just fifteen. I tease him. And he just smiles so sweet, so sweet!"

194

He mimicked a monstrous coyness. And he pursed, in imitation of the China boy's smiling, a mouth like the sessile, fleshy suckers on the tentacles of an octopus.

"I'm sure of it," I said. "Excuse me."

I got out of my car and walked past the slot machine players. The gray almost-gentleman was giving more change to the reeking woman. The dirty Louisiana youth was looking beyond the baby in his arms wistfully at the three valueless symbols in combination on the machine he was playing. But further aft—if ferryboats possess fore and aft—was the big truck of the American Lending Library, Inc., and its pleasant driver. I had expected no such vehicle on the line between Mississippi where one man out of seven would not recognize his own name if written and Arkansas where a better record is still not evidence of great bookishness. Up in Arkansas I had been shown a map speckled with dots denoting libraries established and maintained by the Emergency Relief Administration. But on that hot day on the river below Greenville it seemed and it still seems to me that books transported by truck for profit in the South are a good deal more encouraging than libraries set up by those trying to spend money usefully as a substitute for naked relief. The driver complained of the roads, not of the illiteracy. And he was not afraid that relief libraries would take the profits from under his job.

The Arkansas shore loomed close and green before us. I drove ashore and south toward the Vicksburg bridge. On the way I was pleased, no less than by the sight of a truck load of books for rent, by the discovery of a blacksmith shop —one of many I found out later—in which a huge half-naked black man beat a ringing out of iron for the feet of plantation horses and mules. I like to think that books and beasts together mean a happier, safer South.

22

THE MADAME'S MEMORY

I FOUND the Civil War (War Between the States to you, dear Cousin Lucy) in the South only by accident. To most Southerners at last, it is as remote as the War of the Roses. But to Vicksburg, which is commercially dying slowly between the river and the high waterside hills which canyon the town, the war remains in battleground and cemetery and to these, Vicksburg hopes, the spending living will still come. The same carefully tended war is to be found in the vicinities of Richmond and Gettysburg and attended by the same preoccupation for present profit. Certainly when the United States guards the graves it also mourns, the grass grows greener than in the poorer countryside around. Even the sun, as through the circle open to the sky in the dome of the big Illinois Monument, seems to shine brighter on the Federal dead. I came to this green and sun across the long bridge from Louisiana into Vicksburg at the time of the opening of the second Assembly General of the Descendants of the Participants of the Campaign, Siege and Defense of Vicksburg Society. And so far away from the battle even in the South are we, that though the families of the more than hundred thousand participants have undoubtedly experienced normal growth since 1863 I had no difficulty in getting a room with a bath in the Hotel Vicksburg, where patriotic ladies wearing bright baldrics waited for the descendants. I could feel their cordiality quickening as I came across the lobby, cooling as it developed that once again the traveler was merely the traveler, not the filial patriot. But Harris Dickson, gentleman and author, who is as kind as he is wise, a world man in Mississippi who knows that Mississippi is world enough for any stirring mind, took me in hand and presented me to patriots in white linens and flowered chiffons. Long after the reception in the cemetery— bright the ladies and pale the punch—he gave me one of the same mint juleps which he gave to Col. U. S. Grant the Third. (The mint is not crushed.) J. C. Pemberton, grandson of the Confederate who lost Vicksburg, lost a julep. He did not reach Vicksburg until next morning.

Charming gentleman that I am sure he is, I did not meet him. I did not even miss him or the formal ceremonies in which he came to take part. Indeed, Harris Dickson seemed to me to contribute more to the richness of Vicksburg than the Civil War does. And his deep porch certainly seemed to me richer in the warmer Mississippi meanings than any history paraded out of the past for the sake of a present Vicksburg. Later on I found, too, that life now on the back piazza of Hope Farm and on the court at Green Leaves in Natchez is pleasanter than all the museuming in the big houses which the cotton snobs of old Natchez had built before the war in an amazing competition in architectural pretentiousness. Dickson talked of the river, of mechanical cotton pickers, of Negroes, of levees and crevasses, of share-croppers, of Tung trees, and of an old Negress he had found beyond gas boat and mule team trip at the lost Brierfield of Jefferson Davis. She remembered Jefferson Davis, she said, and Dickson was convinced from the internal evidence of her tale that she was more than 120 years old.

And of floods: People along this section of the river once believed that they were in no real danger unless there was a conjunction of the high waters of two or more of the big rivers delivering water to the Mississippi. But the last flood was a single river flood and it all but destroyed towns which had felt themselves secure before.

The Cherokee rose, indigenous to the Mississippi country, is one of the three roses of the world from which all other roses have grown.

"Natchez is the great Southern novel," he said, "but I can't write it. Nobody can write it yet. More people have got to die."

John Hudson, the New Orleans *Times-Picayune's* Mississippi man, recollected that as young reporter he had covered a famous and sensational murder trial in south Mississippi a good many years ago. He spoke of a suspect in the case and laughed shortly. "The man, queer and solitary, lived in a big, old-fashioned house and it was the dirtiest place I ever saw. You could scrape the lice off of his bed by the handful and every time I went out there I had to have my clothes burned. I asked him how he stood it. He said they didn't bother him." Hudson laughed again, an abrupt laugh below the mustache like a scrap of fur which increases his resemblance to Robert Louis Stevenson. "He said that bugs would not bother you if you slept on your stomach so they could crawl over you, but if you slept on your side and prevented them from passing, they would eat you up. I never tested it."

From the opposite darkness on the porch Lawson Magruder, Delta planter and brother of an admiral, spoke of a certain piece of land. "It is like a desirable woman who has everything a woman needs and everything a man wants."

"I heard," I told him, "that there is no love of the land in the Delta in the earth and family sense, only as property like money."

"It isn't true," he said, with some feeling. "It isn't true."

"I heard," I told him, "that when planters have a good year they don't spend the money improving house and land in the Delta but on pretty ladies in Memphis."

"That's not so."

A young doctor spoke of the amazing dimensions of a water moccasin he and some friends had come upon while fishing further south on the Pascagoula River. "It was as thick around the middle as a girl's leg above the knee."

And talk came around again to Harris Dickson and to flood in New Orleans and, from cafés in New Orleans, to Paris and New York and a place called Gerstenberg's in Washington. He remembered coming there one night tired and lonely after years of absence and he recognized only the descendants of the old great Danes sleeping still with their noses between paws under the heavy tables. And at last an old waiter named Gustav. He made him take his apron off and have dinner with him, and both he and Gustav complained to the manager about all the change that disturbed them. "Oh, we had a grand time," he said a little wistfully. "A grand time."

And time has done something like that to all of Vicksburg. On one side is the river on which the great boats no longer move. And on all other sides a cemetery bands it, crowded with the dead and with the neat iron tablets which tell every move live men made so long ago. Warehouses sit on streets where the lawn of the old Klein mansion once ran to the river. The Syrians have come. They press close against the Negroes around Brother-In-Law's Barber Shop and Catfish Row. A filling station crowds close to the screened porch of the Butts house on Cherry Street. Little that Pemberton surrendered or Grant won is left. But the continuity of Vicksburg is maintained at 12 India Street (to alter its name a little). It does not require a philosopher to wonder how many generations of little girls have ministered there to how many generations of men.

Vicksburg is a quiet town though church bells ring it on Sunday mornings as full of sweet noise as Perugia at vespers. Its citizens come home and report that the preachers are good men even if a little wordy; but down the river hill of the town and outside the concrete levee with a gate in it, the Salvation Army group, composed mostly of uniformed girls, sings loudly and unmelodiously to the accompaniment of brassy music while the boats go and come across the narrow channel of the river between Vicksburg and DeSoto Island which, conveniently, is a part of the State of Louisiana. There Tom Morrissey runs his houseboat saloons, one for white, one for colored. To them the two boats, *Haig* and *Haig,* run on a schedule uninterrupted by the Salvation Army. And there I remember an unwashed mother suggested that her daughter—then dancing with great energy—might be disposed to go along with us. The implications of her suggestion somehow seemed infinitely evil beside the ordered almost country-prim sinning for a living at 12 India Street.

Tornado and the wash of the river may have carried away the Natchez-under-the-Hill which was so long infamous even on the shores of the Mississippi. Tyrone Power, the British actor, in 1836 reported the "dancing-shops, bar-rooms, faro-banks or roulette tables" and the "numbers of half-dressed, faded young girls" who "lounged within the bar-rooms or at the doors." The preacher, Timothy Flint, reported the tornado which struck it in 1840. But if Natchy-under-the-Hill, as Power called it, is gone The District in Vicksburg remains. It runs along Walnut Street from Jackson and between the river and the hilltop where sits old Christ Church. On Sunday afternoons in the streets below the church prettiest women sit rocking and waiting on their porches. The color range is complete: the women range almost in a chromatic scale from pale baby-faced little tow-heads to Negresses black as licorice, and there are red heads and high browns between. But the women of 12 India Street are not to be seen sitting on porches. It has no porch. Instead it sits flush with the sidewalk on one of the steepest hills in a hilly town. It rises behind a scabrous yellow façade three stories, the first of which has heavy solid yellow shutters on the windows.

"It is about a hundred years old," Baxter said. "There was an army officer who came here for duty at the engineering experiment station. He said he had heard of 12 India in the Philippines."

"It is almost proverbial in Mississippi," Person said, "how many prostitutes come from Smith County. It's an all rural county and 15 miles from any railroad."

(Smith County: Total population 18,405. Per cent urban, 0. Per cent white, 80.4. Population per square mile, 29. More than half of the total population, 24 years old and younger. Percentage of tenancy, 51. Value of all farms, $2,981,313. Value of tenant farms, $992,948. Spendable income per capita, $58.50 in 1932; $96.00 in 1935.)

We ascended a steep narrow unpainted flight of stairs to a floor which contained two big rooms one on each side of the landing. In one two very poorly dressed country boys were talking quietly to two girls. They might almost have been relatives calling. The girls might have been relatives receiving. And in the other room we met the Madame. I have forgotten what she said her name was. A dumpy little woman with none of the vigor of person or of tongue which I have always thought would be essential to an executive position in a bawdy house. There was no evidence of flame in Madame or evidence that flame had ever burned in her. She reminded me of a little fat storekeeper in Raleigh with whom I had discussed the still flourishing trade among the Negroes and poor whites in snuffs.

Person asked if he could buy a drink for the girls, and there was not the least doubt that he could. Indeed, I suppose the old system by which the girls get a cut on all the sales they help make must have prevailed there for the mere suggestion brought the girls flocking from every direction. Even the two who were talking with the country boys in the next room came in to receive the beer which was then the only legal alcoholic in Mississippi. All of them sat about the walls like shy children.

It was an ugly room upon which not the least money or effort had been expended with the idea of improving its appearance. The chairs were such as are customarily rented from undertakers. And the girls who sat upon them made no more offering to vice than the primitive fact that they were female. They looked, indeed, very much like the childish clerks to be seen in many Southern ten cent stores. All of them were fully covered and cheaply clothed. As far as I could see there was not the least effort to make old sin attractive. The whole place seemed not so wicked as terribly poor, unimaginative and a little pitiful.

Certainly if the old time river houses were as uninspiring and unalluring as this one, they have been vastly romanticized. Possibly, however, the type of women who made the old houses famous prefer now to move in such unofficial houses as the big hotels which North and South, so police tell me, have willingly or unwillingly received the diaspora of the districts.

A Negro maid brought the beer and with Mr. Baxter and Mr. Person I drank to the ladies. They snickered at the gesture. But they drank, too, and stared at us as children do at unexpected and unfamiliar guests. Madame drank her beer a little wearily. Very far off I heard a church bell ring for Sunday evening services.

"I suppose you get a lot of young men on Sunday nights," I suggested.

"Not the young," she said. "We don't get many young men. It's older men who come here, many from the back country and the plantations."

"You surprise me," I told her.

"Yes," she said and smiled over it. "The older ones. And they are better business, too."

We drank our beer with little natural chit-chat to accompany it. "My friends tell me your house is a hundred years old."

"It's old. I don't know how old. I rent it from Mr. So-andso." She rubbed her plump cheek with a plump hand. "I don't know how old it is. But I know it is old. I was a girl here twenty—twenty-five years ago. And one night I was with a man who said he was in the house during the siege. He told me he paid for his entertainment with a silver spur he'd found where some Yankee dropped it in the mud. They'd have loved him better for bread, he said. Everybody was hungry then, soldiers and girls. That was a long time ago."

"Yes," I agreed. But not so far away, I thought.

The girls who had come in from the other room said thanks for their beers before they went back to the country boys. The Negro maid promptly brought the bill for the beers to Baxter.

"I think he was from Georgia," the Madame went on. "But I'm not sure. You know there are so many men. . . ."

"I know," I said.

And the Madame blushed.

The three of us went down the street stair to the precipitous hill upon which the old house sat. And the breeze blew fresh and cool from the river where the Salvation Army girls were singing and *Haig* and *Haig* were steadily sailing back and forth carrying the thirsty to the island named after the great captain who had discovered this river only to be buried in its waters. And that, like the evening of the Madame's memory, was a long time ago.

GOVERNOR'S PLAN

"Boys," asked the Governor of Mississippi, "what was it?"

The newspapermen stood about him listening to the report of the week-end's fishing trip. And I, the visitor listening with them, regarded at the same time Hugh White, who as Governor has set out to balance the ancient agriculture of Mississippi with a new industrial development.

"We were sitting out there in the boat, when one of those farmer-fishermen came along and showed us where something had grabbed a set hook he had and broken the cypress limb which it was tied to." The Governor lifted a thick and hairy forearm. "The limb was as big around as my arm. Some of our folks saw the limb on the water and grabbed it. Whatever was on the other end of it spun them around so fast that they would probably have been upset if the line hadn't broke. What was it? I've been fishing in Mississippi for forty years and I don't know. What was it?"

He gesticulated his question with his cigar. He is a fat man with straight graying hair, a thick body, brown hairy arms, an emphatic manner. But he speaks his vigor out of a little mouth. He looked me over calmly when one of his office staff introduced me and told him I was interested in his "Balance Agriculture with Industry Plan."

"No," he said. "No. I'm sorry. No. I've just gotten back and I've got to make a speech tomorrow and I haven't got time to talk with you about it. I'm sorry."

Distinctly I was disappointed. Early that morning in Vicksburg a noisy knocking on my door had announced the expansion of my touring company from one to three. To ride through the Deep South with me had come my brother, Dr. Worth Bagley Daniels, of Washington, D. C., a physician satisfactory as a traveling companion because his interests are not all bounded by the human hide, and his son, Worth, Jr., a twelve year old red head with the body of a Percheron, the appetite of an anaconda and a passion for playing slot machines with his father's or my money. We drove the fifty miles to Jackson.

"I'll be here an hour anyhow. Take the car and go see what you please."

And now the Governor was being very emphatic about his present inability to talk about his plan.

"I'm sorry," he said again as if he really were.

"So am I," I said. "Do you really think you're going to get industries worth having by subsidizing them?"

He glared at me and at the word "subsidize."

"All the states are subsidizing," he said, "one way or the other. We're doing it openly, honestly. You can call it subsidy or not. The rest are trying to do the same thing."

I waited silent.

"I don't ask the people of Mississippi to grow one less bale of cotton." He smacked the top of his desk with a hairy hand. "Not one less bale. I don't mean to make Mississippi an industrial State. But I want some balance. It's the only way we can escape from this poverty at the bottom of the country."

"You think the factories are coming?"

He reached grimly across his desk for a paper.

"They're coming. And I'll tell you why. I can't tell you where these figures come from but listen. Fifty-nine per cent of all the industrial migration is due to labor racketeering and the like."

He chewed at his cigar.

"Down here we haven't got the disturbing elements in our population they've got up North. Don't you worry, the factories are coming. The only question is which Southern States are going to get 'em. I mean for Mississippi to."

I watched his cigar complete a parabola from wet mouth to beaten desk.

"But when you get the industries aren't you going to have the same 'labor racketeering and the like'?"

The Governor smacked his desk. "No."

"How are you going to prevent it?"

"We have always prevented it," he said with an elephantine shrug.

One of the Governor's subordinates laughed and the rest of us grinned in understanding if not sympathy. The Governor leaned forward with his thick arms on his desk.

"It all goes back to my town of Columbia," he said. "Some years ago I was about to start a sawmill near there. You know I was raised with the smell of pine timber in my nose. Well, I was about to set up my mill where the timber was, about 12 miles from town, when some of the men of Columbia came to see me. They said they would give me a piece of land adjoining the town but free from its taxes and control if I would establish the mill there. After thinking it over, I agreed. Since then, of course, the timber has been cut off but we've gotten other industries to take the place of the sawmill payrolls. And here we're trying to do the same thing for Mississippi that we did for Columbia."

He went on talking, talking, and the impression grew in my mind that he was not a very sensitive man, not a particularly wise man, but an essentially honest man trying by his lights to do something for Mississippi. Certainly Mississippi needs some way out of darkness. With all or most of its wealth growing on one stalk (85 per cent of its wealth is in agriculture; 83.1 per cent of its people are rural) five cent cotton means actual starvation on the land. Declining cotton markets may mean a starvation in transition. What industry it has possessed was associated with a disappearing virgin timber. In the five years before I talked to Governor White, his State had lost more than two per cent of its population despite a high birthrate. Mississippi is poor to hunger, to ignorance, almost to despair. The Governor's plan of escape, as he outlines it, is simple: Any Mississippi community, upon petition of 20 per cent of its citizens and the approval of the State Industrial Commission, may hold an election. If two thirds of those voting agree the community may issue bonds for the acquisition or erection of factories for industries which may be exempt from ad valorem taxation for five years. The community may sell the plant, lease the plant; sometimes even under some conditions it may practically give it away.

(In the Governor's own town of Columbia, Thomas L. Stokes of the Scripps-Howard newspapers reported that while the Governor was Mayor the Chamber of Commerce by public subscription raised $80,000 to build the plant for the Reliance Manufacturing Company of Chicago, a company which was organized in 1898 to use convict labor in Wisconsin. The company was to become owner of the building if it made a payroll of $1,000,000 in five years. That it has already done. It was also exempt from taxes for five years. The Columbia plant is only one of 16 operated by this company in the United States. About 720 people were employed in the Columbia plant, Stokes reported, 85 per cent of whom come in from the country to make the dress shirts and pajamas which the company produces. The State Planning Commission reported that in 1935 the per capita spendable income in Marion County, in which Columbia is located, was $198 a year, an average which must include the Governor's income from his timber fortune and the spendable income of the least tenant farmer, who has much less than $198 to spend, as well as the income of that tenant farmer's daughter who may work in the garment factory. Such an average spendable income in the Governor's own county throws illumination on the Governor's statement that frequently one factory worker will earn more than the total family income from the farm had formerly been. This demonstrates not good wages in the subsidized factories but the pitiful return from labor on the Mississippi farm. Wages in Southern garment factories—and not only in Marion County and Mississippi—are often so low that they represent not a differential between the North and the South based on living costs, skills, railroad rates, etc., but the complete absence of any true labor market for the much eager, intelligent, trainable labor in some sections of the South. Even exploiters are sometimes surprised at how little they need pay.)

"There may be better plans," the Governor conceded, "but we haven't been able to find them and we can't wait forever for them to be found. Mississippi is too far behind to wait. And these other Southern States aren't waiting. It doesn't seem to me to be far from towns furnishing light, water, heat, fire protection and so forth by municipal ownership and control and through taxation to furnishing places in which citizens can have work. If work isn't necessary, I don't know what is."

Neither I nor any of the newspapermen in the circle about his desk intervened to prove or deny that the provision of jobs is a necessary function of municipal corporations. I wondered how many times they had heard this lengthening speech for which the Governor had not had time. And I wondered, too, if the Governor realized how near such a plan might on its shining surface seem to come to State Socialism, far off as actually was the lending of community capital to old-fashioned capitalistic exploitation.

The Governor snorted, "Subsidy! It looks like sense to me, like down in Columbia when they got me to put my sawmill there."

And then suddenly he seemed spent. "No," he said. "No. I'm sorry. But I've just gotten back. I've got to make an address tomorrow. And I haven't got time to talk with you about our plan. Some other time."

I said again, "I'm sorry," and I wondered how long he would have talked had he had the time.

"I'll show him what we're doing, Governor," promised Howard Suttle, young Mississippian who in the past eight years had participated as newspaperman-publicity maker in seven general elections. Politics is one industry Mississippi does not have to import.

We told the Governor good-by and with the two Worths who had exhausted the possibilities of the Capitol of Mississippi, we went to see how Mississippi stirs out of her old lethargy. And that stirring is nowhere better to be seen than in the office of L. J. Folse, Louisiana Catholic in sternly Protestant Mississippi, who has by his own admission spent years denying the almost national lying that goes on steadily, he says, about Mississippi.

"Why, people have made it a business to defame Mississippi. They've devoted their lives to it."

There was the man who wrote and the paper that printed his statement that he had been afraid to get out of his car in Mississippi because of the snakes. He made a picture of a writhing earth. In all his years in Mississippi Mr. Folse never has seen a snake. He does not deny that there may be some. Irishman that he is, he does not contend that Mississippi is as snakeless as Ireland. But somehow he almost gives that impression.

He is eloquent. He is informed. He not only knows Mississippi from The Weaver Pants Corporation in Corinth to the Southern Kraft Corporation in Moss Point, but as executive director of the State Planning Commission he also knows the meaning of the dumping of a bucket of water in New York State or Montana on the long line of the State which borders its river.

This thin gray Irishman, lively, intelligent, opinionated, but human and humorous, seemed to me to put life and possibility into the Governor's plan which looked in the Governor's talking and analysis like a species of solemn folly almost designed to secure for Mississippi the worst types of industry, and to provide a veritable picnic for promoters. But Folse is not merely concerned with urging towns to issue bonds to build factories for industries, moving, as the Governor said, largely on account of labor aspects of industry which may be wages and hours as well as unions and racketeers. He is concerned as chief planner for Mississippi's future with river and water and forest, with agriculture and fishing and all the varied aspects of a long State.

And Mississippi moves: Fifteen years ago when the first stock law was passed men shot each other and blew up dipping vats unable to see that the law was designed to save the State from the cattle tick. Now the same individualism and tradition makes difficult teaching the people that they ought not to burn over their lands, a process which has destroyed forests, aided erosion and done the earth no good. So Mississippi moves slowly: it is caught in poverty between eroded hill and sea plain swamp, back of the river and cotton, in pitiful tenancy and in an independent farming which is sometimes only a recurrent half-starving in independence. It is only belatedly becoming aware of a diversity of resource.

"But—" said Folse, and I felt the same attitude which I had found in Lilienthal's garden in Norris, "but once the people are made to understand—whether it be the dipping of cattle or the burning of fields—nine times out of ten, they will decide right."

Beyond this faith in the decision of the democracy of Mississippi, he frowned. The people were not always able to choose. They did not always possess the free choice David Lilienthal demanded for them.

"The people of the North," he said, "have studiously kept the South in the business of producing raw materials by a deliberate and fixed disadvantage in freight rate differentials which made it impossible for the South to compete in the production of manufactured products. That's one big reason we're poor. Of course we ought to produce more than cotton but they tied us to cotton—tight. That's one big reason why we have to offer special advantages to industry. The North set our slaves free but the North made the whole South slave. We've got to be freed."

But not all Mississippi, not even all Jackson, was solely concerned with the maps and charts, plans and talk of escape from the State's deep old poverty. Young Suttle drove us across the dirty, greasy Pearl River into the Free State of Rankin where then in a succession of cheap, tawdry little houses the ladies and gentlemen of Jackson drank and gambled in naked violation of the law. Almost everybody, it seemed, was "fixed" and happy except a district attorney who had taken the law of Mississippi seriously. Juries would not. But under Mississippi law the chancellor, or equity judge, could padlock houses shown to be nuisances. But quickly beside one padlocked house another unpadlocked rose. And in them all liquor was cheaper than it was 50 miles away in Louisiana because there was no Mississippi tax to be paid. In the afternoon the roulette wheels were not turning. But dressed and ready for the evening was a Southern gentleman out of a book, already fingering the house's chips which would go, not to enrich or ruin him but to stir the play of the backward and the timid who might join the nice old man.

Nor has all Mississippi faith in plans or charts or the ponderous hopefulness of the Governor's speeches. We said good-by to Suttle and drove south through a worn hill country. There seemed to be almost as many tomato plants as cotton plants on the road to Hazelhurst. And I was grateful for company between Hazelhurst and Natchez when a tire blew out. We fixed it and stopped at Union Church, a tiny community about a country cemetery where the dead are more numerous than the living. An old gentleman with a mass of white curls ordered our spare tire fixed. And while we waited I saw Mr. Cato. Half whispering on the porch of the store he said something to a Negro that sent the Negro off guffawing. He leaned back against one of the thin square pillars and gradually the grin left his face. He regarded our car.

"My people came from the Carolinas," he said. "From the Scotch settlements."

"Along the Cape Fear River," I suggested.

"I don't know. My name is Cato. I never could figure it out. Cato is a Dago name."

"I don't ever remember hearing it among the Carolina Scotch."

"There used to be thirteen families of Catos around here. But now I'm the last one."

I went into the store and bought a Coca-Cola. The two Worths watched the operation on the deflated tire.

"I tell you what I think," Cato resumed while I drank. "I think some Scotch Queen had Italian musicians and that one of my ancestors stayed in Scotland until his descendants were all Scotch but the name."

That seemed to me entirely probable and I said so.

"Yes. There used to be thirteen families of Catos round about Union Church and now I'm the only one."

He did not seem so much disturbed as anxious to tell an interesting fact.

"And last week I sold the original place of my Grandfather Cato. I'm the last."

He smiled over it. And we left him smiling when we drove away, past the big fan-shaped country cemetery about the old church on the road to Natchez and the river.

24

LOST PRESENT

In those days the ladies and the gentlemen rode their thoroughbred horses in from the surrounding plantations to the theater which was built in a graveyard. And after the play on the evening of February 11, 1835, Tyrone Power, who had come up the river to Natchez from New Orleans on his American tour, met an old acquaintance, John Howard Payne. Mr. Payne, wandering always, improvident always, had come down the river from St. Louis to Natchez seeking subscriptions for a literary magazine which he proposed to establish in London. Neither the Irish actor, whose hilarious playing of Larry Hooligan O'Halloran made the world laugh, nor Mr. Payne, whose "Home, Sweet Home" sang the world's homesickness, were aware of any special significance in their meeting. But the very casualness of their coming together in Natchez, which never produced a great man but to which then all the great went visiting, gives point to the fact that in that unusually cold February and in the years immediately about it Natchez was at its little time of perfection based on cotton money, nigger money and river trade.

That was the same year in which S. S. Prentiss of Natchez, the Southern silver-tongue who was born in Maine, was to establish his reputation as an orator in the Mississippi legislature. And that year, too, John A. Quitman of Natchez, Southern soldier and statesman who was born in Rhinebeck, New York, was president of the State Senate. The big houses on the wide plantations spread back from the river, their doors open in eager and eternal hospitality. Aaron Burr had come plotting. Henry Clay came politicking. Jefferson Davis came courting. Tyrone Power had no trouble stirring laughter. Peddlers came selling easily paintings which Power said were "worse pictures than are offered to connoisseurs at a pawnbroker's sale in London." Some of the pictures remain. But there was no nostalgia in Natchez then to need Payne's so sad song. Home, sweet home, is generally simpler than the pretentious houses which surrounded Natchez. There was a moment in Mississippi. It passed. And not even Mrs. Balfour Miller can bring it back to life again.

"His success, as might be expected," Power wrote of Payne in his journal at that moment, "has been most encouraging."

All Payne's projects were encouraging, but somehow that was all. His pockets were forever empty, and six years after he met Power in Natchez he went off, glad to have the job so far from home, as consul to Tunis and never saw home, sweet home, again. Sad, strange coincidence, Power was lost at sea the same year Payne sailed for Africa. And the year before that a twisting, terrific tornado had struck and destroyed the well-known wickedness of Natchez-under-the-Hill. In 1850 Sergeant Prentiss was dead at the age of 42 and buried under the moss-hung live oaks at Gloucester Plantation. Governor Quitman died, too, a few years afterward, in the fifties. Frederick Law Olmsted looked at Natchez with the bristling antagonism of a democrat and an abolitionist, saw young men drunk at the hotel and pigs running loose in the public garden on the bluffs, and compared Natchez in the fifties (population, 18,601; children in schools, 1,051; books in public libraries, 2,000; and seats in the churches, 7,700) with Springfield, Illinois (population, 19,228; school children, 3,300; books in public libraries, 20,000; and seats in churches, 28,000). Lincoln of Springfield had not even been nominated for the Presidency. Olmsted chose his town for comparison only because its population was nearest to that of Natchez of any town in the free states. But Natchez was not even aware of Mr. Olmsted who was entertained at no plantation but talked instead to an Italian confectioner and a German inn-keeper. The gentlemen of Natchez were spending their money on greater and greater houses. And in the sixties when the call to arms came the painters left their brushes in the buckets in the vast architectural atrocity, a Moorish castle in American woods, which Dr. Haller Nutt was building at Longwood. They never picked them up again. Neither did anybody else.

But in 1932 Mrs. Balfour Miller, handsome, childless, full of energy and mistress of old and quietly lovely Hope Farm, organized the first Natchez Pilgrimage as an activity of the Natchez Garden Club. She went, slim in her crinolines, inviting Mississippi, the South and America to "Natchez Where the Old South Lives." That year in Natchez and elsewhere the Old South was practically starving and Yankees as well as Southerners with the price were more than welcome. And they came. They filled the Eola Hotel. They followed the costumed ladies of Natchez through the double doors at Gloucester, under the six high fluted columns at D'Evereux, through the garden of gazebo, box, azaleas and japonicas at Arlington, even under the cast iron balcony over the door at Homewood where now (except at Pilgrimage time) Mrs. Kingsley Swann, rich Yankee settler, turns back the tourists with a vigor amazing (and amusing) to the natives. The whole affair was a great success. Newspapers far away rejoiced to print pretty pictures of costumed Natchez ladies standing decorously in doorways, and, less decorously, flying in swings just high enough to show that there were limbs of flesh beneath the billowing skirts of dimity. The City Bank and Trust Company of Natchez, which knows good business when it sees it, presented to Mrs. Miller a silver tray engraved in token of the highest civic service. The years marched: 1932—1933—1934—1935—1936—and all went lovely as a bride descending a wide mahogany staircase in a Natchez mansion. Then schism ran like a crack in old masonry through the Natchez Garden Club and suddenly—a stranger may think also a little sadly—there were two garden clubs and two pilgrimages, but no more mansions and only one Natchez. The town lay wide open and wounded when we visited it.

I remember we came into Natchez with the darkness and after dark walked through its wide empty streets past a smell of horse manure and hay, and big abandoned cotton mills to the park which sits with the town high on the bluffs and high over what long ago had been Natchez-under-the-Hill. I recalled that Olmsted had found there a man, bearded and smoking, and a woman with him, and beyond them hogs grunting. Tyrone Power, from the park, had heard in the darkness quarreling down under the hill and two shots and a woman's scream. The past back to them did not seem very deep in the darkness. Full of quietness now was the town behind us and the wide night over the curving river between us and the lights in Louisiana. A boy and a girl on a bench were as quiet as they were close together when we passed. Further on a man rose as we approached.

"Got a match?"

Worth gave him a paper pack.

"Thanks," he said and lit a red face above a shirt that ended abruptly without either collar or tie.

We walked again in the morning. There was a house of ancient line and brick. It bore the huge, bright legend: "Magnolia Laboratories and Packing Company—home of the KFM fly and mosquito spray." Along the street before it the oleanders were in full bloom. I regarded their bright crimson flowers and narrow pointed leaves carefully.

"These are oleanders, aren't they?"

"Certainly, they are," my scientific brother said. "I know that much myself, though I'm generally, so far as flowers are concerned, like Dr. Ray Lyman Wilbur. He made a great reputation with his hostess by identifying a tiny yellow flower in her garden as *icterus neonatorum*." He laughed. "That's jaundice of the new born."

Young Worth read the lichen-grown inscription on the Confederate monument:

> From each Lost Cause of earth,
> Something precious springs to birth,
> Though lost it be to men,
> It lives with God again.

The monument had been erected in 1889, a quarter of a century after the war. Young veterans must have been in their forties then. What a day it must have been for them! It was built nearly fifty years before the morning we looked at it. Beyond it in the shade of the live oak trees a man wearing the conventional well-washed khaki of the Deep South was mending a net and beside him a woman was suckling a baby. We went on from the park the little way to St. Mary's Cathedral where wedding music sounded through the stained glass windows. Two women gave us samples of a headache remedy and young Worth claimed and pocketed all three. Before the Cathedral two Irish policemen were standing. And one of them gave me what seems to me to be the clearest explanation of the quarrel between the ladies of Natchez over the presentation of Natchez's lost grandeur in its lean present.

"The Garden Club," he spat and said, "took in folks that didn't even have a flower pot. They run it. And some of the folks that own the biggest places need the fees the tourists pay to see them to eat on."

Perhaps the policeman was prejudiced. Anywhere else in the world, the withdrawal of the home owners from the Garden Club and the withdrawal of their old mansions from the homes displayed might have been a cool selfishness. But in Natchez pride and poverty, big house and little purse go remarkably often together. One Natchez mansion is owned by a Yankee millionaire, and one by a Coca-Cola bottler, which is the Southern equivalent. Perhaps half a dozen are owned by persons well-off by the little Southern town standards of Natchez (which is 5,000 persons smaller than it was in 1850). But the majority of the owners and inhabitants of the great houses of Natchez need the money which the pilgrimages bring them, a few of them must wait for the quarters of the tourists to buy bread—or a bottle. Therefore, maybe the division of the dollars between home owners and club treasury was the basic reason for the withdrawal from the Natchez Garden Club in May, 1936, of a group of owners of antebellum houses. The original Natchez Garden Club divided the money from the pilgrimage, one-third to the club for "the preservation, beautification and restoration of historic Natchez" and two-thirds to the owners of the homes shown on the tours. In the new Pilgrimage Garden Club, organized by the seceding homeowners, after the payment of all expenses, three-fourths of the money goes to the homeowners and one-fourth to the club for some civic purpose. So probably the money is the basis of dissension in this matter in Natchez as in a great many other matters in the great wide world. But also important was the matter of control within the first club. There are over a hundred members even now in the Natchez Garden Club, but the houses worth visiting are limited to perhaps less than twenty-five. The flower-potters certainly might be in control. From such a possibility of a tyrannical majority ladies in Natchez seceded in 1936 as did gentlemen in Natchez in 1861. Thus far the results of the 1936 secession for both and all have not been disturbing. Indeed, two pilgrimages grew successfully in 1937 where only one grew before. But there is anger at home and laughter abroad. And the realization grows even in Mississippi that there was similarity between the civic schism at Natchez and one which threatened at Mound Bayou where the all-Negro town established by Jefferson Davis' body-servant celebrated the fiftieth anniversary of its founding in 1937. The two-garden-club affair follows ludicrously close on the multiplication by division of Baptist churches and similar institutions in the small town South.

One thing I know: whether or not the secession of which she is a part is wise, Mrs. Balfour Miller has not only served to make the world aware of Natchez, also in Natchez she was a guide whose hospitality was only equaled by her energy. She led us in courtesy and kindness about the Mississippi countryside which is Natchez. Only a few of the houses are in the diminished town. Most of them sit, as is proper to the past, in the midst of plantations where still in a species of freedom Negroes grow the cotton which built the mansions. From the big town house of Stanton Hall to the plantation places of D'Evereux and Linden and Gloucester we went, to Richmond where Miss Theodora Britton Marshall (Pedodie to Natchez) dispenses history and antiques in her basement shop. And then on to Dunleith, which has been loaded with an ugly, heavy tile roof, and Elmscourt and Arlington to Landsdowne where young Worth, weary of the past, snatched eagerly at the opportunity to stay and swim with a young one of the Marshalls who inhabit it. But Mrs. Miller took his father and myself on to the monstrous pavilion in the woods called Longwood. The road to it was shut for construction and to reach it we had to go down the long narrow back roads cut like corridors in the hills. The sides of the road cuts are as erect as the walls of a room for such is the nature of this earth that it crumbles in erosion when sloping, stands perpendicular without washing. Dark and shadowed, such roads are lovelier than the mansions. Tree and vine and moss cover them. The sun falls through like coins on the earth. And suddenly on such a road we were lost. But the road emerged from the darkness of its own cut into the sunlight beside a wide field where a group of Negroes were chopping the weeds out of the cotton rows. Mrs. Miller asked them the way. And an old crone and a young yellow fellow, with notched teeth and eyes in which pupil and iris and ball all seemed run together in a grayish brown jelly, were voluble in giving directions. Around them other Negroes, while not speaking, stopped their chopping and regarded us with a pleasure in interruption that approximated delight.

Mrs. Miller asked the old woman, "Do you know where there's any Reb-time furniture?"

"Naw, mam, I sho' don't," the old woman said.

"What about an automobile diagnosis of that man's eyes?" I asked my brother.

"That isn't hard. Congenital syphilis. Did you notice his teeth, how they were notched? They are called Hutchinson's teeth. And his eyes."

"Is he blind?"

"He has vision enough to chop cotton all right. I don't know how much else."

"Is it curable?"

"It would have been. He could probably be helped now."

We turned back then and found our way to Longwood, still unfinished more than 70 years after the workmen put their tools down to go to war. But Merritt and James Ward have lived in it for years. While we looked at the house Merritt came in a great hurry up the road through the woods and, half breathless still, recited for us a set speech about his ancestral house. It would be hard to imagine a more hideous country place than this bulbous and octagonal Byzantine creation in the woods of Mississippi. Nutt's Folly they called it after its builder, Dr. Haller Nutt. It is a name that should stand. As a Southerner I set down with pleasure the fact that the architect ("artitect" Merritt called him in his speech) was from Philadelphia.

That night we sat under a big lyre-shaped punkah which once little black boys kept swinging to drive off the flies. But there were no flies on the porch or in the garden at Green Leaves the night we were there. We saw the china Audubon is thought to have painted but which sadly, if he did, he failed to sign. And other lovely things belonging to the Melchoir Beltzhoovers. The men talked. Balfour Miller spoke of the Negro phrase, "my cuzin on de sho'er side." The sure side, naturally, is the maternal one. And I remembered Mrs. Miller's phrase "Reb-time." Young George Marshall questioned out of a life close to the earth in Mississippi whether or not the live oak is indigenous to that country. Someone spoke of a strange breed of dog on the other side of the river, the Catahoula hog dog, a bluish hairy creature with glassy eyes. We talked about plantations not far from Natchez where Negroes are born and die, labor and live, without ever having a settlement with the landlord whose tenants only they are supposed to be. I know there is no pleasanter place in the South than the green court at Natchez within the walls of Green Leaves, nor any better talk or pleasanter people than Worth and I found there.

All down the Delta I had heard the story of the eccentricity of Natchez. And it is there. But by no means only eccentricity. Indeed, I had the feeling that Natchez is not half so eccentric as it is lonely and remote and uncertain of itself. Poverty is a wonderful preservative of the past. It may let restoration wait as it ought not to wait, but it will keep old things as they are because it cannot afford to change them in accordance with styles or preferences. In Natchez the living occupy the past. And I am not at all sure that the living now are particularly

decadent within the huge shells of past grandeur. They may
have been most decadent long ago. Some of the houses, as
D'Evereux, are as simple and beautiful as any Southern mansion anywhere ever was. But it is impossible to see Natchez,
coming at length to the last ante-bellum house built and the
ultimate in hideousness, too, at Longwood, without realizing
that in Natchez long ago there was a vulgar period of ostenta-
tion, when planters built houses and when they bought such
pictures as Tyrone Power saw ("the quantity of raw material
used up in the work being a great consideration here with
lovers of art"). They knew a good horse in old Natchez; they
were ready with laughter for the antics of an Irish actor. But
they bequeathed their descendants no aristocratic confidence
of superiority in Natchez as they sometimes did in Charleston, and in New Orleans, in Richmond and in Savannah. Or
maybe the trouble is that Natchez has been poor—uninter-
ruptedly poor—too long. And whenever I think of Natchez I
remember, too, how that young woman cried on the steps of
a great old house: "Damn antique! Damn ante-bellum! I want
some modern conveniences. I want to live!"

And I remember how she went up the steps with heels
clicking on the old stones. Then Worth and I drove back
through the country darkness to the town.

25

GHOST IN LOUISIANA

HUEY P. LONG
1893–1935

Sleep on dear friend
And take your rest
They mourn you most
Who love you best.

HUEY LONG was two years dead when I read that epitaph in the long shadow of his towering capitol. It was chiseled on one face of the cheap little funeral urn on his flat concrete tomb in Baton Rouge. But Huey Long then was not too dead to be hated, not too dead to be adored. He was live enough to stalk like legend through Louisiana. Between the hills and the marshes he has become both the damned and the redeemer.

Seven vases of flowers sat about the urn. They were not such ribbon-bound, formal flowers as a State would put above a hero. Rather they were such bunches in such vases as the poor or children might gather and bring.

"These are the fewest flowers I ever saw here," said a young man who had brought two women, one young, one old, to see the grave. "You ought to seen the flowers here on the day of the anniversary of the free text books. I never saw so many flowers. You couldn't even see the grave."

He shook his head in a memory full of wonder.

"The plain folks of Louisiana ain't forgot Huey Long. I reckon they won't."

Nobody has forgotten him. Nobody will soon. I found him first in Louisiana as tangible as an adversary in the mind of an old gentleman in the parish of felicity, West Feliciana, where so long ago Audubon watched and listened while a mockingbird sang from a gum tree. They are poor there, poor and old. And the elderly gentleman spoke, with a bitterness which death had not in the least interrupted, of Huey Long. His hand shook and, listening, I felt that he had a right to speak well or ill of the dead since he was almost one of their company.

"Sir," he said, "he was a scoundrel." But the word left him unsatisfied, and he counted slowly epithets as a good Catholic might count prayers. "Dog. Pig. Snake. He ruined this country. I thought when he died: It is the last, thank God. I was mistaken. Down to the last little seamstress on relief, you've got to belong to his crowd or be punished for it. Maybe it's worse now. They have made peace with Roosevelt and have Washington money as well as ours. But they don't spend it in Feliciana. I know. I am not so old and blind that I can't see swine."

He spat yellow tobacco from under a moustache which remained miraculously white.

"He was a damrascal," he said.

But Huey Long was not entirely to blame for his troubles and the troubles of West Feliciana. In one year, the old gentleman told me, the boll weevil made a $40,000 change from black to red in the ledgers kept on his planting. Actually the little voracious bug almost ate the parish up. And long before the boll weevil came, in the same neighborhood an intelligent traveler had recorded a native opinion that once this was reckoned the garden of the world, "the almightiest rich sile God Almighty ever shuck down; gettin' thinned down pow-

erful fast now, though; nothin' to what it was." That was before the Civil War. The soil had begun to be worn between
the grinding stones of land selling for a dollar an acre in
Texas and Negroes being worth a thousand dollars a prime
field hand in Louisiana. The same process of cheap land and
dear labor had worn the lands of the Carolinas and Virginia
and Georgia. There was no sense in saving Louisiana fertility
then, and when the time came to save it, it was already half
lost. And both men and land were cheap and poor.

The day we rode that country the scrub pine and wild roses
grew together upon a land which once must have made the
riches to build some of the great houses and plant the vast
gardens and avenues of trees which now are open—eagerly
open—for a modest fee to the tourist looking at the past.
Scrub cattle move through the stunted second growth woods.
Off the main highways silence lies on the land like night. I
remember how loud the sound of Worth's knuckles was on an
unpainted farm house door when we stopped to ask our way,
and how much louder was the sound of the old field bell
which he rang. Then at last came another old man—old as the
gentleman who had talked of Huey Long—but stooping and
cadaverous and barefooted. He told us the way back to the
highway and while we turned in the dusty yard I saw a young
woman staring out of the shadows within a window. She disappeared quickly, as if she had been caught in a shameful act,
when I met her eyes. But the old man stood leaning, thin and
yellow, against a thin unpainted pillar watching us disappear
in the dust of his road.

It is a sad land, that old section along the river between the
barren hills of the hill billy parish of Winn where Huey Long
was born and the still fertile alluvial plantations bordering
the sluggish bayous in the south. Once in Feliciana gentlemen from Virginia and the Carolinas modified their living
gently with the graces of France and Spain. Perhaps there are

excellent plantations still somewhere behind the roses and the pines, the swamps and the bayous; but the rolling land is too uneven for airplane dusting against the boll weevil (even if the planters had the money to pay for it) and every year for decades the cultivated hills have lost a little and a little and a little more of the topsoil which is the essence of its ability to support life—not to speak of the graces.

Terrebonne is another land in the same State. It lies across the instep of the boot of Louisiana from Feliciana. But this parish of the Good Earth has by no means been a land of riches. Sometimes even it must have seemed to its Cajun fur trappers, oyster tonguers, shrimp seiners and fishermen that *le bon Dieu* had forgotten them. And devout, even superstitious as they have remained, they have in some cases in poverty had to forego the expensive services of priests and begin their families by a simple ceremony in which the bride jumps over the handle of a broomstick in the presence of three witnesses. And, occasionally, as the good physician and gentleman of letters, Dr. Thad St. Martin of Houma, has suggested, brides were so big when they came to jump that they found difficulty in jumping the stick at all. It did not greatly matter. But such Cajuns, of course, as André A. Olivier of St. Martinsville insists, are not typical. But they are there and they have been desperately poor.

"Terrebonne Parish," declared the energetic and enthusiastic Julius Dupont of Houma, "was the back door to China before Huey Long came."

Mr. Dupont, man of thinning hair, horn-rimmed glasses, is manager of A. M. and J. C. Dupont Department Store, biggest store in Houma and biggest probably in the whole Teche and Cajun country. The Duponts have been in the store business for 81 years. The founder came out from France with a bundle following a priestly relative who had come out with a crucifix.

"We're growing bigger by serving better," Julius Dupont told me.

Certainly as manager of such a business he was not a poor little fellow who needed Huey Long to lift him out of poverty. But he believed while Long lived and he believes now that he will be better off as the people of Terrebonne are better off.

"Water's wet, fire's hot, two and two make four and Huey Long was right."

Mr. Dupont, who is a member of the staff of the Governor of Louisiana, a member of the board of trustees of Louisiana State University, a member of the Southern Policy Committee, and a Rotarian, is a firm believer in the possibility of a fairer and better world for everybody in it. In this Southern Louisiana country he was one of those chiefly instrumental in forcing the adoption of a fur trapping code and in keeping the ethics in operation after the code passed with N.R.A. He followed Huey Long's program for wealth shared.

"Huey Long," he told me, "changed Louisiana from a hell hole to a paradise. He was the emancipator. He brought light. He gave us the People's Highway, route 90. Along with his administration came the Intercoastal Canal. He set Terrebonne free. But disregard the material things he did and his service in ending ignorance would be enough to make me praise him."

I pointed out the detail that Huey Long deserved no credit for the Intercoastal canal, a Federal project planned and begun long ago. Indeed, the advance of Terrebonne like the fall of Feliciana is an event which was growing to occurrence years before a Kingfish cried from the capitol. Once its bigness as the largest county in the United States was regarded as a bigness of impassable swamp and unapproachable sea. But its fish and its furs as well as its fertility made it ripe for open-

ing before Huey ran in his road to take Cajun votes and produce out as well as carry new wealth in.

Dupont stirred in impatience. Yes, he knew that Long was
not entitled to all the credit, but he dismissed that detail. He
went on, eloquent.

"Of course, the hypocrites—that's what I call them—they
think they are the aristocrats—they curse him. Most of my
friends do. Some of my family can't understand why I'm for
him. Well, he woke Louisiana. He had guts. If Hoover had
been re-elected, there would have been an explosion in the
United States, but not in the South. Southerners haven't got
the guts."

"Why don't you think so?"

"Well, Southerners have been just as bad off as other people, but did they do anything about it? No. You think about
it. The place where people resisted when they were taking
their homes away from them was in Iowa. Other places, too.
They weren't in the South."

He paused for emphasis. I hoped that he would develop
further the thesis of an unresisting South incapable of explosion, but he went back to his central theme.

"But Huey Long woke Louisiana up. Oh, I know what
they say about him. I know. Huey Long had to deal with rats.
They were in politics before Huey Long and he found them
there. He had to deal with them. Said he bought legislators
like sacks of potatoes. He bought them for the people. They
used to be bought for the corporations. Huey Long had to
deal with politicians in practical politics. What did they expect?"

He slapped the top of his desk.

"Yesterday is a memory. Tomorrow is a mystery. Now!
NOW!!!" He halted dramatically. "That's what Huey used
to say. I remember hearing him say: 'Many are walking.

Some are buggy riding. Some are in automobiles. But I'm flying.' Huey Long moved Louisiana forward."

Then he seemed thoughtful.

"Maybe," he conceded, "we moved too fast in the last eight years; certainly we moved too slowly for centuries before that."

He tugged open a drawer of his desk. "I want to give you something. Now listen to this." He read from a corded folder.

" 'God willed, God ruled, God commanded Destiny to make him great. He was the victim of every form of persecution and abuse, struggling every moment of his public life under the cross of misrepresentation; sacrificed to blind prejudice, but these only served in violation of precedent and convention to lift him higher and higher to the stratosphere of greatness. These tortures seemed to mark his course. They increased his necessity. His unlimited talents invariably aroused the jealousies of those inferiors who posed as his equals. More than once, yea, many times, he has been the wounded victim of the Green Goddess; to use the figure, he was the Stradivarius whose notes rose in competition with jealous drums, envious tom-toms. His was the unfinished symphony.' "

He put the book down, slowly. "That's Huey Long. That's the truth. That's literature."

And he handed me with his compliments the funeral oration delivered by the Rev. Gerald H. K. Smith over the grave of Huey Long on September 12, 1935, two days after he died in Lady of the Lake Sanitarium, four days after young Dr. Carl E. Weiss shot him in the narrow corridor of variegated marble outside the Governor's office in the huge capitol at Baton Rouge. And perhaps it was from the hour of that speaking that the legends began to grow. They have grown lushly since.

Louisiana is a State almost designed for the growing of

legend as it was a State almost perfectly planned for the growing of Huey Long. It is not a true Southern State for all the
Negroes and the heat. It is in spirit and character rather a
Caribbean republic. Its traditions are not truly French and
Spanish; they are instead the traditions of hard Anglo-Ameri-
cans softened by pleasant and relaxing Latin ways and the traditions of the Latins toughened in ruthlessness by the meeting with the Anglo-American pioneer.

"It is a mongrel State," said one of the wisest men I found
living in it. It did not seem that to me but I did feel that for
too long Louisiana as a State lived in a darkness around its
brightly lighted city. Wealth from the land went to New Orleans for joyousness. And poverty remained unlighted on the
land. Ignorance remains there, an ignorance of soft Catholic
superstition and of jerking Protestant evangelism. But there
has grown swiftly a rootless realism. Huey Long was its
prophet. And the yellow-skinned, malarial-looking man from
Alexandria spoke in its terms when on the ferryboat at Baton
Rouge he told me the first legend about Huey Long.

"Huey's as dead as a mule with his belly blowed up," he
said.

And that, in case any gentle reader does not know it, is
dead. I could almost feel the buzzards circling over that dis-
tended body. But I wondered if the man, who had used this
disturbing figure from the fields, and some others did not
want Huey Long and Huey Long's influence to be dead in
Louisiana.

"You're damn right, I do," he said.

But Huey Long is there beyond the ferry in the wide road
that runs straight and smooth between timbered swamps and
canals full of erect, fragile water hyacinths to Opelousas
where perhaps Huey Long's murder was born when a young
doctor married the daughter of a politician. Some of the
worst housing in the South sits on the banks of the loveliest

flower-filled canals, which must sometimes, too, be filled with mosquitoes. And where the swamp-forest separates the sugar cane fields show the deepest furrows and the highest rows of the farming South. Beyond Opelousas there were more horses and buggies on the road and more cattle in the wide flat fields. There were derricks raised in the search for oil and more oil. But where the oil has already been found the tenant houses still have no glass or screens in the windows, only board shutters to keep out the chill or the mosquitoes.

"Of course, you've heard," said a young plantation manager who had taken his agriculture at Cornell, "that Huey was killed by his own bodyguard and not by Weiss at all. One story was that Huey had begun to think of himself as President and so, greedy for power, was in the way of those who remained greedy only for money. It's a fairly familiar story. But, of course, untrue. Weiss used a 32. Huey's boys toted 45s. It was, they say, a 32 that killed Huey."

"Pierre," his younger brother suggested, "maybe they haven't heard the story that Huey did not die at all. But instead was taken back to the capitol and that somewhere between the observation tower and the ground he is kept in a prison by his 'friends.' Some say he is not a prisoner but a lunatic. The Cajuns say that when the wind is just right in Baton Rouge you can hear him. He seems to be making some kind of speech."

I ordered more beer. We had all eaten as many crabs as we could hold and the table in Delahoussie's restaurant in New Iberia was tumbler deep with their red shells.

"And what about the cult of the Second Coming of Huey Long?" I asked.

"Well," Pierre said, smiling, "it is a waiting that will require little more patience than that which went along with his sharing of the wealth. When Huey returns, riding on a golden cloud, the poor will be eased of their burdens, and, if every man is not a king, at least, those who wait are confident, that they will have more than they have now. Most of them could not have less. Some of them have picked out the property of their expectation, I understand. 'Dat's goin' to be mine den.' "

He laughed.

"Now, you must have a beer with us," his brother said.

But of course Louisiana is not merely the memory of Huey Long. Next day, like good travelers, we went to St. Martinville where young Worth was intrigued with a deputy sheriff with big pistols in his belt and spurs at his heels, astride a most weary horse. Behind him in the old St. Martin's Church three little Negro boys and one girl were praying at the principal altar. They scampered from their prayers and an old Negro bent with difficulty to his. At one side stood a huge and hideous grotto and virgin which the Church had labeled: "Grotto de Lourdes—built by an octoroon, a native of St. Martin. This is a work of art, a masterpiece." And behind the church the Evangeline Oak on the edge of Bayou Teche wears a sign, too: It is $500 fine to tear off its bark for souvenir of the lady who so long ago was separated forever from her lover and who forever loved him true. André A. Olivier, proprietor of The New Army Store, is as true to their memory. His establishment is piled high with Cajun history and Cajun souvenir. And he gave us a card in advertisement of Judice's Café.

"What about Rousseau's Café? I saw his signs."

M. Olivier shrugged elaborately.

"Oh, yes. Yes. Rousseau's is good. But you know he married his wife in Chicago and if you want Creole cooking . . ."

It is a rich earth. Cane and rice and oil and peppers and salt. At noon the Tabasco sauce plant on Avery Island was open and empty with no sound anywhere except the pigeons cooing in their cages. Across the road the egrets muttered to

233

each other like lazy white ladies too closely crowded together in an ill-kept slum. But without such guarded roosts on the edge of his Jungle Garden which Edward A. McIlhenny began to provide for them in 1892 the egret might have disappeared. We watched them come home with the sunset, the egrets, the herons and the ahinga. Tiny turtles stirred in the pond with only their beaks at the surface. Blue lizards ran and battled (perhaps it was love-making) in the grass. And with the darkness the bugs came off the water and out of the shadows of the finest botanical collection in America. We fled.

It was in another garden in New Orleans that I heard the last of the Huey Long legends—perhaps the end of the legend. I was talking to a young lawyer between the clamors about a badminton court and a swimming pool.

He told me: "Terror was what drove him. Maybe you haven't seen it. It isn't often seen tied to brains as in Huey's case. But there is a lean, utter, muscle-jumping terror that you'll find at the protracted meetings of Methodists and Baptists and Holiness folk in the hill country and sometimes even at revivals in the little towns. It is dry and hard and violent as country laughter and as humorless as country screaming. Before that night in Baton Rouge Huey used to say that when he was a boy up in the Parish of Winn they went to every funeral within ten miles. He never got over expecting to go to his own. I think perhaps that he always thought of death in terms of scrawny poor folks being buried in pine coffins in the red clay of Winn in the summer time when they had to bury them quick."

"He didn't choose a very safe life," I suggested.

"No. He was too sensitive for that. He began afraid. From the beginning he always jumped first. No enemy was too little to get. So he made enemies and power and fear. Why do you think he kept the bodyguards by him? He didn't keep

234

Joe Messina and Squinch-Eye McGee about him for compan-
ionship. He kept them because he was afraid. He played
clown because he was afraid. And I think he died for the
same reason."

He lit a cigarette slowly.

"The sensibilities filed to such a point that made him a
good rabble rouser also shaved his courage thin. He was
afraid of people; he was afraid of the devil; and he was panic
stricken at the thought of death."

Slowly he blew the smoke out across the garden in the direction of the badminton court.

He remade the story for me.

The fairly narrow hall behind the elevators and in front of
the Governor's office in Baton Rouge was thick with his bodyguard that night when Huey Long was shot by Dr. Weiss.
The guards didn't help Senator Long, though they killed
Weiss. But for a little while the bullet in his abdomen seemed
almost to quiet his nerves. It was reported that he gave an
order that no statement was to be made to the press. It was
also reported that he said slow and dazed, more bewildered
than terrified, "I wonder why he did it." But quickly afterwards he lay, partially dressed, waiting for the doctors on a
roller or table in an operating room in the Lady of the Lake
Sanitarium.

"I don't think," my acquaintance said, "that there was anything to the report that the operation was bungled. It was
current in Louisiana at the time, as current as legends that
Dr. Weiss drew the lot to kill Long in a drawing of murder-
ous conspirators. I don't think there was anything to it. Hamilton Basso printed it in a magazine in the North, pointing
out its improbability. Maybe you saw it."

The doctors had gathered very swiftly. Examination showed
that the Senator had a gun-shot wound in the abdomen and
that the bullet had gone through and through the body. The

examining physicians sent the patient to a private room and kept all visitors away from him. He was in what they called a state of shock for which they instituted usual and accepted treatment. By 'phone they called the most competent physicians in New Orleans and Shreveport, some of them Long's special friends, urging them to come by plane. Meantime, an anesthetist and a pathologist were summoned. And meantime, also, the doctors in Baton Rouge had to make, while they waited, the decision as to whether or not they should wait. They waited impatiently. After two hours none of the out-of-town surgeons had arrived and Huey Long was bleeding internally. He was getting restless. His pulse was faster. His blood pressure was falling rapidly. Once more they 'phoned New Orleans and found that the doctors there had not been able to get a plane. They were coming by car, which requires about two hours. Another of the physicians had just left Shreveport, also by automobile.

It was a hard question they faced. Were they to wait? They were, in general, as competent to deal with the case as the men coming from the other cities. Their experience and their learning told them that the earlier cases of gun-shot wounds of the abdomen are operated on, the better are the chances of recovery. They had a very serious case on hand and a very important patient and they certainly did not want their patient to die. Were they to wait while he bled?

And so they decided to operate and advised the patient of their decision. He agreed. Somehow even the decision seemed to reassure him. The operation was performed. The operating surgeon was assisted by two others and a fourth doctor watched steadily the pulse and blood pressure. As the operation advanced the doctors discussed the surgical procedure. But the patient did not do well on the table. After the operation post-operative treatment was instituted. From Charity Hospital in New Orleans young physicians came, two sur-

geons and two physicians, so they could alternate, one surgeon and one physician as a team to remain with the patient
at all times. When one team became sleepy the other relieved
it. He was restless; sometimes he whispered unintelligibly;
long times he stared at what none of the rest of them could
see.

The young doctors stayed beside him, the older ones came
and went until Senator Long died at 4:10 A.M., on Tuesday
morning, September 10, thirty hours after he was shot. Later
that day there was a formal announcement for the press: "It
was the unanimous opinion of all the physicians in attendance that the cause of death was shock and loss of blood due
to the gun-shot wound in the abdomen. One of the things
agreed on at the beginning was that there would be no over-
treatment. He was given the same treatment anyone else
would have been given." That statement is in the files of the
papers. It is perhaps undoubtedly true as a doctor's statement,
but the legend is still in the corridors of the Lady of the
Lake Sanitarium, a legend as tangible as terror, that it was
fear that killed Huey Long.

But whatever killed him, two days later the Rev. Gerald
H. K. Smith shouted above the grave before the Capitol:
"His spirit shall not rest as long as hungry bodies cry for food,
as long as lean human frames stand naked, as long as homeless
wretches haunt this land of plenty." He was heard in the
bayous and in the hills. Nice people in New Orleans accepted
the triumvirate of Mayor Maestri, Governor Leche and Sey-
mour Weiss as cynically as they had accepted Huey Long.
The blood has run out of Caesar but here are Antony, Octa-
vius and Lepidus, an Italian, a Creole and a Jew. Life and
politics go on in Louisiana as in Nicaragua and Haiti and
Santo Domingo and after the same patterns Americanized.
And pretty girls in nice flat New Orleans gardens run shouting after the feathered shuttlecock. Comus comes. The mint

in the juleps at the Boston Club is crushed before the whisky is put in, or not crushed, as the drinker wishes. But beside the green bayous and on the red hills Huey Long is a spirit, as stripped of comedy as of flesh, that moves as John Brown's spirit moved. And like John Brown's it is a spirit which may leave red tracks in the grass and the sand and across the flagstones to the big house door. . . .

There is a ghost at large in Louisiana and not even laughter has laid him.

26

THE OLD TOWN

THE young, brown Negro in the Boston Club put a veritable vegetable bunch of mint into the bottom of the tall glass. He crushed it. He put in sugar. He packed in ice. He put in two and a half jiggers of whisky and the frost grew like mold upon the glass. It sat a long time on the round table about which we sat, all men behind the white façade of the old club, safe from any intrusion of the swiftness or modernity on wide Canal Street outside—safe almost from the heat. Dr. Rawley Penick told a hilarious tale. My brother told one. We laughed. And then a gentleman boasted quietly.

"You're all right until your number comes up. I know. I've survived war and typhoid, yellow fever and cancer of the kidney. My number hasn't come up yet."

"Luck," I said.

"Fate," he told me.

He sipped from his glass.

"Every night when I came home," he said, "I'd make water on the dirt floor of my garage. I don't know why but that night I went upstairs. And when I looked at the stool it was blood, pure blood. I guess it was just luck that I went upstairs. I went right out and made them promise to tell me the straight dope. No use lying then. They took out a cancerous kidney. That was years ago. I'm here yet. My number hasn't come up. I'll be here until it does."

He laughed. But he went out and left me not laughing at all. Someone told me the rest of the story. It was pleasanter.

Long ago when he was young and had not begun to look for a rising number, he was a member of the exclusive carnival society which chooses Mardi Gras' queen. And one night he celebrated the birth of his daughter and attended a meeting of the society at the same time. His head may have been a little cloudy, but his legs and his tongue were steady enough.

"Gentlemen," he cried, "I give you the carnival queen for 19——. She was born today. The prettiest girl in New Orleans."

He laughed and drank and all his companions drank with him, laughing. That was a long time ago and when the year came 'round like a number on a wheel none of that group was so young as he had been before. A good many of them, indeed, were dead and resting from carnival in the graves which sit on instead of in the low, wet earth. The gentleman had not done so well, as money alone counts, as some of the rest of them. His daughter, I think, had not even made a formal debut. But some remembered. New Orleans is not a great town for sentiment. The French tradition is, there as everywhere, to plan in advance every detail of spontaneity, to give with a lavish emotionalism that counts every centime and get every centime's worth. And that is one tradition the Americans have not upset. But this time when the year came up like the number on the wheel the older members chose in remembrance the girl to whom they had drunk at her father's merry toasting when they were all young so many years before.

And New Orleans is like that; it believes in luck and occasionally it sees it. It has not forgotten what the Old Octopus, the well-beloved Octopus, the Louisiana Lottery, taught it before it died and went to Honduras instead of Heaven. There is no way up from the new unpaved streets or the old paved alleys except by luck. A black boy or a yellow girl in the old days might hold a winning lottery ticket. So might the Creole girl and the octoroon, the old soldier and the young cotton clerk. Now if the lottery is gone the desire both to win quick and to be romantic as long as any vestige of youth remains persists. I noticed that the Negress servant of my friends had her nails lacquered red as any heiress'. In a town in which voodoo is harder and harder to find they might have been recently withdrawn from bloody entrails of beasts of augury. They passed the chicken. She and her pomaded boy friend still hope for a winning. The numbers racket persists in New Orleans as in every other Southern (and Northern) town. One day one may win. Meanwhile deep black poverty remains. And the first sign that caught my eye in the long sprawling streets of the Negroes as we came into town said: "Hair washed and pressed—35 cents."

Not all poverty is black. Nor all hope. Every night the lower middle class of New Orleans, clerks and school teachers, housewives and little house-husbands, fill the big gambling casinos which have reduced the stakes at keno and craps and roulette and bird cage so low as to catch the mass of nickels and dimes and quarters which every night they bring to play. Henry Ford would approve of the theory if not the practice. And the slot machines. Nowhere have I seen so many of the old side-lever, one-armed bandit type as in Louisiana. Persons whisper behind their hands that all of them belong to political power. They whisper also that one candy must be bought by every storekeeper who does not wish his taxes raised. Power, they report, owns baseball clubs and policemen sell the tickets. Power is going to buy a brewery and Louisiana is going to drink its beer. Or else! But if the wolves are masters, certainly the sheep dropping their nickels and dimes and quarters into the slots and leaving them on the green tables seemed contented enough. And stupid beyond necessity. And cheap. The Old South in New Orleans is dying like a mansion turned to sleazy boarders.

The Vieux Carré retains a loveliness in its decay. Old wrought iron balconies cling rustily to ancient dwellings flush with the sidewalks. Covered passages lead darkly to the green and sun of old courts. But the same tribes of antique dealers and tea room keepers and those who sell cheap booze in old rooms have crept in. Greenwich Village made the word for it. And despite the lingering magnificence of the Place d'Armes, despite the Old World smell of men and women (the Black and the White together) at mass in the Cathedral, incense and flesh and sweat, the French Quarter stems now directly from and for the Tourist Trade. The old French Market remains and changes. New sanitary stalls are rising between the stinking cells, but the area is less French now than Mediterranean, and its reeking smells are more reminiscent of old Constantinople than Les Halles. The food remains excellent at Antoine's (Oysters Rockefeller—Pompano—a Graves wine, very good indeed—and Crepes Suzettes) but the Antoine reputation grows in a South in which the black hand at the skillet must be, but is not, restrained from greasing in hog flesh and frying every product of field and pasture and sea. At the corner of Bienville and Bourbon Streets hangs the sign of old French Quarter history: "The Original Old Absinthe House." It adds: "Dancing—On Tap Jax Beer—Established 1826." And one block further on at the corner of Conte Street and Bourbon Street is the sign: "Old Absinthe House Bar—Established 1826—See the First Bar Established in New Orleans." I passed them both by and went on back to the Hotel Roosevelt, once Huey Long's land, home still of Huey Long's Ramos Gin Fizz and where, though not a single Negro servant is visible, in the air-conditioned dining room they serve a Mammy Dinner.

I found friends there who know New Orleans and at lunch they told me among other things two typical New Orleans success stories or success myths. There are hero-haters as well as hero-worshipers. New Orleans talks in the terms of a *Chronique Scandaleuse* that is to be found elsewhere only in Paris when young monarchist politicians discuss the private lives of Socialist statesmen. Neither thrift, nor perseverance nor industry is the motivating power in any of them.

New Orleans tales: Number 1. A generation ago an astute immigrant of ambition landed in New Orleans. After a few years he accumulated enough to go into the furniture business; and in that business he developed an interesting technique. He sold furniture on the installment plan to little *filles de joie* who had only their bodies as their capital. And each week he would collect the installments due. But when the little frail ladies had paid all but a small remainder of the purchase price, the furniture dealer appealed to certain friends in power and the wicked woman was raided, carried off by officers of an indignant law, and there was the furniture left behind. There was nothing to do but take it back and sell it again. And sometimes the same bed which began to be sold to slim, golden-haired young women who smiled for a very select clientele of gentlemen ended creaking in the cribs where women stood at half doors shouting for patronage. Naturally the family fortune grew and grew. Or at least that's the tale.

And Success Story No. 2. Once in an up-state town there was a fancy lady in a sporting house (to use two delightful phrases) whose charms won the affection of a wealthy gentleman. He took her out of the house and set her up in every comfort. But the gentleman had to go about his business. And the lady was lonely as some like ladies have been lonesome before. She found a young man who filled her loneliness and her heart. She helped him rise, and clung to him when he had risen. Their continuing relationship, now blessed by the church, stands in New Orleans as evidence of masculine appreciation or feminine adhesion. People are not exactly sure which.

"It's a mongrel town in a mongrel State," the writer said. He made a wry face.

"Oh, no, that's not fair," the young professor protested. "Louisiana has been helpless before political crooks because it's divided: Protestants against Catholics, and Cajuns against Creoles. Once also the city was against the country but Huey Long patched that up, using an ax as a tool. Of course, the Huey Long crowd was bad, but don't forget that the crowd that preceded Huey adopted a whole new State Constitution without submitting it to the people. They had tricks then, too. They did it under legislation which permitted the Governor to name a block of delegates to the Constitutional Convention—enough of them."

"I'm the only man who thinks so," the newspaperman admitted, "but I'm expecting a blow up from the inside. It's the only place where it can come from."

A young Nordic in livery brought me a telegram.

"I'm going to see the Governor."

"How dumb is he?" asked the professor.

"As a fox," said the newspaperman.

"Oh, I gather that he's a pretty decent fellow, recognizing the world in which he dwells," the writer declared. "He was 'a nice boy,' the son of a respectable French family here in town. He was young as lawyers go, but a good fellow who liked to hunt and fish. Huey Long found out, too, that he could be both a good fellow and keep his mouth shut. That's a combination as precious as rare. I think we're lucky with Leche considering what we might have."

"I hate to run off like this."

"Give him our love."

It was a long drive over the steaming hot streets to Governor Leche's house on Pelham Drive in a flat suburb. My taxi driver lost his way somewhere beyond a canal and a cemetery and found it certainly only when we both spotted at once the big car wearing the Number One license plate of the State of Louisiana. In that hot weather I took no chance on walking and told the taxi driver to wait. He folded up immediately for a nap in the shade.

The civilian guard who let me into the not very prepossessing villa of the Governor had his coat off in the heat and so fully displayed was the pistol which he wore in a holster at his belt. He asked my name and swung his arm in casual direction to a room at the side. A uniformed State policeman, also coatless, was lolling in a chair in the hall. I doubt whether Emily Post or the State Department's division of protocol would have considered them perfectly dressed or equipped to act as first and second man in a Governor's menage. Interior decorators—or anyone else with a little taste and time—could have improved on the content of the house. The long room in which I waited was furnished with the lack of individuality which is expected in hotel rooms or rented cottages. While I sat in the heat and listened to the coatless, armed men talk the place seemed less like a Governor's house than a gangster's hideout, swiftly furnished for swift abandonment if necessary.

The State policeman got up slowly and with effort and began to get into his coat, talking the while to the plain-clothes guard. Somebody, he was saying, deserved what he got. What did he expect? Didn't the plainclothes man agree? That individual nodded that he did but with a head movement so sparing that he also indicated that it was too hot to think much about it one way or the other. In his coat the policeman looked disappointed. I waited, watching them, on the hotel lobby couch. The policeman went out the door and off somewhere beyond the view from the window. And at last I went up a nice, curved stair built against the half-circle wall of the front hall to the second floor and the Governor s room.

Governor Leche I saw was a big man, close to forty, with heavy stubble-bearded jaws, and dark hair. In a white iron bed, with only a sheet over him, he had on that hot day as unpleasant a cold as I ever observed. In the heat of the room the perspiration showed at the armpits through his green silk pajamas. His nose was red and wet. He roused and shook my hand. He crushed out a cigarette.

"I don't know why I smoke these things. I can't taste them."

A cocker spaniel stared at me from under the bed. In the bed the Governor spoke about the South and the plans of various states in the South to develop themselves and their resources. I mentioned the Mississippi plan of Governor White.

"Oh, yes. We've got a tax exemption plan, too. But I'm not wedded to any one plan. I'm interested in everything. We've got to build; that's natural. We've got one of the richest States in the world here. We've got everything. And we've got to build it up, any way we can, every way we can. This country, too."

The cocker spaniel under the bed barked briefly at my strange foot. And retreated, frightened by his own barking.

"You know a farmer," the Governor went on, "if he is sensible either puts part of his farm in soil-building crops every year or buys fertilizer. In either case he is taxing himself in order that he may profit by improved land later." He blew his nose. "Now we have in America 100,000,000 people who make the great human soil of this country. Now perhaps 25,000,000 people can improve themselves but in the long run all will be better off if the 100,000,000 are improved and enriched by the use of taxes as the wise farmer's land is by soil-building crops or fertilizers."

He waved his wet handkerchief over the completion of the demonstration.

"I'm writing a column," he said abruptly, "in *The Hammond Vindicator*."

"I've heard of it."

He was pleased.

"Some friends of mine bought the paper. I took a little stock. I write a column for it every week. We're getting a fine circulation."

"I understand so," I said. "I hear that it already has one of the most remarkable small town plants in the country. I heard about it upstate."

He nodded.

"That's right," he declared. "For a weekly paper it's doing fine. Fine."

"They tell me that the advertising lineage is wonderful, too. I'd like to know how you do it."

"Well—" said the Governor, "well of course, I'm just a small stockholder but we're building up a great circulation. We're giving away a pure-bred bull to the farmer that writes the best letter on the value of livestock. Like that, and other ways like that we're building up a great circulation. And naturally if we have the circulation we get advertising."

He flicked his handkerchief at the cocker spaniel who had come out from under the bed to stare at me, prepared for peace since I had no disposition to play at war. Then he lit another of the cigarettes that he could not taste.

"Livestock is the thing. No livestock is taxed in Louisiana and this is going to be a great livestock State. And livestock is a way to prosperity."

"Yes?"

"Of course, all prosperity is relative. A Negro with 75 cents may feel rich while an oil operator with thousands may still feel poor."

"What about Huey Long's program? Are you going to carry it on?"

"Of course. We are carrying it on. Huey Long provided free text books; under my administration we've provided free pencils, paper and supplies."

He shook his stuffed head.

"But Huey loved to fight. If he didn't have a fight he'd find one or make one. I don't like to. And I don't look forward to greater power." He looked at me and spoke solemnly. "When I get through as Governor I'll be glad."

I think he believed what he said. That day it was pleasant to be wistful. He looked out of the sun-filled window at the breathless trees. His big jaw set.

"Don't believe everything you hear in Louisiana. Lies grow here. Probably no State in the Union ever was afflicted with a meaner poison squad than was Louisiana during and since the regime of Senator Long. *Grimm's Fairy Tales* were replaced in Louisiana by grim fairy stories, and unless you listen to some of them your imagination could not conjure up such concoctions as were spread throughout the State."

His eyes turned back into the room, a little wearily I thought. Then the spaniel pulled at the sheet and the Governor struck at him with his wet handkerchief again. To the little dog it looked like a game and he barked. The Governor leaned back on his pillows, grinning dolefully. He was hot and stuffed up and tired. He felt too rotten then to fight even with the spaniel.

"This is the nastiest cold I ever had."

"You've got to live through it, Governor. As far as I've ever been able to find out there's no cure for a cold like yours except a long life."

I told him good-by. It was a long way back from his house through the hot flat streets to the all but lost house of some people I knew on Dauphiné Street. The dirty front and the old blinds chained together gave it an abandoned look. But within the court between the house and the old slave quarters was another world, old, private, quiet and green. It seemed almost cool although the householder wore only his underwear and his lady was dressed in a bright costume like a bathing suit.

She spoke of a broken love affair, the second for the woman. "The divorce doesn't make any difference. He's still in love with her. She's a Lesbian who doesn't know it. I told him: 'Forget her, forget her! Don't you realize she's not a woman?'"

We sat talking in a long room behind shut blinds, hidden from the street and the sun. It was nearly dark when I left but still hot and while I walked damp in my linens in the long Louisiana dusk I saw a sign on a little ice house between the Cabaldo and the French Market. It pleased me and I wrote it down. The South understands it and New Orleans. It read like this:

> Ice is best;
> Forget the rest.

I laughed and went looking for it, broken and packed in a glass.

27

THE ROAD BACK

As WE rode out of New Orleans that Sunday afternoon a priest in his vestments stood on the steps of a big, unchurchlike building beside the road to Gulfport and Biloxi and Mobile and, with hand uplifted, prayed over the sunlit heads of a multitude of Negroes.

There was a roadside sign: "Crawfish for Sale, Day and Night."

There was another sign: "Brooms and Mops made here by Pat Richards, blind man."

Along the lovely road between the gulf and the live oaks and the magnolias there were cemeteries, with pines in them wind-whipped like the stone pines of Tuscany, and a Methodist Assembly Ground. The waters of the bay were dotted with the sails of little boats. Where the road turned for a little time inland were the eternal changeless rows of weathered gray houses of poor people, black and white. I remember the long milk-heavy breast which a Negro girl on a streetside porch was giving a baby, and the cattle which stood knee deep in the wide coastal meadows under the pecan trees. Further on there were grapes and satsuma oranges. We learned from a seagoing salesman who was only incidentally a fisherman that the striped bass stir in the shadows of the Tchouticabouffa River and that off Goose Point on Cat Island the tarpon wait for bait of live mullet. At Moss Point was one of the first of the plants of that paper industry which is more and more seeking its pulp supplies from the pines of the South and stirring new argument about trees being cut down in the South. But on the Gulf Coast the plant emphasized rather the forests than industry. Most of the way along "the largest sea wall in the world" well-to-do folk have houses which face Yucatan and the Antilles far away. They sit white under the trees and on their piazzas in the warm sleepy breeze sit gentlemen like a friend to whom I sent a book.

"Soon," he wrote me, "I shall be at the White House in Biloxi for an ill-earned vacation, and this book will come in handily. When I go on a vacation I do not fish, I do not hunt, I do not swim. I just sit on the front porch, smoke seegars, drink highballs, belch and talk big to all the wayward matrons who may saunter up. Naturally in such circumstances I have a great deal of time to read and meditate. That is how you fit into the picture—I'll read your book at Biloxi."

But reading is not required. There could be no pleasanter place for doing nothing, an art in which the South is reported to excel. The breeze blows in from the gulf through the magnolias and the mimosas and is very sweet. The winter is warm and the summer is one long siesta. So much the advertisers of a South, up-and-coming even when it can scarcely stifle its yawns by the sea, might legitimately say. But the professional advertisers of Mississippi, working hard themselves and looking across the flat, windless—and muddy-bottomed—gulf to Florida are almost pathologically eager to impress a weary world with the *dolce far niente* spirit of these shores. On gulf blue paper they have printed: "Mississippians probably spend less time making a living than the people of any other State. The real work year for the cotton farmer is hardly six months. He plants in March and picks in August, and has quit cultivating—'laid his crop by'—in July. He has time for hunting and fishing in winter, enough for picnicking in the summer, and all he wants for celebrating the harvest in the fall. Because his work keeps him in the open he takes full advantage of the pleasures of a country life whose natural attractions men cannot artificially imitate."

Such a statement may bring the Yankees, as subsidies may bring the factories, to Mississippi. But not all the people of the Cotton Kingdom need like the suggestion that cotton farmers spend the scantest time earning a living. This reputed leisure is almost indistinguishable from a regional laziness. It carries the suggestion that the South is satisfied with the poverty which is its share of the national store. There are young up-and-comers in the South prepared to admit anything in exchange for one tourist as there are some ready to subject their neighbors to any exploitation to get one factory. This amounts to admission of the truth of the old slurring statement of Samuel Crowther, business writer from Philadelphia, that the cotton farmer is well paid because he makes a few hundred dollars a year for about four months' work. The actual countable days necessary to the culture of cotton are limited. And some farmers are unemployed for too long a time each year. Then they are men lost, not leisured. Fortunately, an economist born in Mainz, Germany, has not allowed Crowther's statement to stand when even Southerners, mistaking a sneer for a purr, were ballyhooing it. Erich Walter Zimmermann of Chapel Hill has pointed out that Crowther "proves a dependable mathematician but a most unsympathetic observer of a human tragedy." In effect, Dr. Zimmermann says that this commercial carpetbagger's consideration of cotton shows that he can add but not understand or feel.

Dr. Zimmermann adds the truth about cotton that "the periods of slack work come in midsummer—July and August —and in midwinter—December and January. No crops are grown on which labor can be utilized during these periods

of slack work. Of course, in the farthest South winter vegetables can be grown in the slack winter period. Some grass
harvest comes in August, but it is not important. The picking season is the limiting period for labor on cotton. At the
same time corn should be snapped, oats should be seeded,
sweet potatoes should be dug and grass harvested. It is not
surprising, therefore, that where cotton is a very profitable
crop these other crops may not receive much attention."
Not in recent years have cotton farmers, the black and white
rank and file, profited enough to permit them to move for
a season to the milk-warm waters of the gulf. More often
than not—particularly since the boll weevil came—cotton has
only seemed a profitable crop—the apparent only profit crop
in a land habituated, hoping and ignorant. Flesh and earth
are often sold with the staple as gold is sold from the mine.
And a breeze-cooled leisure is less often seen in the cotton
country than August-temperatured anger between tenant
and landlord who, cheating brutally on one side and craftily
on the other, are actually the victims of an old bewilderment
rather than of each other. Cotton is not king; cotton is cheat.

But the road goes on, greenly skirting the Cotton Kingdom,
where not only men but whole families are needed when
cotton needs labor, and the gulf on which the cotton of the
labor of children and women and men was borne away to
the world. It runs on under royal palms, past pines cut for
turpentine, past mimosas in bloom, past a fat blonde woman
smoking a cigarette on the roadside and into Mobile through
which so many bales of cotton have gone from the limited
labor of lazy men to the world. There long ago the sensible
daughters of France staged a "petticoat insurrection" against
too much corn meal in their diet. It needs repetition. That
was two centuries away but it was not a great many miles
away that Dr. Joseph Goldberger used Mississippi convicts
in the study of pellagra to show that men in the cotton

country were starving while they were eating. But Mobile's history is hard to remember beside the dinning memory of the song about how high the eagles fly—"In Mobile—In Mobile." Now my friend there, an exile from Montgomery, who knows Alabama from Fort Morgan to the far side of Scottsboro, says in tones of great sadness, "O Mobile, O Mobile."

"Oh, yes, of course, you know it's the five-flag town. Who doesn't? Also it's alien, and as corrupt and content as Philadelphia ever was. Of course, it's horribly old, like Charleston, but it has some new elements in it. It is isolated spiritually and politically from the rest of long Alabama, but it is counting on the State-owned docks to save it economically, after its decline as a great cotton market. It is the most parochial community of importance in the State. Its newspapers and politicians have no passion for anything but matters of local interest. They do not know there is a League of Nations, and they think Woodrow Wilson was an Athenian demagogue."

My friend was undoubtedly unjust. There was something in the combination of the iron balconies and the Kress stores that appealed to me. And beyond the monument to Raphael Semmes, the picture of the sea stood at its best in two four-masted schooners in the harbor. The steel tramps beside them seemed tramps indeed. There, as in every American seaport that summer, on the docks were gondola cars full of scrap iron for the Japs, the Germans and whoever else would buy. Beyond the town a truck had spilled potatoes on the highway. Cattle stood, hot and still, in the shallows of Mobile Bay. And beyond the bay the road ran through pine lands quickly back to cotton again. And there I found the man, black as asphalt, who knows as participant what Samuel Crowther saw as well-paid shiftlessness, what the advertisers of Mississippi describe as leisured living, and what only the supposedly coldly scientific German economist recognized as a human tragedy.

In appearance he was such a man as might have been fetched with a ring around his neck out of the stockade in Dahomey two hundred years ago or be found today chopping cotton and singing loudly to himself in a field farthest from the big road in the blackest county in the old Black Belt. He was, as I said, as black as asphalt, as black as old scabbard leather; his hair was short and kinky and his lips were as wide as my thumbs. His arms hung long to tremendous hands. And his laughter came loud and cackling like defensive idiocy which Negroes erect against the dangerous answering of white men's questions. The man who had brought me to this laughing black was himself the color of finished maple. I had met him by chance at a school. His hair was longer than mine; it was pasted close to his head. Not a kink showed in it and it gleamed. He was, I considered, almost as far off as I was from the mind of the Negro sharecroppers of Alabama.

This black man to whom he took me looked like one of them. His clothes were better. His shoes were whole. He was a graduate of a great Northern university. But when I saw him I knew that he could go down into the canebrake without stiffening or silencing the men of the canebrake by his appearance. He was brother to blackness. He was cousin of the jungle. But he could also emerge from Negro lower depths of America with ability to understand what he had seen and to discuss it with men, who could never see it, in the civilized terms common to all educated men. He had gone roaring with laughter, slapping a thick thigh with a black paw when I first asked him about tenants and unions and conditions in Alabama. He was so noisily pretending that he irritated the maple man.

"You need not worry about Mr. Daniels," he said a little sharply.

Slowly the black man stopped laughing, watching me and wiping his sweaty face with a white handkerchief which blazed in contrast beside it.

He spoke swiftly, soberly. "Of course, conditions are better in some sections than in others. And they are some better, I think, than they used to be almost everywhere. Almost. But some of the Neegroes still have not even got enough to eat. Their houses are falling down. You'll see them propped up with poles. If they get anything on some plantations, the planters take it away from them. You know a lot of planters made their tenants sign over to them their government checks. The government knows that. But I haven't heard of anything being done about it. Maybe the government can't. I don't know. On some places the Neegroes are kept all their lives in debt and terror. They are scared." Except for the fact that he pulled the first vowel sound in Negro out long his language was as free of fault as any white man's I met in Alabama.

"But some landlords are fair."

"Of course."

"Is it true that even on such places the Negro tenants are lazy?"

He laughed.

"That's what the white folks say when they're sittin' on the porch."

"That's where I heard it," I admitted, grinning at the old but effective defense.

"Some Neegroes are lazy," he said seriously. "Some are hungry. Some are sick. Yesterday I saw a man with no more for breakfast than a piece of fish no bigger'n my thumb and a piece of corn bread the same size. I was going by his house and saw that. He had to eat, and children hungry, too."

"Why don't the tenants tend gardens of their own?"

"Some do. Some landlords don't want it. Some don't give time for it. And, of course, some Neegroes are just sorry."

"And they say cotton's a lazy man's crop?"

"I heard that but I heard it from folks who never had grown cotton. At least not in the fields. There are slack times. But when the time comes to work, the whole family has to work and sometimes folks from town, too. Cotton needs work just when other crops do. People who don't know anything about cotton won't understand that. It's easier to holler, 'Lazy Nigger' and 'White Trash' than try to understand. A lot easier."

He paused. "They could do more for themselves and their landlords, too. But they are ignorant." He added devoutly, "As hell."

The light brown man nodded in agreement.

"On the worst places they're worked so steadily that they don't have time for themselves."

"Where are the worst places?"

He considered.

"All over Alabama. But the meanest Neegroes and the meanest white folks live in Nonesuch County."

He looked about him, instinctively fearful, as an Italian might look in Italy who had said Mussolini's name out loud. He lowered his voice.

"There's one planter there who's killed something like fourteen men—Neegroes and whites—and never been to jail for it."

"What's his name?"

He all but whispered it.

"How does he get away with it?"

"I don't know."

"People are afraid of him," said the mulatto.

"The union organizers and the Communists," the black

257

man told me, "they know where things are worst. They know which are the meanest planters. That's where they're working. I went to one county and found out that a Communist had used my name."

He rubbed his big jowl with his hand. The memory of fear was in his eyes.

"Two times I've had to look down white men's gun barrels. I don't like it."

He pulled his breath into his big barrel chest in noisy sigh.

"I don't see why white folks haven't got enough sense to spend the money, so we can have enough Neegro farm agents to teach the Neegroes how to make more so they could have more and the planters more, too. The white farm agents haven't got the time or won't take it. And these Neegroes are ignorant. You don't know how ignorant these Neegroes are. They ought to spend the money to teach them instead of keeping them hungry and pushing them toward the unions and the Communists. I don't see why they don't."

Afterwards I told what this black man said to a bitter young Jew, radical and red-headed. "I don't see why either," I said.

"The hell you don't," he cried. "Farm agents cost something. You don't need farm agents to teach niggers how to chop cotton. The planters are the taxpayers and they're growing cotton, not fattening niggers. You know that."

He was contemptuous of my insistence that even the most hard-boiled planters might be moved by enlightened self-interest.

"Not in Alabama; it's an emotional problem with most planters, not an economic one. Nigger is nigger. Cotton is cotton. And both forever the same."

I could not understand his bitterness. In the Deep South the Jew shares no prejudice with the Negro. Indeed, in most Southern towns, except where many Jews have recently come in, the direction of racial prejudice at the Negro frees the Jew from prejudice altogether—or nearly altogether.

"And about this short work-year—there's something to that. The Negro has learned that generally no matter how hard he works, he is only going to get a living—a not very good one. Beyond a certain point, not very high, he isn't working for himself at all. Just for the landlord. He's black but he's not blind. Laziness like laughter is a weapon of defense. And the nigra uses it to a fare-you-well."

"And do you think any planter would kill nine, twelve, fourteen—whatever the number is—Negroes?"

"Certainly, what do you think he'd do, kiss 'em? This is Alabama. The papers and the politicians put on acts, but we like to kill niggers."

He was spreading the violence a little thick, I thought.

"Every morning before breakfast?"

He grinned. "No, really. There are people who like to kill them and they get away with it."

But my confidence was not restored in my friend's statements. To a polite and intelligent group of men and women I told what the black man had said. They accepted him as qualified but not entirely objective witness. They thought that perhaps he had exaggerated conditions in the State and in Nonesuch County generally and in particular the malignity of the planter. My hostess was dismayed.

"He exaggerates. I know the man he's talking about. He's as mild a looking man as you ever saw," she said. "Of course—" And she suggested that still some behavior by such a man was a mystery that she did not hope to solve.

"The county," a young lawyer declared by way of adding a little light to darkness, "is largely made up of worn out land, hard to farm successfully. And I think it is one of the blackest counties in Alabama. Isn't it, Colonel?"

"It is," declared a brown-eyed man. I suppose he was about

fifty. He looked merry, self-indulgent, wise and kind. "There are several counties like it. And several men like the one your nigra described. Among the nigras the report of murder attaches itself to ruthless white men like moss. Every nigra that slips off from his wife may be whispered around as murdered. Still and yet and under all the whispers there's some truth. I'm not the counsel for the defense of this man or his county—or other like men or counties," he paused. "And slavery is still in force there, but not generally profitable, I understand."

He grinned over a situation which he did not approve but over which, he indicated, he refused to become indignant. He looked, indeed, like an intelligent physician discussing a malignant condition, but enjoying his cigar nevertheless.

"The Negroes there are today where they were 40 or 50 years ago, except that they are less numerous, although they are still more numerous than the whites. It is a plantation county that in the past has known considerable wealth and culture. In the last hundred years it has sent many a beautiful woman to schools in the East and to Paris. With the arrival of the boll weevil in 1915 the county began to decline and sign mortgages."

Carefully he knocked a long ash from his cigar.

"The landed aristocracy is making a last stand there. It is a perfect delta county of other days. It is in no sense a redneck county. It is basically aristocratic—" he paused— "brutal, unimaginative but genteel."

His hostess and mine smiled at his enumeration of the characteristics of the aristocrat. She did not argue about them. Nor did I. But I wondered if in the cotton country he ought not to be leisurely as well.

"A considerable number of white land owners there have made fortunes. Many of these have lost their fortunes, but are still holding on. A few white men are still making money.

Among them is the man who is said to have killed nine or
ten persons, most of them Negroes. But he is an outsider.
Some of the old-timers said he was a scrub who scrouged in."

He laughed at his own phrase, but without amusement.

"He owns many acres, but rents some others. I understand
that he has skinned not only the niggers but his neighbors.
He may be a killer. I doubt it. Certainly he is a nigger
whipper."

The hard muscles of his face relaxed.

"He has whipped more niggers than any other man in the
county; yet he has to run niggers off his place. Somehow,
they stay with him. The darkies tell this apocryphal story.
'When Mr. Nemo ridin' on he hoss come in de fiel' whistlin'
"Nearer My Gawd t' Thee," you better look out, nigger—
you're gonna be whipped.' "

He bowed to our hostess.

"Katherine, you must pardon me: Mr. Daniels, he's the
greatest sonofabitch that I ever heard of, but if you say anything about him, he may drive to Raleigh in his car and
shoot you on sight."

Once more he deliberately removed the ash from his cigar.

"After which," he declared, "he will buy the jury, paying,
I hear, a fair price."

I laughed, not wanting to be shot.

"And come home to rest, I suppose, between picking and
planting on the gulf."

"Exactly," said the Colonel. "And of that much at least I
approve."

28

STAR IN THE PAVEMENT

MONTGOMERY was the first capital of the Confederacy. I suspect that it will also be the last one. Yankees in the skins of Virginians stir in Richmond. But the gentlemen of Alabama, incited by both geology and good sense, erected Birmingham between themselves and all that North, stinking with the sweat of its eternal activity, to which Tom Heflin, gaudy spokesman for a quiet people, referred so often when he bellowed in Washington of Wall Street. Tom-Tom Heflin, he was called by H. L. Mencken, who from Baltimore applied an evangelical violence to the denunciation of those who so easily offended his Episcopalian prejudices. The name may be excellent. Heflin's drum-beat, Smith-silenced, may still have been the voice of a folk hero booming the instinctive antagonism of a people. These Alabama folk, I think, openly boast of Birmingham above a sneaking preference for other patterns of life than those which Wall Street through Morgan through U. S. Steel through Tennessee Coal and Iron through local overseers have imposed upon this Saar of the South. In Birmingham the Yankees and God, who is presented as a deity who realizes the value of a dollar, are in control, and Alabama there is composed of country boy and nigger who work in the mines and the steel plants. But in Montgomery, set in the pavement of the porch of the Capitol is the brass star to show where Jefferson Davis stood when he said good-by to the United States as the first and the last president of the Confederate States. Behind that

star a Southerner now sits with plenty of talk and time beyond two crowded anterooms where Alabama waits with
patience and pleasure.

That morning Governor Bibb Graves was not in any
hurry. Nor were those who waited for him. An almost incredibly old Corsican, diminutive as Napoleon, found a ready
listening to his stirring, oratorical, unintentionally amusing
reminiscences of a war 70 years still. A placid woman, tow-
headed, waited to ask the Governor for a parole for the father
of the fat and contented baby which she rocked without effort in her wide lap. She looked as if she might have been
waiting a week and would not be disturbed if she waited
another. In the second anteroom there was a sudden burst
of loud laughter. Here was the politicians' club. The chairs
were comfortable. There was ice water. The brass spittoons
sat like golden balls upon the floor. In both rooms every seat
was occupied by those who looked hopeful, those who looked
hungry and those who seemed to be merely resting in the
Governor's chairs. One little man was peacefully sleeping.
Restless only were two smooth men in dark suits, well-
tailored, newly pressed. They had brief cases in their laps.
One of them looked as if he had suddenly discovered that
the room smelled bad. Next to him a farmer sprawled with
the earth of the Black Belt still clinging to his big feet.
Near the door were three Negroes, an old Uncle type, a
skinny black woman with conjure-colored eyes and an uncertain, unhappy yellow man of city type. He looked as if
he had escaped from the South. I wondered what he wanted.
And I wonder now if in that slow-moving stream he ever
reached the Governor's door. A long lank sallow man with
a twitch on the right side of his leathery face came in and
surveyed the crowd before him, undismayed. He saw friends
and waved a hat as worn as his face at them. He joined a
waiting group and the talk went on. The laughter exploded

above another joke. And the tow-headed woman went on contentedly rocking her baby.

Fortunately Grover Hall, editor of *The Montgomery Advertiser,* Pulitzer prize winner and one of the saltiest individuals in the Sou.h, steered the way for me through the crowded Capitol. He had 'phoned. Now he found Pitt Tyson Manor, the Governor's secretary, who was that same year to become the national president of the Young Democrats. The Governor was in the midst of a conference on freight rates, but we were to go in in a very few minutes. Meantime Manor showed me the Confederate monument and introduced us to some of the politicians, congregated in the second and smaller of the waiting rooms. Judge Hall, of course, as one who has been editor and associate editor of the capital city morning paper for more than a quarter of a century knew most of them. He helped introduce me to them. We bowed to each other in the initial formality which everywhere marks the informal South. And before we had time for talk, the Governor's door opened. We were inside.

The men of his freight rate conference kept their seats. The Governor merely swung his chair about and faced us over a wide desk on which sat a huge jar of peanuts. Under thin white hair he has an expressive, red face and the mouth of the orator and tobacco chewer. There is the quality of the actor about him which most of the older politicians in the South possessed and which the younger ones are losing or hiding or dramatically altering as Huey Long did. The Governor wiped the mouth which his countrymen say is the most talkative in Alabama. He spoke in terms of the subject of the conference behind him.

"The United States is divided into empires on the one hand and satrapies on the other by the freight rate differential."

I remembered what L. J. Folse had said in Jackson. And

Donald Davidson had pointed to the warring imperialisms of the North and the South in which the North had prevailed and, prevailing, had appropriated the Federal power to reduce other regions, South and West, to the positions of complaisant accomplices and servile dependents. One aspect of that seizure had had to do with freight rates.

"The satrapies," the Governor went on, "are bordered by a line beginning at Norfolk, running to Roanoke, and thence along the line of the Norfolk and Western to the Ohio River, and down the river to the Gulf. All this country is progressively at a disadvantage in transportation costs in comparison with the rest of the nation. And what's the result?"

Both Grover Hall and I knew that he had not only the question but the answer. We waited.

"The result is that the Southern manufacturer must make up the differential out of the cost of buildings, out of the houses of his workers, and finally out of the wages of his workers. And what does that mean?"

Again we waited.

"It means that a Southern industry is worth very little to the community because the workers can't hardly keep even at the commissary let alone have anything to spend for the movies or at the store. I want to see the workers able to spend money in Alabama. Industry won't be worth much to Alabama until they can, and industry has to take the freight rate differential out of his wages to exist in the South."

He wiped the corners of his mouth with his tongue.

"The war—" he said and in the first Confederate capitol I realized that at last "The War" had become the World War— "The war taught us that producers without consumers are dead balls in the tall grass."

We nodded. Behind the Governor the gentlemen with whom he had been conferring were going on talking among themselves.

"Right after the war, we sold our wheat for a high price because the rest of the world didn't have any wheat. Then when they grew a new crop the price fell to the bottom. Similarly after the war, we had a monopoly of man power. All that is changed. Other nations have a new crop of men and they haven't got the burdens of the old ones that we have. If we are going on we've got to make the South a consuming area."

He shook his head emphatically.

"Yes, sir. I'm becoming a nationalist fast. The South must be able to consume, and it can't consume so long as competition keeps down the worker's wages in order to meet the freight rate discrimination."

"Freight rates don't explain all wage differentials," I suggested.

"Well, no. Maybe not always. But the freight differential has got to be cut out of all wages if Southern industry is going to compete."

"You don't think that the lower living costs in the South offset the freight differential?"

"Certainly not," he said. "We all know that."

"Not all your manufacturers will admit it," I said.

We got up to go. The Governor took a handful of peanuts out of the big jar on his desk and urged us to help ourselves.

"I always was a great meat eater," he explained, "and when the doctors told me I'd have to stop eating meat on account of my kidneys, I found that eating nuts took away my craving for meat."

They were raw and unsalted.

"Don't forget. This freight rate business is the heart of the whole Southern problem. It explains nearly everything. Poverty. Low wages. Bad housing. We can't move till we get free. We've been fussin' among ourselves about it. Alabama is interested in commodity rates. You all over in the Caro-

266

linas and Georgia are interested in class rates. But we got to work together. The differential is harder on some parts than on others but we've got to think about the South."

We went out through the more than ever crowded anterooms. Everyone there seemed as comfortable and patient as before. A Negro servant handed around little paper cups of water. The tow-headed woman was rocking her baby and the uncertain mulatto still stood in the door. No matter if half of Alabama had warned me of the Governor's loquaciousness, I was a good deal impressed by what he had said. Back in Mississippi, Folse at the State Planning Commission had referred to the freight rate differential as if it were the product of an invisible conspiracy. And in Alabama that same summer George R. Leighton, assistant editor of *Harper's Magazine,* had looked at Birmingham, had found it an exploited colony of the East, and had put some tough questions to that North which is always so articulately sympathetic at a distance about the South. He looked back to find present questions and answers: "There was less traffic south of the Ohio than above, so higher rates were allowed the Southern railways. Rates north of the wall were lower than they were south of it. But was it possible that both the Northern and Southern railways were controlled in the same banks? Was it possible that the great railroad investment north of the wall must be protected at all costs, that the migration of manufacture to the South must be watched lest Northern traffic be threatened? Was the Northern steel investment so great that it too must be protected along with other great industrial establishments dominated by the same banking houses? The disorganized textile industry might balance cheap labor and high freight rates and move to Alabama and elsewhere in the South, but what else? And, finally, what about the Interstate Commerce Commission? For better or worse, the bulk of the wealth, population, and industry, the very gut of the

American economy, lay north of the Ohio and east of the Mississippi. Must the Commission, acting in the public interest, take no action that would threaten this section? Was it, in sum, possible that the course of economic history had made the stability of 'the American system' depend on that region and that, simultaneously, it was to the advantage of finance capital in New York that it remain so?"

The answers to those questions must be written in the history of the South and of America. They may indicate that the cruelest aspects of conquest were not involved in Reconstruction in the South but in the use of national power to entrench sectional advantage elsewhere over the South. But those questions were not to be answered in Montgomery that day. In the first place it was too hot and beyond that I had to go to investigate the claims of my wife as to line and dimension of the house of her ancestors. The old house on Madison Avenue is lovely. Not even the electric sign of the undertakers now in occupancy nor the chapel, where the window of the stained glass figure of Christ can be covered with a curtain at the funeral of Orthodox Jews, could hide that. The short, gray undertaker remembered my mother-in-law. They had gone to school together long ago. Hospitably now he showed me through the house where she had been a child. That day they were installing air conditioning. The contractors were finding that all the inner walls were solid brick, nearly a foot thick. And with piping to put in, they cursed to find it.

On the sidewalk Hall turned and looked back at the old house.

"Undertaking establishments in the cities," he said, "but you tell me: Where are the old mansions of the South? In the country?"

"There are some in Natchez and Charleston, Savannah—"

"Oh, yes. That's right. But I said in the country on the

plantations. Drive from Montgomery to Hot Springs by Meridian and Vicksburg. That'll take you through the Black Belt of Alabama, including the Canebrake, and the Mississippi Delta. And all along that way there is an almost complete absence of pretentious country homes, either of the present or the past. Is it all legend?"

"A good deal of it. You see more big houses below Vicksburg. And some of them reflect mighty little taste. New rich and po' white together. Sometimes they do go together, you know, even now."

"I kept worrying about those missing mansions; now I've got the explanation."

"What is it?"

"First modern highways run along new routes," he said. "They ignore the old roads. Often they ignore even the small towns along the way. They cut straight through. Now the old roads are side roads. And it is on the side roads that the fine old houses were built and that is where you will find them."

"I know that's true in some cases."

"And the second thing is that the old-timers tended to build their fine houses on the bluffs of rivers so that they might be close to transportation lines. Thus in Alabama there were once many fine homes facing the bluffs of the Alabama and the Tombigbee in the Black Belt, and in the Delta country mansions were built on the high side of the Mississippi and Arkansas Rivers."

"And besides there weren't ever as many mansions as we've been taught to think."

"No. I guess not. But we travel too fast to see the ones that there are."

He looked at Leake's mortuary mansion once again.

"Well, let's eat. We're the living and the eating. It is not our fault that all the red roses are cut down."

We went down Montgomery Street to a place kept by a

Sicilian named Ridolphi, who was sent to America with a label on him at the age of seven. He serves food a good deal better than that generally to be found in the South. Southern cooking is a household art which withers in restaurants and is not to be found in hotels which import their chefs from Philadelphia or Trenton or such places. But Grover Hall gave in advance his unqualified praises to the food being prepared for us while we sat under the fans and drank cold beer. Montgomery, I considered, ought to serve good food since the legend is that it owes its position as capital of Alabama to menu cards. Originally, according to Jefferson Williamson's story, the capital was at Wetumpka, as the head of navigation on the Coosa River, thirty miles from Montgomery, which was then known as Yankeetown, or New Philadelphia. Enterprising citizens started a campaign for removal of the capital and built a hotel called the Exchange, to help their cause along. But there seemed to be a clear majority of the legislature in favor of Wetumpka. On the day the vote was to be taken, however, handsomely printed bills of fare of the new hotel at Montgomery were given each legislator as he sat eating a miserable dinner in the Wetumpka hotel. The menu cards from Montgomery, listing all the delicacies of the season, were quite a contrast to those at Wetumpka. And when the vote was taken, lo, Montgomery was the new capital. And Wetumpka in 1930 had a population of 2,357. It was a fate which should frighten but I doubt whether it will. It is too easy to fry everything in lard. And frying things in lard may be more important than freight rates.

"Your Governor is not merely garrulous," I said.

"Certainly not. But a strange man. Graves was never most widely known as a lawyer, but both as an artillery colonel in the war and as Governor he has shown real metal. He loves to talk—no doubt about that—but he does have something to say and that's a great deal. In fact, I suppose it's everything."

"I like Southerners who talk," I said. "I like men who talk. Generally it is the stupid who are silent."

He laughed. "Don't depend upon it."

"No."

And I remembered that while Southerners had talked for fifty years of a past full of heroes, of a world in which tragedy was a noble neighbor, men from New York and Boston had devoted themselves quietly to the fixing of freight rates. It was not the soldiers but the clerks who directed the movement of the American story. In the South, strangely, the men, who had come down to set slaves free, had gone home with victory to make the whole South economically inferior and dependent. And where all were kept poor the white man learned to steal from the Negro as the Negro had learned to steal from the white man when there was not enough for both of them. And then thin-lipped persons looked at the South as they rode through it to Florida and thanked a thin-lipped God that their capital was Boston and not Montgomery. The worst carpetbaggers stayed at home.

And yet. I caught myself. In the complicated South, all that is wanted is the simple remedy. The war. The Negro. The boll weevil. The birthrate. And undoubtedly the fixed inequity of the freight rate differential is important. From the politician's standpoint it is perfect. It is basis for stirring, noisy fight against enemies, none of whom vote in the South. A fair freight rate structure is necessary to an advancing South but not all the greed, not all the inequity, not all the exploitation, not all the protection of vested interest is Northern. There are Southerners, too, as voracious as the tiger and as equitable as gamblers who demand no more than to play with their own marked decks.

29

MOUNTAIN AND MOUSE

As I CAME over Red Mountain, past the big aluminum-painted statue of Vulcan and down the long hill into Birmingham I remembered old Joe Poe who had been coming to Birmingham, too, and who had seemed so lost on the dusty road between Chattanooga and Scottsboro. I had come a long time round since I had seen Joe, and I wondered vaguely what had become of him. Certainly there was room in the long, sprawly city below to hold him or to hide him, even, less probably, to give him work. But I forgot Joe as promptly as I had remembered him. That day the air was crystalline in the sunlight and the only smoke in it was far off over the forges. Birmingham did not look as young as I knew it to be. It was a good city to look down upon in the morning from the mountain top at the end of the road from Montgomery. And later when I came back at night it was even lovelier, and greater being lovely, wide and long and lit at intervals far off with the dull red flames of the forges.

It was cool on the mountains where the great houses of the well-to-do are, or, at least, there was a little breeze in the Alabama heat. But there was no breeze in the city. In its pocket in the mountains, it baked. Perhaps it was the heat at the hotel, perhaps I had come upon a frontier between Southern manners and Northern service, but at any rate Birmingham was the first city I came to where the bellboy, a white one, failed to thank me for my tip. I went downstairs and though the dining room was empty, in another room I

could hear the Rotarians or Kiwanians or some such beginning their luncheon with the robust singing of "America."
Outside the midday streets were almost empty, and I was impressed, too, by the air of emptiness which grows from so
many vacant lots. After Birmingham's swift growth it was
easier to understand the acres of vacant building lots in
Muscle Shoals. Birmingham's business district spreads unnecessarily but hopefully wide. I walked across it in the sun.
But in Birmingham vacant lots are not so much areas of
despair as shares in promise. And in North Alabama it is not
strange that the hope exists that what has happened once
may happen twice.

I sat down, hot and weary in the coffee shop of the Thomas
Jefferson. Why Thomas Jefferson in Birmingham, I do not
know. Then I did not care. The restaurant was empty but
it was air-conditioned, and I got promptly my chicken salad
and iced coffee.

"It's hot," I said to the blonde waitress.

"Yes. I guess so. It was when I came this morning. But last
summer this time I was in a plaster cast and that's hot. I
mean it's hot."

She fingered her curls and wrote my brief order. I ate in
cool and quietness. But at last I had to go again into that
sun. I took a taxi the brief way to the office of *The Birmingham Age-Herald*. Upstairs they pointed me the way to James
Chappell's office, and there I found him in the yellow shade
of Venetian blinds, the editor and general-manager and the
intelligent goodfellow whom I had seen last in the very early
morning at Hot Springs. I sat down without interrupting
the editorial which he was reading. Its author sprawled in big
patience in a chair. It was, I gathered, about the Duke of
Windsor and his then new Duchess. Chappell approved and
out its author carried it to the printers. We talked about his
Alabama, about Grover Hall down the road, about the

273

Scottsboro boys, about steel and unions in Birmingham, and about white men and black men in the Deep South. And he invited me for dinner.

I spent the time between in the coolness of the Tutwiler bar with young and intelligent Charles F. Edmundson, who was just then leaving the Scripps-Howard *Birmingham Post* to become an editorial writer on the *St. Louis Post-Dispatch*. We had the cool room to ourselves except for two middle-aged playboys and their beautified and giggling playmates. I spoke of William Mitch whom I was to see later.

"I understand that John L. Lewis sent him down here because he couldn't trust the labor men on hand."

"That's my understanding," Edmundson said. "He can trust Mitch. He looks to me like a Methodist preacher but my wife—she's a coal operator's daughter—she thinks he looks like a thug."

"I'm going to see him," I said.

Then we went in talk from industrial Birmingham to black Alabama. Edmundson told a terrible story. He had seen it as reporter. About the time when farmers in Iowa were resisting foreclosures during the depression, something of the same sort happened in Alabama but to a different, tragic ending. Down in Middle Alabama two deputies went out with the legally proper papers to take a mule and a cow away from some hard-working Negroes who had borrowed money on them from a hardware dealer or some such time merchant. They had fallen down on the payments. So the deputies came to get the animals. The Negroes knew that without the mule they couldn't make a crop, and without a crop they would starve. So they resisted foreclosure. There was an exchange of shots in which the officers were slightly hurt and several Negroes were seriously wounded.

Then followed the hunt for the Negroes and Edmundson

went down to cover it. From all the little towns and the countryside around armed white men gathered and the hunt went
forward in school buses. Somebody had to be hiding those
wounded Negroes. The posse meant to find them. There was
not only anger and excitement in the school bus in which
Edmundson rode. There was liquor, also. And he recalled
with revulsion a little drunken barber who could hardly hold
his gun but pointed it menacingly at every Negro questioned
along the road.

And then at last the news came that the wounded Negroes
had somehow gotten to the hospital at the Tuskegee Institute. Officials there had promptly notified the sheriff. He had
come and taken them out of the hospital and locked them in
jail. Edmundson went there and heard them breathe, a wet
dreadful sound, labored and bloody. Slowly they died. And
remembering it, he declared that he thought the incident indicative of the lengths to which Tuskegee, and some other
Negro institutions like it, go in the effort to maintain the
best relations with the whites in Alabama. He was afraid the
incident was typical even if unusual.

"You mean an educational ideal true to Ole Massa."

"Yes," he said. "You know some of the Negroes at places
like Fisk look down on Tuskegee."

"Yes," I said. But Tuskegee had seemed rather impressive
to me, and realistic. It appeared to recognize that valuable
as the academic education is, the Negro has desperately immediate educational needs: how to farm and eat, how to be such
a waiter as can resist the pressure of the country white girls
on his job. "Yes. But they couldn't operate in Alabama unless they carefully held good race relations."

"No. And Tuskegee Institute is a good source of income
for the town of Tuskegee, Alabama. But the people at Tuskegee could have 'phoned the Governor. If they had gotten in

touch with the right white people, guards could have been put by the beds in the hospitals, rather than letting the Negroes bleed to death in the jail."

"Of course they could have done that. They could have done other wise things." But I wondered if either he or I could appreciate the dry hysteria which probably touches even the Negroes most remote from the danger of the mob in the Black Belt when mobs (or "posses") run past—in schcol buses.

He also spoke of that wage differential between the North and the South about which Northern and Southern manufacturers quarrel, and about which also Southerners quarrel among themselves. Undoubtedly, in the name of a wage differential, some employers in the South had taken advantage of the lack of a market for the surplus labor in the South to pay wages which have no possible relation to a true differential but are only related to the exploitation of hungry people at wages as low as the employer's conscience or the group conscience of employers (which is always tougher than that of the individual ones) will permit. Both of us knew that. But Edmundson said there must be a differential to give the South a competitive advantage in order to get industry. Once industry is established, the wages would rise, he thought. And certainly the absence of any market for labor is the best basis now for merciless exploitation; an academic resistance to a frank differential closer to decency may serve only to support that deeper, hidden differential which is closer to shame.

He left me at the Bankhead, and in a little while James Chappell and his wife came by to pick me up. At their house I met their daughter who I hope may be representative of a new youngness and intelligence in the South. But I am puzzled to place her between missionary Christianity and a hard-headed wish to be of use in a difficult world. Certainly she does not look like a young woman who should make any such puzzle. She should be, I thought, dancing or writing, perhaps dancing and writing. There was something old-fashioned about the shape of her head and the way her hair was fixed upon it. She would have been, I knew, especially lovely had she worn such crinolines as women wore play-acting at antiquity in Natchez and Williamsburg.

Not the least of the virtues of the crinolines was that they gave a girl, slim above the billowing broadness of her skirts, the appearance of moving like an angel without wings, floating, flying. If there were limbs beneath, they were lost in a realm as lacy as dream. There they would be altogether smooth vestiges of loveliness, and never, never mere engines of locomotion. But this girl in Birmingham walked in her straight long evening dress with a forthright and interesting stride. Hedda Gabler moved in Alabama. Mary Chappell was working then on her thesis for her Master's degree at Vanderbilt; she had chosen to write of old William Gilmore Simms of Charleston who had lived beyond his vogue and his time. And when she finished it, she was going once more to teach English and economics on the mixed faculty of a school which maidens from New England had long ago established to help black children up from Alabama darkness. Her striding legs were carrying her like a missionary into darkest Alabama. But she moved with no lugubrious Christianity. In the same county where she would teach, Negroes were still whipped on the plantations, I heard; sometimes they were shot. Black people walked in fear. Even white people walked carefully within the strict bonds of custom. But on the terrace at the Shades Mountain Country Club there was laughter. The four of us sat a long time over dinner, talking. And below us late swimmers splashed and shouted in the pool.

Before I got to Birmingham I had discovered that the South had forgotten the Civil War. Or, at least, had desisted from noisy, angry or mournful memories of it in public. But it still regards a person or a town unable to trace ancestry beyond 1870 with a suspicion of bastardy, a suspicion generally hidden behind a fan, never indicated by more than an eyebrow, but a suspicion nevertheless. And that applies with particular force to Birmingham. It is not so much that the surrounding South is steadily engaged in lifting its nose at the odor of those new rich or old poor which may smell remarkably like each other. As is often the case, Birmingham is far more conscious of the brevity beneath its riches than is the country or the people round about it. So snobbishness is noisier. Wealth glints. Persons who are fortunate enough to belong to the Mountain Brook Club rather than the larger, less exclusive and less expensive Shades Mountain Country Club do not let the hour pass without somehow allowing the news to escape. (I had dinner there with a charming relative; do I boast in the manner I impute to Birmingham?)

It was a strange, new city at which to sit in a house surrounded by trees growing out of land which had been deeded to the same folk who now live upon it in titles signed by President James Monroe. Strange, too, in such a house in Birmingham to find an intelligent, hard-working modern whose vanity is that he is the great-grandson of William, eldest brother of John C. Calhoun. As far as I can discover, William was only Calhoun's brother and the great-grandfather of John Temple Graves II; he is a string serviceable to bring the two together. Certainly it was pleasant in the afternoon to talk with people unhurried by the hungry restlessness of Birmingham and yet far ahead of most of it in understanding of the modern world of which Birmingham, even if unwillingly sometimes, is a part. But no solemn things were said. No one demanded, Whither Europe? When war? Why Fascism? We talked as everyone was talking of the recent marriage of Edward of England and Wallis of America. The ladies were all partisans. All For Love, is a doctrine still held high in Alabama, even in Birmingham. I remember we walked through a green meadow and by a clean stream, and smoke and sweat and poverty and dirt seemed far away. I drove unwillingly back to Birmingham and this less serene present in it.

There are special elevators for Negroes in the Brown-Marx Building in which the huge U. S. Steel subsidiary, the Tennessee Coal, Iron and Railroad Company has its offices. I went to the offices of TCI, as everyone in Birmingham calls the chief absentee landlord, to see Ernest D. Le May, who is a thin, pleasant man in occupancy of a large office as Director of Public Relations. It was he who later sent me to see Charles Fairchild DeBardeleben. Nobody could understand Birmingham without seeing him, Le May said. But Le May talked first. He had begun in industry with the Southern Railroad and he had nothing against unionism, far otherwise, he had been sympathetic toward it since he was a young man: his brothers long ago were railroad mechanics and union men.

"I'm only against Communism. That's what I fought. I always will. And undoubtedly Communism grows from reaction."

Le May went on: The majority of employers in the Birmingham area were far from enlightened in matters of social justice. They had a great deal to learn. The whole South has much to learn. But such criticism, he implied, did not in any sense apply to TCI.

He smiled. TCI was trying to build up the South. He wanted me to know more about its agricultural program. It seemed that the president of TCI was at a party in Montgomery some years ago. A gentleman came up to him and began to berate him on the grounds that while TCI was using 1,000 mules in its mines, it was purchasing all its hay outside the State of Alabama. The President looked into the matter and discovered some interesting facts about Alabama and hay. If TCI was buying hay outside of the South to be eaten in the South, still the South was not growing the hay that it should. He put the veterinarian who was in charge of the mules in charge of an agricultural program designed to increase the purchasing power of the South in general and in particular the farmers who buy TCI products. Dr. Jackson, the man in charge of the agricultural work, came in. Both he and Le May talked in their shirt sleeves.

Le May telephoned Mr. DeBardeleben. "Uncle Charlie," he called him, and made an engagement for me to see him in the afternoon. Before I went out either he or Dr. Jackson gave me a copy of a forthright news release. It was headed: "Tennessee Coal, Iron and Railroad Company Endorses Soil Conservation." And that's flat-footed, I said to myself as I went over to the Comer Building to see William Mitch, whom John L. Lewis sent to Birmingham to do the organizing job because Lewis lacked faith in either the character or the intelligence of the indigenous labor leaders.

Mitch has the respect of newspaper men in Birmingham. I had to wait for him because he has offices also as head of the steel activities of C. I. O. in the Steiner Building and was busy there. With me men waited who were members of the United Mine Workers of America and who looked it. Neither compliment nor insult is intended. Mitch himself looked, as my newspaper friend has said, like a Methodist preacher, a Methodist preacher with a predilection for costume jewelry. A man of fifty, dark-haired and sallow, he wore, I noted, a tie pin, a tie clasp, a watch chain and, I think, a ring. On his walls were pictures of both John L. Lewis and William Green. He explained that Green was an old friend but that the industrial unionism plans of Lewis had his full faith and support.

He had, of course, he said, been labeled as a carpetbagger and a foreign agitator but he did not think that the fact that he had come to Alabama by way of Indiana from Ohio had lessened his influence with the miners. Of course, too, the operators had attempted to make his unionization of the white and Negro miners in the same unions appear as somehow wicked and anti-Southern and a betrayal of the white race. Mitch had replied that the operators had not regarded it as wicked to work them together. He had met the effort to use the old Ku Klux Klan against the union by getting union men on the inside of the sheets.

This man who had organized the white and Negro miners of Jefferson County was as undramatic an individual in appearance as a traveler could find in a day's journey. But he must be a man with a genius for the bold dramatic act, which coming from him acquires especial force. I remember that he spoke of a meeting in a church—Birmingham is proud of its churches—at which a mine operator was scheduled to speak about unions and union organizers. Mitch was not invited. But Mitch attended. He listened to the operator's remarks. Then he got up and made some remarks of his own. He must have looked more than ever like the Methodist preacher in the pulpit. I think he took that meeting for his own.

I told him I was going to see Charles F. DeBardeleben. He smiled mildly.

"Ask him about the mystery man," he suggested. Then he told me about the report which he had had of the mystery man who suddenly appeared, so it was said, in the mine village or deep in the mines to frighten the unorganized miners, most of whom are Negroes. Unfortunately, in DeBardeleben's office I found too much else to occupy my mind and I never got around to the man of mystery.

A narrow-faced individual, with a quality of excitement

about him, I found Mr. DeBardeleben to be a gentleman who spits his words out of bitter lips.

"The South," he said by way of beginning, "is worse off as a result of the Roosevelt Administration than it was as a result of the Civil War. This infernal administration is sending the country to hell as straight as the martin to its gourd. It's the damndest thing I ever saw."

He is not puzzled by these times. They seem simple to him. He can tell when even a President is a fool, a labor leader, a racketeer, or a steel executive, an apostate. (I talked to him before Tom Girdler rose and fought C. I. O. and before Myron Taylor, who accepted C. I. O. for U. S. Steel, mounted up and out.) He banged his desk and under the spot where his fist fell I saw still there under the glass the Landon-Knox label. Mr. DeBardeleben had not deserted them many months after the election. Under his violent fist and his violent words, the label seemed to me a little touching, like a Confederate flag flying where no longer any Confederacy is. The past is sweet.

Looking out of his windows high in the Webb-Crawford Building, it was hard to remember that DeBardeleben is older than all this city. No, not quite. The founding of Birmingham is formally dated from 1871, but even in 1880, its first Federal census, only 3,086 souls were discovered. Charles Fairchild DeBardeleben dates from Prattville and 1873. But as he is in the central line of the city's ancestry, it and much else of industrial Alabama trace their ancestry through a Hessian and a Yankee. Birmingham, despite the uplifted noses of the aristocrats behind their fans and their eyebrows above them, is undoubtedly legitimate child.

But before either Hessian or Yankee, there were geologist and abolitionist. In 1846 Charles Lyell, F. R. S., made a trip of examination with Mr. Brumby, the professor of chemistry at Tuscaloosa. He wrote: ". . . we examined several open quarries of coal . . . even at the outcrop the coal is of excellent quality . . . rich beds of ironstone and limestone bid fair, from their proximity to the coal, to become one day a source of great mineral wealth. At present the country has been suffered to retrograde, and the population to grow less numerous than it was twenty years ago, owing to migrations to Louisiana and Texas, and partly to the unthriftiness of slave labor . . . One of the evils, tending greatly to retard the progress of the Southern States, is absenteeism, which is scarcely known in the North." When in the fifties Frederick Law Olmsted came through the empty country he found a half-naked white woman shoveling iron ore out of a digging, and with her three daughters and a husband. All five of them together then, he found, could make $1.50 a day.

In those years the Yankee was growing. He was Daniel Pratt, born in Temple, New Hampshire, son of a New England farmer. The son became a carpenter and as a carpenter, in that wandering time, he came down to Georgia where he became a partner in a cotton gin factory. In 1838 he settled twelve miles north of Montgomery where in time he built a grist mill, a lumber mill, a shingle mill, a cotton gin plant, a cotton mill and a woolen mill, a foundry, a carriage factory, a tin shop and a store. In 1858 they were capitalized at $519,-000. The Hessian was a captain who landed in South Carolina during the Revolution to serve against the Colonies and his descendant, Henry Fairchild DeBardeleben, was in the 1850's an orphan boy working in a grocery store in Montgomery. At 16 Henry Fairchild DeBardeleben became the ward of Daniel Pratt. He lived in the Pratt mansion and attended school, he worked in the Pratt plants, he fought with the Prattville Dragoons and in 1863 he married one of the three Pratt daughters. In a real sense he became the Pratt son. Pratt sent him to new Birmingham and when Pratt died in 1873—year of the panic—son-in-law DeBardeleben was left the richest man in the whole coal and iron area. After that his fortune rose and fell with Birmingham's. He fled from fear of tuberculosis and back into business again. But he helped to build Birmingham to the population of 132,685 which it had in 1910, the year he died. And by that time his son, the Charles DeBardeleben whom I saw, had already been general manager in complete charge of Alabama Fuel and Iron for five years. And for him as for his father, there were good times and bad times, but the general direction was to riches until the depression, which began in 1929 (earlier in Alabama, some say), hit Birmingham perhaps harder and swifter than any city except Detroit. It is a Birmingham proverb: "Hard times come here first and stay longest." That is said with a species of pride. But the depression, Mr. DeBardeleben told me, was hardly so fearful as the recovery which grew from it.

"Roosevelt is turning the country over to John L. Lewis . . . this infernal administration is using the taxpayers' money to support strikes and feed strikers . . . Roosevelt doesn't understand any business . . . I saw the other day where the income from John L. Lewis' racket amounts to $16,000,000 . . . Myron Taylor betrayed his associates . . . John L. Lewis is a thug and redneck . . . the Congressman from this district is a fourth class comedian . . . this is the damndest administration . . . sending people down here badgering business and asking us fool questions . . . and taking all our money in taxes."

He shook his long head bitterly.

I asked him: "What about unionism in your mines at Acmar?"

He roared at me. "And what are you doing coming here and catechizing me about my personal affairs?"

"I don't care anything about your personal affairs, but they told me you could tell me about conditions in Birmingham

284

from the employers' standpoint, and that's a condition I'd like
to know about."

"You're not going to catechize me."

And he turned to his desk and I understood that I was dismissed. I went out but I went less angry than aware that I had
met a personality. Even then it seemed obvious to me that
DeBardeleben was not merely an angry man, full of bitterness. I knew that he was saying openly and honestly what
a good many business men in Birmingham and the South
believed but as good politicians did not say. I preferred De-
Bardeleben. Furthermore, I knew that as one of the boldest
and loudest opponents of unionism in the mines of America,
he was also one of the last of the old time masters of men out
of the old time South. Most of DeBardeleben's miners are
said to be Negroes and Negroes were used in these mines before slavery was abolished, in a manner of speaking, in Alabama. His community at Margaret Mines near Birmingham
was, I learned, one of the only two mining communities in
America in which a union miner was not allowed to put his
foot. And he is, I was told, a paternalist who has succeeded in
paternalism.

During the whole depression, people said, no DeBardeleben employee—employee is a strange word when there is no
work to be done and no wages to be paid—was ever on the
relief rolls of this "infernal administration." Instead DeBardeleben marshaled his "big family" in self-support. He put
his miners to gardening while other miners elsewhere depended on government for defense against starvation. Union
men whom I asked about the report did not undertake to
deny it but suggested that perhaps the miners were gotten
out of the DeBardeleben mine community and so ceased to
be DeBardeleben miners before they went on relief. I doubt
that. I had the feeling that the truth of the matter was that
DeBardeleben as a benevolent despot in charge of miners

growing cabbages, did an excellent depression job in paternalism. (That was not so rare in the South as in Birmingham. On the land undoubtedly some landlords let their tenants take the full consequences of five cent cotton. But there were others, thousands of them, who carried tenants through the depression as masters once carried slaves through hard times. As a system of social security for those at the bottom in the South such a system has its merits. Sensible Negroes still attach themselves to particular white folks, and sometimes it is hard to tell whether the whites or the blacks in such a persisting relationship are the slaves.) But whatever may have been the results of the DeBardeleben system during the depression, I found no convincing evidence that his "people" were better off at the time I talked to him in paternalism than they would be in unions. But blood had already been shed at Acmar and more blood would probably have to be before paternalism gave way to unionism in the DeBardeleben mines there.

"For 32 years," he told his workers, not long before I talked to him in the community house at the Margaret Mines, "we have stood together against the slaves of John L. Lewis. We've fought them and we'll fight them again. And if the day ever comes when you men have to pay tribute for the right to work, we'll close down these mines and go farming."

Mr. DeBardeleben's use of the pronoun "we" was interesting. It appeared not only in his speech. While he talked it stared from the statement painted on the wall behind him: "We are 100% Non Union and Proud of It." And strangest of all perhaps was the big billboard message signed, not by DeBardeleben, but by "Employees of Acmar Mines." It announced in big letters: "NOTICE—Acmar is a place of work and happiness. All persons are warned that we will not tolerate any agitators or trouble makers." But all those signs, like Mr. DeBardeleben's hoarse, strident voice, somehow seemed unconvincing. William Mitch seemed far less agitated about the present situation than Mr. DeBardeleben did. And if Mitch should somehow organize the DeBardeleben mines despite company string bands, company machine guns, company Negro preachers and company reiterated declarations in the first person plural against unionism, it would not be so surprising to some as it might be to Mr. DeBardeleben. Some thought, they told me, that such is his devotion to his ideal of industrial relationships in a time in which those ideals seem out of date and harshly quaint that Mr. DeBardeleben would like nothing better than to die fighting to save the Acmar and Margaret mines from the men of John L. Lewis. Southerners have died for lost causes before, they said, and been heroes for it. But while personal heroism might be personally highly satisfactory, it would probably do little service to Alabama or the South or America.

Suddenly and very sadly it seemed to me that I had strangely come in Birmingham to the other side of something remembered. Charles DeBardeleben was the other industrial extreme in a South changing and growing older from Joe Poe, old Joe whom I had left at Scottsboro limping. As Joe was querulous and confused, no longer expecting a pension, but needing one: Mr. DeBardeleben was irascible and certain, cursing the times he had come to. It seemed a pity that they would never meet. Joe Poe's bones were always too little, I thought, and are probably now too brittle for work in Mr. DeBardeleben's mines. And Mr. DeBardeleben is too preoccupied in this day when Roosevelt is sending the country to hell as straight as a martin to its gourd to be concerned with Joe. He has 6,500 others, black and white, loyal and muttering, strong and weak, on his mind. And yet without knowing each other little Poe and big DeBardeleben have grown old together and one is no more satisfied with these times than the other is.

"The South is worse off as a result of the Roosevelt Administration than it was as a result of the Civil War."

"This pension ain't nothin'. They wanted me to bring everybody in Alabama up to sign for me. And it ain't nothin' if you git it."

This is a bad present for both, I considered. There is no job in it for Joe, no peace in it for Mr. DeBardeleben. Joe is disregarded and Mr. DeBardeleben is besieged. Joe is shut out and Mr. DeBardeleben is shut in the prison of his mind and within the armed citadel at Acmar, his mine village, by the emissaries of that "thug and redneck" John L. Lewis.

The streets were crowding as offices were emptying, but I walked on with no particular destination. The truth is, I told myself, that Mr. DeBardeleben and Joe are both lost in this moment. The whirling world around them by no means is certainly right. John L. Lewis may be as ultimately destructive as Mr. DeBardeleben believes him now to be. Perhaps Joe Poe was right when he first feared the roar of the machines and mistaken only when he went timidly past them to take up the brooms in that mill in Lindale, Georgia. Certainly they are both sad figures in this present advancing Alabama—little Joe brown as the earth which will so soon receive him like leaf mold—if it has not already—and DeBardeleben white as anger and as furious as the last horseman of a Legion of the Bitter-end. Idealist or demagogue, patriarch or exploiter, Acmar's master is at least possessed of some of the spirit of the giants and is not one of those industrialists who have come up from counting money with hands fit only for measuring linen or weighing sugar or counting money. As I look at the world, he is foolish and mistaken, but I also see that he possesses some of that violence which may be embarrassing in conversation but is essential to the heroes of history and poetry.

He is a mountain and Joe Poe is a mouse and both are

equally lost in these times. Joe Poe seemed a little more complacent. Charles DeBardeleben seemed a great deal more angry. But both seemed old in a world brash as Lewis, hopeful as Roosevelt, pragmatic as Taylor. The two are brothers of each other and of the past.

30

OVERSEER'S CAPITAL

"AND this young thing came rushing home from the party in a taxi all by herself. She ran upstairs weeping and threw herself down on the bed sobbing as if her heart would break. Her mother was gone and I was there with her all alone and I didn't know what to do. After all, I'm just an aunt. But I went upstairs and I said, 'Darling, what's the matter?' She lay there shaking and sobbing, sobbing, sobbing. 'Darling, what's the matter? You must tell me.' She drew in her breath as if she must have the last air in the world, and she said, 'I've been insulted.'

" 'Insulted?' I cried. And there I was all alone with her. 'I'll 'phone your mother and we'll get the men of the family. Tell me about it. Before they come.' I was about to reach for a shotgun myself, but she said, 'Oh, no. Don't 'phone.' 'Well,' I demanded, 'what happened?' She sobbed again but she wiped her eyes. 'When we got there he went into the gentlemen's room and when he came back he had liquor on his breath. I've never been so insulted in my life. So I got a taxi and came home.' I looked at her a long time. She wasn't fooling. She went back to sobbing again. And I said, 'My God, when I was coming along—that was about 1924—the only way a man could insult a woman was to try to pull her pants off and if she knew how to act it was sometime before he got out of the hospital.' She let out a wail at that. Then she said, 'Your generation was the coarsest since the Restoration.' I guess so. God knows I can't understand these children growing up in Georgia now. It's a different world."

Certainly Atlanta is. Long before I heard this parable of our times in Atlanta and the South from an Atlantan of my own age, a red-headed woman immaculate and immediate from the beauty parlor, I had concluded that. She clinched it. I had come across the hills from Birmingham to late lunch of salmon and mayonnaise in the empty dining room of the Atlanta Biltmore with Garland Burns Porter who from our college days together had labored in the service of old William Randolph Hearst for whom he not only sells advertising but for whom also he once played the harmonica to the great delight of the Lord of San Simeon and his advertising executives. I suggested that it was a pity that in the South advertising has been too much a piping in Hamelin, stirring up desire beyond the possibility of fulfillment. He was shocked at the suggestion. As all good advertising men should be.

But he forgave me and he guided me to those long rich hills North of Atlanta where along Tuxedo Road and now grander still along Paces Ferry Road are the palaces of the new masters of Dixie. Never in any earlier South were there such or so many mansions. Indeed, I think that if the James River shore were extended along the Battery and Bull Street through Prytannia Street in old New Orl-yuns and all the fine houses of the older South were set upon that way, they would make no such show as that which Atlanta does now on the hills where dwell the aristocrats of Coca-Cola, the lord of golf, the baron of chocolates, and all the rich, fat city burghers and their sleek pretty wives who grew in the years after the landed folk were cut down like the lilacs.

I wondered what kind of folk these rich were behind the clipped hedges and the fences, all artfully designed to conceal and display at once. It seemed a pity that some case worker could not go into the gates and ask such questions as are properly put to the poor. But in Atlanta and elsewhere the questions and the answers might prove embarrassing. That night in a newspaper office I checked on them in a Who's Who. The latest one I could find about was that for 1934–35, but it showed that of the bankers, capitalists and financiers listed from Atlanta, twelve of them, ten were church members (5 Methodists, 1 Baptist, 3 Presbyterians, and 1 Episcopalian), five were either Elks or Masons or both, and 7 were admitted Democrats, none were admitted Republicans, five were politically reticent. And I compared them with the bankers, capitalists and financiers of Richmond, 10 church members out of 10 gentlemen, and seven of them Episcopalians, at least two of them vestrymen, 1 Methodist, 1 Presbyterian, 1 Catholic, not a Baptist. In Richmond the proportion of Democrats among the plutocrats was even higher, 7 out of 10; Republicans, if any, were equally quiet. The Methodist was also a Mason and an Elk. An Episcopal vestryman was also a Mason and the lone Catholic was a Knight of Columbus. But these details can hardly be considered adequate case histories of the Southern rich in old Richmond or newer Atlanta. I had no time to trace out how much of Atlanta's array of palaces came from Coca-Cola of which it is the capital. But as Chattanooga had taken its greatest wealth from a combination of Coca-Cola and Cardui so at least some Atlanta money had come from the revived Ku Klux Klan which for a while seemed to serve men, as Cardui eased women, as tonic for disturbed, uncertain or deranged virility.

"They don't have lynchings on Paces Ferry Road, do they?"

Porter looked at me as if I had suddenly and quietly gone crazy, and he answered me with a combination of the scornful and the amused.

"No," he said.

It seems a pity, I thought, with so many trees, and so much

room for the congregation of the indignant. If there are going to be lynchings in the South there could be no better place for them, though the scene might look perilously similar to that famous scene in which Marie Antoinette spoke of bread and cake in hungry, angry days. I wondered who, if anybody, in Atlanta would have a witticism for the poor if they should come clamoring at these gates for bread. Probably some practical plutocrat would throw them a nigger instead. It has been done before.

"Let's go to niggertown," I suggested and perhaps a little abruptly.

The way was too brief and too far. I am no roaring radical. Most of the leftists whom I know in the South are both as violent in their talk and as rigid in their thinking as old Uncle Charlie DeBardeleben of Birmingham. But it is too far from Paces Ferry Road to Butler Street as human beings live in Atlanta. This is no secret. The Techwood housing project built with Federal funds along Techwood drive stands as monument to that fact where formerly was an area mildly described as unsightly.

"The sooner forgotten, the better," my classmate said.

Steve Nance (his death in 1938 was a loss to the South as to labor in it.) Told me that it was a success in human as well as financial terms, and Steve Nance knew as much about the poor people of Georgia and Atlanta as anybody in it. But the Negro companion project, he declared, had failed because it was impossible to get rents on decent housing down as low as the incomes of the Atlanta Negroes for whom they were built. Housing is a condition like tenant farming which is a symptom of a deeper, more dangerous ill. Decent farms, decent houses are easy to design in the clear sunlight from the south on the mall in Washington. It is a good deal less easy so to alter patterns of Southern living that they will include not only rows of great houses on the suburban hills but also big

293

Negroes adequately paid and little Negroes adequately fed in the city bottoms beyond the railroad tracks. And not only Negroes. And not only the South.

One of the grandest ironies in the writing about this South of our times is that Erskine Caldwell's amoral Southerners of *Tobacco Road* and Ty Ty Walden's pock-marked farm, and Hamilton Basso's rich and itching Yankees of Aiken have all lived their scrotum and stomach lives within the relatively brief circumference of a circle which has its center at Augusta. Washington, Georgia, about which Steve Nance told me in his office as Southern director of the Textile Workers Organizing Committee, lies in the same circle. Governor White of Mississippi would be proud of Washington. This home town of old tempestuous Robert Toombs, having slipped backward from a population of 4,208 in 1920 to 3,158 in 1930, decided to do something about it. And so, Nance told me in Atlanta, the town contributed $20,000 for a shirt factory through public subscription, and $20,000 more was borrowed for the plant by its "future workers" to be paid by deductions from their wages. These "future workers" and all their cousins signed the notes at the bank.

"And what can I say about it?" Nance demanded. This Southern chief of the textile and garment divisions of John L. Lewis' Committee for Industrial Organization, was a wise talking and cherubic-looking individual, who had at least two gleaming gold teeth in the front of his mouth. "I think such plants which generally pay low wages are uneconomic as they build up future social costs for communities. But even if the workers get only $5 a week that's almost riches to people whose sole family cash income has been only $200 a year. And what should I say about long hours to people who have been working from 'kin to caint,' from the earliest they can see in the fields till the time when they can't see at all."

He spread his hands in question and futility.

"If labor in the South is going to get anywhere, we've got to do something about these tenant folks. The real threat to the American standard of living does not come from the coolie and the Jap but from the poor whites of the South. They are terribly poor and terribly productive. They must be given some sort of standards or no other standards in America will survive."

Nance knew. He had seen them, not able to bring himself to blame them, make one of the biggest strikes he ever led a complete failure though it should have been also by any sensible strike standards a success. As head of the old State Federation of Labor (before quarrel of C. I. O. and A. F. of L. gave Georgia two Federations) Nance led out the workers in a big chain of cotton mills in protest against a wage cut and an alleged new system of stretch-out. As in every strike there was considerable difference between the mill management and the labor leaders not only as to the issues involved but also as to the proportions of the walk-out. Out of about 2,500 mill hands, I think Nance told me that more than 2,000 came out and stayed out. I know that he felt that the walk-out was effective. He contemplated, of course, that Governor Eugene Talmadge would send the troops that he did send. What he did not contemplate was that the mill owners, possessing the capital to do it, would go out on the barren hills of worn sections of Georgia and bring in and train an almost entirely new corps of hands. In two months the militia was helping the mills eject strikers and their families from the mill village. One man was killed in the process: "The examining physicians," said the Associated Press, "said he died from complications resulting from bruises on the head, but added that a weak heart might have contributed to his death." But for Nance the time for contemplating causes had passed. He had 1,600 families on his hands. They were homeless. They

295

were hungry. And he moved them. Today they are not only in Atlanta but in every cotton mill town in Georgia, nuclei for union organizations and for C. I. O. strength. And after they moved, pushed out by the new-trained staff from the country, Nance received a request from those whom the mills brought out of the hills to take their places that he send men in to organize them.

Steve Nance was under no misapprehension about the ease of his task. A printer by trade, he knew that the rank and file of workers in textile mills and garment factories in Georgia are a poor and ignorant folk who need education as much as they need unionization. I remember, that when he spoke of the threat to decent standards which comes from the crowded countryside, I asked him about the Southern Tenant Farmers' Union which I had seen in Memphis and about the Farm Laborers and Cotton Field Workers Union with headquarters in Birmingham. This latter union considers even tenant farmers as possible oppressors and sees "an economic difference between those who have an interest in a crop and those who strictly work for wages on the farms." He shook his head.

"We're working about as far down as you can go right now."

"I suppose you've got some who feel that they've got to have a strike as soon as they get a union, and that there's no use in having a union if you're not having a strike."

He nodded glumly.

"I got a 'phone call not long ago: 'If you'll send us a speaker I think we can have a strike.'"

The recollection set him grinning and the sun gleamed at his golden teeth. He went on.

"I said, 'Son, we're short on speakers and we're plumb out of strikes.'" He laughed then loud.

He hoped to keep out of strikes. He wanted contracts, not

conflicts. But he was wise in knowing that hope of advancement of labor in the South to decent living standards and to consuming power depends upon a wider advance than can be contained in the company of those who seek improvement through unions alone. And I found that fact clearer when I went from his office to that of Tarleton Collier, a fragile person who writes a column about the South in Hearst's *Atlanta Georgian* which is as stout spoken as it is strangely placed. He had just come back from a visit to some Middle Georgia counties where the Federal Government was transferring land upon which men could not make a living to birds which might find it a refuge. Collier had seen the people there and talked to them. They were the same folk, I knew, who were eagerly taking places at low pay and long hours in shirt factories. There were more such behind them, inexhaustibly more.

"Sorry people?" Collier asked himself. It was an entirely rhetorical question. "Why not say sorry land, or perhaps sorry guidance. Perhaps it was not land for cotton or corn to begin with, and certainly not after it had been wasted by years of clean-tilled single cropping; but they clung to these crops because it was a natural and expected thing to do."

Tired-looking and sad, he contemplated those poor people in his memory.

"If something had been done for this land and these people a generation ago, much of the tragedy would have been averted. As it is, they have gone along in increasing hopelessness and their children have fallen into the sterile routine which enslaved them."

But he had not found *Tobacco Road*, he had not found helpless depravity. He had been, he told me, impressed instead with the thoughtfulness and the intelligence of the people. We were impressed together by his discovery that white men in those counties were realizing that their own hope depended also upon the hope and welfare beside them of the Negroes.

"The big houses were gone," he said. "But as we rode in that country I saw a place upon a hill with most magnificent trees about it. 'What a site for a house,' I said. And the man who was driving me said, 'Yes. It is. It was. But the boll weevil had already come through before it burned. And there was no money or need to build it back again. Not even any sense in it.' We rode on beyond it. I never saw such a lovely place for a great house. And it is somehow terribly sad, that it's gone."

And the people who lived in it, or their children, have gone to town, I thought, or moved into smaller and smaller houses on the poorer and poorer land: But the Old South keeps its patterns nevertheless. I found one of its keepers in the erect, religious Negro man who in the elaborately decorated apartment in the Atlanta Biltmore tends the quarters and the clothes of young Randolph Hearst. The servant seemed about sixty. He made juleps, using brandy as a base, in the lively modernistic bar. He had in all his lifetime had but three jobs and one of his employers, dying, had left him a huge Pierce-Arrow which he still drives. He had been employed for young Hearst before that young man arrived in Atlanta to begin the learning of his father's empire. He served an excellent dinner, perfectly, traditionally; and young attractive, personable Randolph Hearst was gentleman and host in the South. I was grateful for my dinner, but I knew, as Garland Porter and I went downstairs in the private elevator, that I was impressed as a colonial who had dined with a prince beginning an aristocratic career in an outlying province of an empire. It is always pleasant to dine at the viceroy's house in his colonial capital. And Atlanta, indeed, is more and more that capital of the South where the overseers of the absentees meet to administer it.

31

GRAVEYARD AND GULLY

THAT Sunday morning was the only time, I think, that I ever saw dew in a cemetery. It gleamed between the little monuments in the neat democracy of death which the United States everywhere makes in its green graveyards. I never saw any place so quiet. Even the birds seemed hushed, waking slowly and reverently. It was hard to think in that quietness of the noise which must have been made so long ago by the soldier-prisoners at Andersonville. What a noise they made beyond Andersonville until poor old Henry Wirz the Swiss swung in Washington in what at this distance of years looks remarkably like a lynching within the forms of law participated in by the President of the United States.

Though he did not know it Hugh Bennett, chief of the soil conservation service of the U. S. Department of Agriculture, routed me out of bed in the Atlanta Biltmore before day that morning. He had told me: "You should by all means see the famous Providence Cave in Stewart County, Georgia, near the town of Lumpkin. This is a celebrated gully probably more than 150 feet deep at the head, yet formed in soil within the past half century. It is but one of numerous similar gullies which have ruined a large area of good land in Stewart and two adjacent counties."

So I rose early in order to have plenty of time in which to see it on the road to Tallahassee. Also I had observed on the map that the same road south ran approximately by the old Confederate prison. And so from the black and misty darkness on Peachtree Street I went down to meet the milkwagons on the road toward Americus. I considered stopping at the new fine-appearing mill village about the huge Martha Mills at Silvertown but rode on instead. Afterwards Albert Matthews, general manager of these big tire fabric plants of the Goodrich company and as such lord of Silvertown, wrote me that probably at the hour when I drove through his baronies he was sunning himself and swimming intermittently at his pool on Crystal Hill. We could have gone swimming together and then looked at mill and town. "Really," he said, "this is a wonderful plant and village." It would have been as easy to stop then as it would have been hard to go back afterward. I went on and turned off following a fat filling station attendant's directions at Rupert. At Ideal (whose Ideal? I wondered) I drove by an old decaying mansion which sat behind its conventional columns almost flush with the sidewalk on the principal street. And it was full morning, though the dew remained, when I drove into the big empty national cemetery at Andersonville. Empty of the living. But I had the company of a multitude of the dead.

That stop on my discovery of the South was entirely one of personal privilege. I doubt whether it has the least significance so far as the present South is concerned, but it was the atrocity center of the Civil War from the Northern standpoint and as one who distrusts atrocity talebearers everywhere I wanted to see the scene of their old anger-building. Men died there rightly enough; the little crosses in this isolated section of Georgia indicate that. The figures are that of the 49,485 prisoners received between February, 1864, and April, 1865, 12,800 died. And after them also Wirz, who had charge under General W. S. Winder of the prisoners, as a contemporary chronicler reported, "died, as thousands of other scoundrels have, with calmness."

It was difficult that early morning in the cemetery and fur-

ther down the road in the prison park where the stockade
had stood to visualize in the sloping meadows such a crowding as· the 33,000 men who once were gathered in the 27
stockaded acres. Now all green the fields slope down to a
pleasant stream. Death and suffering and war seem utterly
far off. There are no quieter places in America. There are no
cleaner places. Nor greener. In the park a cottontail scurried
in the grass. And how far off seemed lice and fleas and flies
and gangrenous sores, and scurvy and diarrhea and death,
and the slowly buried and namelessly buried dead. Sherman
had not come this way but the war was the same. And while
I stood on the edge of the old stockade a Georgia family
stopped in the road behind me.

"Mister, do you know whether they allow picnicking here?"

I turned. There were a fat woman and a sallow man on the
front seat of a dilapidated car and in the rear five solemn
children all eying me.

"No," I said. "They can tell you up at the cemetery, I suppose. There's a lodge there and a keeper."

I went back to my own car to drive away and when I rolled
off the man was talking to the woman and she was shaking
her head. The solemn children were listening and eying the
bright lawn and the stream which cut it pleasantly in two.

I had noticed at Vicksburg as I did again at Andersonville
how green the grass is where the Federal government tends
it. But I was never so impressed by the greenness of government grass as I was when I went on beyond it through Americus where people seemed to know as little about Andersonville on the one side as they did of the big ditch at Lumpkin
on the other. Both cemetery and ditch, of course, are off the
main highways and, increasingly, in the South as elsewhere
places that are off the main roads are out of the world. But I
found my way, and a remarkably pleasant one, along the dirt
roads upon which starched children, black and white, marched

to Sunday School, to Lumpkin where a gentleman who appeared to be nothing less than a senior warden in the Episcopal Church pointed me the way to the caves.

They are, of course, not caves at all. They are ditches. But ditches of the same genus as the grand canyon of the Colorado. Down through the red soil to almost pure white clays the chasms run in the midst of cultivated Georgia farms. They come perilously close to the highway and seem ready to engulf road and farm-house and church. They run beside the road for what seems to be miles. Full grown trees rise from the bottom of these ravines; and in them, too, points of earth rise like clay towers of stalagmites, fine phallic symbols in the midst of an advancing sterility. I saw them with a layman's eyes. And, like a layman, I lay on my belly and stared over the edges which fortunately for me did not crumble under me. I looked far off where the ditches twist and hide themselves beyond farm land and trees.

They left me not so much shocked at land destroyed as puzzled by the character of the destroying ditches. In Stewart County there is no such wholesale erosion as that which around Ducktown and Copperhill makes a whole corner of Polk County in Tennessee look like a desert. That mountain desert grew from the rare phenomenon of sulphuric fumes. The Stewart County ditches grew from careless man and washing water. But the land about them did not seem to an unpracticed eye badly worn soils about to collapse in dramatic canyoning. Instead the big ditches lay deep and open in the midst of apparently rich and fertile fields. Corn, cotton and pecan trees grow near them. And near them, too, I came upon a big barn smelling pleasantly of animal husbandry. There were houses, too, surrounded by such flowers as are generally grown in the country only by such folk as love the earth as well as hope to profit from it. I remember particu-

larly one old time house of classic line and the white oleanders which were blooming before it.

Perhaps improperly I took hope from learning that there
is nothing new about such ravines in Georgia. In this same
section the same such ditches were reported as long ago as
1846 by Sir Charles Lyell, F. R. S. In his volumes on his second tour of geological investigations in the United States he
reported seeing in the neighborhood of Columbus, Georgia,
which is scarcely 35 miles from the present Providence Caves,
the last detachment of Indians on their way to Arkansas. He
added: "Here as at Milledgeville, the clearing away of the
woods, where these Creek Indians once pursued their game,
has caused the soil, previously level and unbroken, to be cut
into by torrents, so that deep gullies may everywhere be seen;
and I am assured that a large proportion of the fish, formerly
so abundant in the Chattahoochie, have been stifled by the
mud." In greater detail Sir Charles described a similar ditch
(still in existence) near Milledgeville, more than 100 miles
away. He wrote:

"Twenty years ago it had no existence; but when the trees
of the forest were cut down, cracks three feet deep were
caused by the sun's heat in the clay; and, during the rains,
a sudden rush of waters through these cracks, caused them to
deepen at their lower extremities, from whence the excavat-
ing power worked backward, till, in the course of twenty
years, a chasm, measuring no less than 55 feet in depth, 300
yards in length, and varying in width from 20 to 180 feet was
the result. The high road has been several times turned to
avoid this cavity, the enlargement of which is still proceeding,
and the old line of road may be seen to have held its course
directly over what is now the widest part of the ravine. In the
perpendicular walls of this great chasm appear beds of clay
and sand, red, white, yellow, and green, produced by the de-

composition in situ of hornblendic gneiss, with layers and veins of quartz, and of a rock consisting of quartz and felspar, which remain entire to prove that the whole mass was once crystalline. In another place I saw a bridge thrown over a recently formed gulley, and here, as in Alabama, the new system of valleys and of drainage, attendant on the clearing away of the woods, is a source of serious inconvenience and loss.

"I infer, from the rapidity of the denudation caused here by running water, after the clearing or removal of wood, that this country has been always covered with a dense forest, from the remote time when it first emerged from the sea. However long may have been the period of upheaval required to raise the marine tertiary strata to the height of more than 600 feet, we may conclude that the surface has been protected by more than a mere covering of herbage from the effects of the sudden flowing off of the rain water. I know it may be contended that, when the granite and gneiss first rose as islands out of the sea, they may have consisted entirely of hard rock, which resisted denudation, and therefore that we can only affirm that the forest has been continuous from the time of the decomposition and softening of the upper portion of these rocks. But I may reply, that similar effects are observable, even on a grander scale, in recently excavated ravines seventy or eighty feet deep, in some newly cleared parts of the tertiary regions of Alabama, as in Clarke County, for example, and also in some of the cretaceous strata of loose gravel, sand, and clay, in the same state at Tuscaloosa. These are at a much greater height above the sea, and must, from the first, have been as destructible as they are now."

It has been more than half a century since Sir Charles was buried in Westminster Abbey; it has been nearly a hundred years since he published this statement of the effects of what

we ordinary folk in these times call erosion. Those years are
disturbing and encouraging. The destruction of soils where
the forests have been cut down has been proceeding for a
long time. Therefore, at least, it is no new threat to our existence. Therefore, also, it takes a long time for knowledge to
impress itself upon a people even when it is bread-and-butter
important in their lives. Probably, we should not even yet be
considering erosion in Georgia if lands were selling now for
a dollar an acre in Texas. But the cheap, fertile lands are
filled up. And the ditches run now through a land tragically
important to the people who live upon it. How tragic has
been indicated by the studies of Dr. Howard W. Odum, native Georgian now at Chapel Hill, who has shown that no
less than 61 per cent of the country's eroded lands are in its
Southern regions, lands which lose annually an estimated
twenty million tons of potash, nitrogen and phosphoric acid.
Such a loss means an unsatisfactory substitution of five and
a half million tons of commercial fertilizer at a cost of $161,-
000,000. How much this is is indicated by the fact that the
consumption of the rest of the nation was only about two and
a half million tons. Also the South which pays out so much
for fertilizer has been able to spend only a little more for the
education of all its children than for this one costly item in
its agriculture.

But on that Sunday afternoon that rived land did not look
tragic; the people upon it seemed not at all wasting survivors
or wasted remnants of a human order that had departed from
depleted and eroded soil. Far otherwise, land and people—
white folk and Negroes—seemed to me that day vigorous and
arrayed for pleasuring. Indeed, I wondered if Sunday finery
betrayed me in judgment of the people who walked those
Georgia roads. In accordance with an old Southern custom
the South has always put all the wealth it could put its hands
on on its back. Ladies came smiling and well-dressed from all

but empty houses. Architecture, putting most of the money on the columns at the door, followed the same pattern. Catharine Van Court has reported of Natchez that though the food cupboards might be scantily supplied, the guest boards never lacked cake and wine. Like all respectable Southern customs, it applies to both races. As for instance the new love of locomotion—and speeding.

Here they walked. There were few cars. The Negroes were not riding. Nor were all the white people riding whom I met on the roadsides. But the women and the children particularly were good to see. And all of the women, white and black, wore clothes of the same fashion as I had seen in Atlanta. The young are no longer sunbonneted. The chain stores, whatever may be their other vices, have brought color and style to the country South. Their dresses may not wear so well. Their sandals may not be so well suited even on Sunday to dirt roads in June. But they have made a better looking people and a people who obviously will not be content in a retreat to subsistence agriculture attended by relinquishment of the goods and gadgets of industry.

The roads of Georgia are not considered Pomander Walks. Indeed, Erskine Caldwell has made them seem instead grisly ways to the bone pile. But that day I rode I saw more good looking women, black and white, than I have seen on any Easter morning on Fifth Avenue. They walked, smiling, alone, in couples, in companies. They were pleasuring, fed and unfrightened. Certainly never anywhere have I seen so many good looking colored women, not in New Orleans, not in Harlem. Some of them were good looking after the white pattern, slim, fragile mulattoes. But particularly I remember seeing one big young woman, black as moonlessness, who might have come out of a jungle. Her hair stood out from her head. She had on a blue blouse and a red skirt and she looked beautiful as what she was.

I wished as I rode that we knew more about the racial differences among Negroes. "A nigger is a nigger" may satisfy the intellectual as well as emotional demands of some Southern persons. But Africa is as big as Europe and there was undoubtedly as much difference among those Africans who were shipped to these shores as among those Europeans who came. The difference between a Coromantee and a Gaboon was as marked as that between a Spaniard and a Swede. In Mozambique alone one student determined the presence of 31 different human shades from dusky or yellow brown to sooty black. And in back country Georgia the chromatic scale extends all the way from the blondest people on earth to the blackest and the infinite variety of combinations between them. Certainly anybody who rides through back country Georgia and sees the different types must realize that the conventional flap-breasted, narrow-hipped, straight-shanked Negro women are merely the least attractive of an infinite variety. Undoubtedly there is a possibility that such creatures predominate. They look even now like slaves and like the creatures to bear slaves. Such black folk are probably in the majority because they accepted slavery without struggle. Indeed, in Africa for centuries they may have been the slave and drone races, the helots of handsomer and prouder people whose very pride made them poor survivors of the slave trade. And there are beside them such white creatures as bear—and bear properly —the names po' white, po' buckra, white trash. But if that Georgia road was any sample, these folk—the triangular-breasted Negroes and the squirrel-mouthed whites are rare in the South as they have always been rare in a world of vain and vigorous folk everywhere anxious to love and eat.

There were more and more pecan trees by the roadside. In Thomasville on Sabbath afternoon a town band played concert at the courthouse. And their brassy music broke the late afternoon quietness. I grieved to see that there were more musicians than listeners. That seemed sad but the musicians appeared undisturbed. They went on playing and Thomasville echoed with the notes of "I'll Take You Home Again, Kathleen." I rejoiced in it. And I parked at the curb to increase by at least one the audience that was needed for listening. But after a little I rode on again and Florida began, even in Georgia, beautifully with the reappearance of Spanish moss and the increasing frequency of high palm and big fern. A hot rain fell and the pavement ran into Tallahassee slick between roadsides heavy scented in the dark.

32

SWANEE ROAD

PERHAPS it is true, as Mr. Kilmer said originally very nicely and as countless ladies have reiterated shrilly since, that only God can make a tree. But a man made the Swanee River. The river which Stephen Foster took, misspelling it, from a map where he searched for a better two syllable stream than Peedee, does not run merely to the Gulf from Okefenokee Swamp and its alligators and moccasins and shy, poor white people on occasional prairies and Negroes in the dark shade of its black gum trees. It runs rather from homesickness into memory. Its sources are diverse as its singers. Those English Crimean War soldiers who sang it so long ago had never heard of Florida but they also had childhoods far from the Black Sea shores and beyond the aging of the old folks at home. It is the river behind all of us with shores simple as sand. And it is not Southern though it may border Southern living on the one hand, as Stonewall Jackson's river, beyond which was the shade of the trees, may border the other. It is a river to be sung, not seen. But God's triumph is that it may be seen without suffering. God has made a river lovely as a song. I saw it and I know.

I came deeper and deeper south to the really little town which is the capital of Florida. And in the conventional columned Southern mansion, I found Governor Fred P. Cone who had been confined to his bed because his feet hurt him. He looked older than most of the Southern Governors I had seen. In the little upstairs sitting room of the Executive

309

Mansion he rocked in his chair and told me the trouble with his slippered feet.

"Is Florida a Southern State?" I asked him.

"What?"

"Is Florida still in the South or have the millionaires carried it off?"

"Florida's Southern all right. Why, North Florida and South Georgia are about the same, same folks, same ways of making a living. Florida is a Southern State sharing the fate of the South. Of course, North Florida and South Florida are different. There are a lot of Northerners in the South and they're different from the old farm and plantation folks in the North. They usually say down here that Ocala is about the dividing line."

So I rode south in the strange certainty that if I went far enough south I should find the end of the South and a new North below it. On that road I went by drainage ditches in which grew not only water hyacinths like those I had seen in Louisiana but also white water lilies profuse and fragrant, and a very erect flower like a lavender cat tail. One whole lake near Cross City was in amazing and beautiful bloom—and all wasted on native Floridians.

But not all is garden in Florida. For miles on end wasteland runs to the roadside. The tourists had fled through these wastes from the heat. But no tourist will ever go south beyond Cross City without being aware that he is approaching that Swanee River of his song. An enterprising filling station proprietor had appropriated the name in the hope of selling more gasoline, hot dogs and soft drinks on its shore. Lovely even beyond the expectation Foster stirred, the Suwanee River moves dark and quiet, twisting between its tree-lined banks. It is not only beautiful. It is not only the greatest luck that a river, chosen for the sound of its name, should fulfill every wish of seeing. It is also excellent in a South of red rivers to come at last upon one clear and dark together. It is not the only one: wherever Southern rivers run back through swamp and forest the waters run clear or stained only by decayed vegetable matter, like some streams in Europe, as Sir Charles Lyell observed, which flow out of peat mosses. But where the ax has cut the forests, the waters wash the land, and the rivers run red as a bleeding to the sea. And anemic is the earth and the man on it left behind.

I spread my map upon the ground and squatted above it. Below the Suwanee the Waccasassa River flowed into the Gulf and south of the Waccasassa, the Withlacoochee. There was the village of Yankeetown. I looked at the map again. The Suwanee runs to the Gulf as the southern border of a new county named Dixie. And for a moment the conjunction of Suwanee and Dixie seemed geographically obscene, like quadroons in Harlem crooning to fat white men about a Dixie to which they could only be taken if they were tied. And even in summer it seemed to me that the road to the south smelled like the acid sweat of thin-blooded people who flee from the cold. I rode on and in June I sweat as I drove like a Georgia convict digging under a gun.

Flat Florida is a strange land. The sun is there certainly, summer as winter, though this day I rode just ahead of a thunderstorm. And the wastelands continued.

"This is such a barren," I said to myself, "that nothing would grow on it but a millionaire."

But below Williston the wastes bloom and the highway may run between a desert and a garden. There is a theatrical quality about groves of citrus fruit surrounded by royal palms, and a dramatic quality, too, about the flat, treeless, apparently entirely unproductive earth before and beyond them. Some of the little towns have splendid tree-lined, moss-hung streets. Neither the palm or the pine are much good for shade. But what dense black shade there is under the orange trees. There is too little of it. Generally the sun beats down bright and blinding in a country deliberately devoted to the sun and the winter. In St. Petersburg, store windows were sealed with heavy brown paper against destructive summer sunlight. Hotels were shut. Benches were empty upon which in winter old men sit baking their bones. And the hotels that were open were built for winter. The big fans in the center of the ceilings of bedrooms which are standard equipment in Mississippi Valley hotels were not to be found in Florida. The restaurant in the hotel was shut for summer, but there was a restaurant still running up the street. The towns were indulging in siesta months long. And in the midst of it big red Hibiscus bloomed on the roadside by Tampa Bay.

I went on south. The land was Southern; but the people were gone. Summer had driven them away. I was not entirely sure that I had penetrated the bottom of the South and into a new North beneath it until by the wayside I came upon the sign:

"Alpine Goats."

I knew that I had not ascended even a slope since last I had seen the sea. Nowhere does Florida rise above 300 feet. So I turned in the drive bordered by some slightly diseased looking royal palms. At its end a very giant of an old woman in knickerbockers stood watching my approach. Her gray hair hung in a long, lank bob about her head. She regarded me without speaking after I stopped. I got out of the car and made my best Southern manners.

"I was interested in your Alpine goats."

For so large a woman she spoke with a strangely thin, high voice.

"They were my sister's."

"Is she here?"

"No. She's dead."

"Excuse me. Of course, I didn't know." I muttered it.

"The goats are dead too," she said. And then cried suddenly, "Do you think that's a mere coincidence? Do you? Do you?"

I stepped back, frankly frightened. But abruptly she was no longer fierce. She looked as if she were going to cry.

"There aren't any goats. And I'm going back to Philadelphia. We ought to have gone to Pasadena. I told her so. She never would listen to me."

I backed away apologetically. She stood in the drive, big and gray and alone and a baby and she wept. I knew I was more cowardly than chivalrous, but if time has taught the Southerner anything it is that chivalry may be meddling and meddling may be dangerous. That's a selfish learning. But I knew I was out of the South and I turned north in Yankee Florida to get back into it. I hurried between the decaying gates of East Coast real estate developments where the jungle has run across the building lots to the edge of the road. At St. Augustine paper Dixie cups are provided at the sulphurous Fountain of Youth which failed to preserve De Leon. Between St. Augustine and Jacksonville a bird, like a buzzard but smaller was trying to carry off a turtle that had been smashed between asphalt and automobile tire. Jacksonville was crowded like a city that lives all year round. And beyond it the coast of Georgia spread in marshes like a country that is only alive and no more. But even in this benumbed extremity I knew I was safe in the South again. I rode and sang: "Way down upon de Swanee Ribber, far, far away . . ."

I am sure I sang it out of tune.

33

PLANT THE PINES

THE scars on that boy's face in Darien were sickening. He stood conspicuous at the bridge head with a red flag in his hand, halting motorists while repairs went forward on the bridge. His scars were more arresting than his flag. While I waited he stood with one foot on my running board and I talked to him, looking far beyond him and his terrible torn face to the little town that is left where Fanny Kemble's bitterness whipped this Georgia shore. She must have been a woman both talented and evil-tempered in her righteousness so to sting the planters of this land with her descriptions for the abolitionists of their depravity and oppression. But one thing as well as woods curtained with yellow jessamine she remembered in pleasure in this country which was to her in 1838 "the abomination of desolation." She wrote of "fragrant bathtubs made of cedar" which she preferred to "the finest Staffordshire porcelain." To make them the Negroes had cut cedars down. To clear the rice field squares in the tidal swamps, they had also cut the cypress and the gum trees. And further up the rivers afterwards the sawmills and the turpentine mills had come. The forests of long-leaf pine were cut down. The faces of trees were needlessly hacked to draw down the resin. Behind them was left in all reality a land without hope, such an "abomination of desolation" as angry Fanny Kemble had seen. And competition and hurricane, destructive tide and disappearing Negroes had let the water into the rice squares, and sometimes the salt marshes, beautiful and sterile, now seem marching inland to meet the ravished land where all the forests have been cut down.

I drove that road behind the winter islands of the millionaires and the summer shores of vacationing Georgians, and beyond the cut-over barrens where more and more pitiful white people live in the counties where once Negroes so outnumbered their masters that they remained long African for lack of another civilization to imitate. And as Tobacco Road is close to Aiken, so behind Jekyl Island the most ignorant, pitiful and poverty-stricken whites in Georgia seek a living where razorback hogs eat the roots of pine seedlings, and their owners each year deter reforestation by the annual burning of the dead wire-grass in the mistaken belief that thereby better spring grazing is afforded for their few scrawny cattle. Many of them are scrawny humans hardly fit for oppression. I remember the description of the condition of one of them which a distinguished Georgia physician gave me on his porch behind pillars on one of the squares which in decorous green procession interrupt old and dignified Bull Street in Savannah. A boy had been brought to town: The doctors and the hospitals are wide apart behind the Golden Isles of Georgia. The doctors who remain in the little towns are old men without successors. This boy, sent to Savannah, had malaria, hookworm, pellagra and from malnutrition his thigh bone had pierced his pelvis.

"Coastalitis," the doctor said, "is a terrible disease. Curable maybe, if there were schools and doctors, but the young doctors don't want to practice in the little towns where they can't have the laboratory facilities which they have been taught are—and actually are—essential to the medicine they are learning. The old physicians were better in the country. They practiced by intuition but more and more the younger men are dependent on the microscope and the chemical analysis. It's hard to have them in the little, little towns. A few marry nurses and make their homes their laboratories, but the distances are longer and longer between the doctors."

Across the Savannah River in the Carolinas I knew that the Duke Foundation under Dr. W. S. Rankin was trying to work the problem out with the development of county hospitals where practice would be centralized: the patients would come to the doctor as pupils go to consolidated schools. But there is a man, scientist, too, in Savannah who believes he has the cure not merely for this Southern coastalitis but for other aspects of that poverty of the South which in farm and town has made the South the ill-kept backyard of America where old, ugly things are kept which long ago, in a decent, sanitary community, should have been thrown away. And he believes that his own cure extends all the way from barren land to poor cities, from earth to industry. His specific is trees—not trees for shade such as those in Savannah which give the old seaport a pleasant shadowed quality. But trees to grow, to be beaten and cooked into pulp for paper and cloth and cellophane.

I went down the cobblestone hill to the unpretentious Pulp and Paper Laboratory on West River Street to see Dr. Charles H. Herty who was born seventy years ago in Milledgeville, Georgia, where Lyell the geologist saw the big ditch which had grown because the trees had been cut down. I had known Dr. Herty since the time when his boys and the Daniels boys were Dekes together at Chapel Hill. And long before that I had heard his name in connection with trees. When I was going to school the geography books spoke of North Carolina as producing tar, pitch and turpentine. Now the trees and the naval stores trade are gone. But Dr. Herty in those days was already teaching the South to use the less destructive cups in place of the old box system in collecting the crude turpentine from the scarred pine trees.

Now in Georgia since 1931 he has been experimenting to

demonstrate that from the pulp of the pine (and other woods) can be made both newsprint paper and rayon. Furthermore, the pulp can be made from trees grown in less than a decade on Southern lands which, while poorly suited to agriculture, are admirably adapted to the growing of pines. On thousands of acres of such land bent-backed Southern farmers have been essaying the impossibility of making a living growing corn or cotton. They have only starved while they hastened the washing away of the last remnants of topsoil. But the pines, given a chance, will grow not only to restore the earth to ultimate fertility but, as a result of Dr. Herty's experiments, also to a market for trees which will provide cash for the countryman, new jobs for workers in towns and a new tax-paying, wealth-making industry for the South.

While Dr. Herty took me through the laboratory, showing me the steps from the loblolly pine log to the finished newsprint paper and rayon yarn, he spoke in terms of his faith that the cheaper wood, lower-priced labor and nearness to essential supplies, including hydro-electricity and fuel would make inevitable a transfer of the wood pulp industries to the South. Already I knew that kraft mills in increasing number were establishing themselves in the South in order to find the wood supply which is being consumed in the northern areas of slower growth trees. But Dr. Herty insisted that before very long Southern rayon mills would at great saving be using Southern wood pulps and that Southern newspapers, and others also, would be printing on the products of the Southern pines. I pretend to no proficiency as prophet or qualifications as chemist; but there is at least a contagious and convincing quality in Dr. Herty's enthusiasm. And, having ridden through the pine barrens I was more interested in the possibilities of escape than the processes of industry. And it was on the land that Dr. Herty's experiments have stirred the first controversy. It is the old controversy between those who believe that the people must be ruled by law and those who believe that if the people have a chance to make an intelligent choice their choice will be intelligent.

Dr. Herty had seen intelligent choices made. He told me about the 86,000 acres around Cogdell, Georgia, acquired by Alex Sessoms, an old sawmill man and nephew of that Alex Sessoms who 25 years ago was one of the first to use Dr. Herty's better turpentine cup. He has done nothing toward reforestation except keep the fire out and protect the natural regrowth.

"So far as the eye can see in every direction," Dr. Herty said, "thousands of acres are covered with young seedlings whose deep green foliage bespeaks rapid growth. The reproduction is so dense that from time to time it is thinned in order to get the proper diameter growth."

He told me also about James Fowler, "a country boy," who at Soperton, Georgia, has planted 12,000 acres in pines. The old turpentine expectation was 15 trees to the acre, but young Fowler has 450 to the acre, planted like an orchard. It was he who in 1933 brought a truckload of logs to the Savannah laboratory. They were thinnings from his land on which slash pine seedlings had been set out. They were all seven years old. From them an excellent grade of newsprint was made which proved to be, Dr. Herty said, lighter in weight but stronger than regular newsprint when tested in comparison with paper furnished by one of the leading metropolitan dailies. On this paper was printed the first edition of a newspaper (*The Soperton News*) on material made entirely from young Georgia pine by the standard methods characteristic of a newsprint industry.

Such reforestation for profit, Dr. Herty believes, is the best basis for the reforestation and for the protection of the forests of the South. Teach the Southern landowners, he said, that there is profit in trees and they will grow trees as they grow cotton. Little regulation to protect the forests will be needed then. The self-interest of the landowners will provide greater protection than a whole book of laws or army of forest wardens. Education, not regulation, he insists, is the way to the protection of the remaining forest resources of the South.

The Forest Service is not so sure. Its members agree to education. They hope for good results from self-interest. But the problem is faced in the middle of a race between those who are grabbing what is left of the forest and those who are educating. It is not at all certain that the educators are leading—or even that they can catch up before the remnants of a vast forest heritage are destroyed.

"You, of course, are familiar with the facts as to the recent expansion of the pulp industry in the South," said Joseph C. Kircher, U. S. Regional Forester, who has his offices in Georgia. "The end of this period of expansion does not seem to be in sight. Our early period of timber exploitation by the sawmill industry, which swept the South from the Carolinas to Texas in a few decades, removing the virgin timber which was here as the accumulated growth of generations, left untouched as a general rule the small timber which now is being taken for pulpwood, poles, posts, tobacco wood, and even for low grade lumber. The small portable sawmills now are cutting immature timber that was considered to be of no value by the lumber industry of yesterday. Demand is causing the utilization of smaller and smaller timber. Locally it is as if a shortage of mature beef were forcing the population to depend on calves for meat."

He went on:

"Forestry agencies, Federal and State, have failed as yet to induce the majority of landowners and forest industries to look upon timber as a crop. The general practice still is to liquidate the timber, large or small, get the cash and let the future take care of itself regardless of the fact that it is easy to prove that it pays well to reserve ample growing stock for further quantity and quality growth. We have failed even to accomplish forest fire protection although no intelligent person doubts the folly of permitting the present widespread destruction to continue."

The American seemed to be still the legitimate child of his ancestors. And he appeared to be no more aware than they were that there was an end to the land to be exploited, that there might even be a limit to the trees to be cut down.

"Education and demonstration," Mr. Kircher continued, "are widely recognized as means of promoting better management of forests. This approach to the problem is good and deserves far more attention and financial support than it now is getting. Extension work in forestry by Federal and State agencies should be strengthened and expanded. There is a growing weight of opinion, however, which holds that education alone will not provide a complete remedy. Adherents to this viewpoint can cite the failure of the forest industries to impose self-regulation in their operations. They can point to the further fact that many managers of wood-using industries know the importance of sustained-yield operations, yet are liquidating partly because of the feeling that if they do not take the young timber someone else will. The pulp and paper industry right now is hesitating to bind itself to conservative cutting on lands from which pulpwood is purchased because, as the pulpwood men say, the young trees they leave will be cut promptly by the portable saw-mills, the polecutters, or someone else."

That someone else is a prominent American, North and South. He is the manufacturer who may pay lower wages and so undersell the virtuous. He is the taxpayer who may lie to the tax assessor and so increase the burden on all the rest of us. He is the acquaintance of the business man who figures, shrugging, that if he doesn't cheat these simple people, somebody else will. He is the man who cuts down the trees. But he seldom gets a chance to beat the virtuous to his snide tricks. They are almost always there first, shrugging while they destroy.

Mr. Kircher asked a question.

"Does it not seem that there may be a need of some measure of public regulation in the interest of the wood-using industries themselves as well as the communities whose economic welfare is dependent on the permanence of the industries and the forest resources on which the industries feed?"

He did not quite answer it.

"I must confess that my mind is not made up as to how this could be accomplished. I am sure, however, that some way must be found to put an end to the old practice of quick liquidation followed by stranded communities and relief rolls. My fear is that the slow processes of education and demonstration will prove inadequate in bringing about the necessary changes in time to prevent irremedial damage."

But that big question lies beyond the plant on River Street in Savannah. Dr. Herty has shown, he believes, the South to a way which will improve its lands, help its people, give it industry and wealth. He is the chemist. The length of human life being what it is, Dr. Herty cannot carry the results of his researches into full development. Indeed, if he were to live to be a million, the development of his researches on land and in factory would not be his task. He is the chemist, the researcher. Beyond him must be promoters and, rarer and more necessary in the South, protectors. Somehow by educa-tion or restraint, the Southerners must recognize the South as a land with a future, and not merely a land with a past. Recognition of the meaning of a future will include conservation as well as extraction, consideration for land and people as well as profits and promoters.

So I thought as I went back through old Savannah to the huge, rambling, pleasant old De Soto Hotel. A paving project sent me detouring through back streets where Negroes sat before their wooden houses built close to the street. There are fewer of them now in Savannah than there formerly were, just as there are fewer of them in all the Georgia and South Carolina Low Country. Savannah has not grown rapidly. Indeed, pleasantly and in the shade and in the big rooms behind the brass knockers it has almost stood still. But what growth there has been has been white. The Negroes who remain are still crowded close together. And with the wharves the colored folk, shouting across the alleys unaccustomed to so many cars, give Savannah the color of its present as of its past. The dust did not disturb them—or the heat. But there was dust in my throat when I got to the hotel. The sun fell on the high stoops of the old houses and there was a good deal more of the day.

"Where," I asked the girl at the cigar stand, "is this big plantation, The Hermitage, that I see advertised?"

She arranged her magazines.

"It isn't here any more."

"Did it burn?"

"No. Mr. Ford took it away."

"And where did Mr. Ford take it?"

"I don't know," she said. Obviously also she did not care.

"Maybe to Dearborn?"

"Maybe. But I'm not sure. I'll 'phone and find out for you."

"No. Don't bother. If he took it, it's gone."

And that night the physician who told me about the boy whose thigh bone had shoved through his pelvis, spoke of

Henry Ford and the work he had done for people about his plantation in Bryan County.

"I think Henry Ford has done more good than any man since Jesus Christ," he said.

And if so, I considered he was entitled to a plantation, or even to Georgia. He might both plant and protect the trees.

34

PATTERN IN THE STONE

I HAD never been to Charleston in the summer before and on the day I came, so far as most of the people I knew were concerned, it was as empty as it used to be in those lost summertimes when ladies and gentlemen fled for their very lives to the up-country and the sea islands. The bay glittered metallically and the streets steamed. But the killing malaria had departed. Gone, too, were the numbers of turkey buzzards which once were so numerous above the town that even in winter Sir Charles Lyell counted nine of them perched side by side, like so many bronze statues breaking the long line of a roof in the clear blue sky. And he was told: "You are lucky in being here in a cold season; if you had come back in summer, you would think that these vultures had a right to the whole city, it stinks so intolerably." That is perhaps slander a hundred years old. Certainly I saw no buzzards in Charleston. But the heat remains. Sensible people, if they can afford to get away, do not remain.

In the Low Country now in summer, not only houses in Charleston, but plantation houses in all the country round are shut tight by millionaires from the North who own them and who come down only for the winter season, for the shooting, and, if they are not only rich but lucky and presentable as well, also for the balls of the St. Cecelia Society. Millionaires are the successors of rice. They are the cash crop. They dung an earth worn barren. They rejoice in the posssession of acres flooded by waters through old broken dykes. And most of them are welcome. They are not only in the Low Country of South Carolina. They are on the islands off the coast of Georgia. There was one of them—there may be more—in Natchez. There were a number of them about Thomasville, close to Florida, in South Georgia. They have flocked to Virginia as to the nearest South. And in Kentucky the Southern gentlemen behind the white fences, the blue grass and the juleps are almost always persons from New York, Chicago or Detroit.

"I believe the neighborhood around Lexington," Barry Bingham, able, young editor of *The Louisville Courier-Journal,* and a cousin distant but pleasant, told me, "has been almost entirely taken over by absentee landlords from the East who want to have some acres of Bluegrass on which to raise horses."

In Washington at a tobacco hearing I had heard, however, that even the millionaires began to plant burley when the price rose to 35 cents a pound. Which proves that even a millionaire is not averse to making an honest dollar.

Barry added: "The same kind of condition exists around Charleston, South Carolina, where so many strangers have moved in to take advantage of a picturesque and charming community. This strikes me as one of the unfortunate things that is happening in the South today."

I shared Barry's feeling and fear, until W. W. Ball, lively and hard-headed editor of *The News and Courier* of Charleston, showed me that there was another way of looking at this migration southward of the Yankees which has taken place in approximately the same years as the migration northward of the Negroes. Rich white man and poor black man passed on the road. The Negroes would not swap Harlem for Horry, and the Northerners, sometimes becoming more Southern than the Southerners they displace in the Big House, add rather than swap, Monck's Corner to Manhattan. The change is significant. in 1910 in South Carolina the Negroes were in the majority by over 150,000. Their majority was 45,000 in 1920. In 1930 the whites were in the majority by more than 150,000.

"I think that is the most notable thing that has come to pass in my recollection extending back sixty years," Mr. Ball told me.

Of the millionaires, he said: "Numerous wealthy Northern people have purchased abandoned rice plantations and lands adjoining. Many have restored or built fine houses. As a 'bridge' I think this has been of much service to the State. If these vast acres come into demand for agriculture, they should be taxed according to value. Pending that, their occupation by rich men is so much net gain."

Similar ideas moved the plantation owners, who saw the possibilities of continued rice planting disappear slowly and then swiftly with the increased incidence of tropical hurricane. Indeed, former Governor Duncan Clinch Heyward, who sold his plantations to A. Felix du Pont of Delaware, has written in *Seed from Madagascar* (University of North Carolina Press—1937), the story of the last days of rice planting in South Carolina, of his concern for the Negroes left on the abandoned land who would be faced with starvation unless something could be done which would give them work. Millionaires at the moment were the only something in sight. And millionaires in the South Carolina Low Country are as excellent a cash crop as middle-aged Christian Philadelphians of means are on the Delta Cooperative Plantation at Hillhouse in Mississippi. And both the dispossessed tenants of Arkansas and Mississippi and the aristocrats of South Carolina, who escaped the mortgagee by way of the millionaire, are equally lucky to have found them. The discovery that they will grow in the South is a rural event not equaled in South Carolina since it was discovered that seed from

Madagascar would grow in the Low Country and that Negroes could do all the hard work.

But the virtue of the people of the Low Country has been that while they have sometimes sold their houses to the Yankees, they have not felt it necessary to throw themselves into the bargain. Similarly in Charleston while many ladies have sold their antiques (the old taboo against trade is relaxing in the exact proportion as trade expands) to persons from the North, it has not been a part of the transaction that the purchasers also be invited to dinner (two-thirty to three-thirty is still the standard hour). They remember always that at Charleston, as Mr. Rutledge Rivers told me, the Ashley and the Cooper Rivers come together to form the Atlantic Ocean. I laughed with Mr. Rivers over his witticism of the waters, but there is truth below the layer of laughter. I even suspect sometimes that the sea stands back respectfully and in a little awe at the Battery. Certainly I know others do. I remember the wistfulness of a fellow North Carolinian. We are historically the residents of a vale of humility between two mountains of conceit. And this North Carolinian reported that there were only two kinds of South Carolinians, those who had never worn shoes and those who made you feel that you never had worn shoes. It is also true of the Virginians.

But some things are disappearing in the South Carolina Low Country as well as the rice. Indeed, some old things are gone as indigo. In the change the trade in antiques, which began when Miss Amelia sadly and secretly parted with ancestral spoons in order that papá (behind each "p" the "a" is short) in his declining years might have the best imported sherry, has advanced to a well organized commerce. The salable or purchasable antiques of Charleston were practically exhausted long ago, and the best and soundest old South Carolina antiques are now imported from England where a greater supply exists. There is no trickery in this. In the good native shops the antiques are what they are reported to be. Chippendale is Chippendale. Original is original. But tourists who expect a sideboard relinquished in tears by the impoverished aristocrats may be disappointed. A lady's pretty hands may once have seemed to be soiled by trade; but, dirty fingers or not, the ladies are in business for a profit. They deserve one.

Undoubtedly today quaintness is an industry in Charleston. Charleston is wiser than poor disappearing Darien down in Georgia where huge roadside signs hailed the motorist with the invitation to stop and see a real ex-slave, Liverpool Hazzard, who belonged to the Butlers to whom Fanny Kemble refused to belong. The technique of Charleston is the same as that so successfully pursued by Miss Greta Garbo and Mr. Charles Lindbergh. A graceful weariness attends the tourist trade. But on the Battery there is a skyscraper to hold them. The aristocrats who own the gardens are every spring packing them in at one or two dollars a head. Even an aristocrat knows a gold mine when he has one. And, if the main tourist entrance is through the garden gates, why should not other gentlefolk seek an honest penny feeding the creatures, renting them rooms, selling them sideboards, mammy dolls, pralines, gasoline, oil, tires, hot dogs, old portraits, carpentry work, legal services, medical attention, the air, and assistance with ancestry.

"My dear, her people are in trade . . ."

"Well, who isn't, Aunt Arabelle?"

But Charleston is neither the production of a millionaire with the most excellent intentions as Williamsburg is; nor the remains of a pretentiousness that wholly collapsed as is Natchez. Charleston is what it was. Its houses are the old houses; and their occupants often enough are the descendants of the old occupants. So it is differentiated from Williamsburg which is excellent archaeology, but only archaeology. Williamsburg is a reproduction and would be so labeled in any honest Charleston shop. And Charleston possesses not only a past but a past which is rich in character and quality. Its follies were great ones. And its gentlemen were not merely rich men riding on the backs of slaves. Undoubtedly on the rice plantations there were nigger whippers who mistook themselves for gentlemen; and sometimes, not often, Charleston made the same mistake. But there were also men—and women—who were not merely well connected and not merely rich, but important beyond such trivia, intelligent, creative, figures fit to march in such a pageant as that in which moved, through a mourning city, the black horses pulling the catafalque of Calhoun. And their race is not merely living; it is also aware and awake. Neither the rednecks, nor the Syrians, nor the Irishmen (sometimes they strengthened them) nor the Greeks, nor the Negroes, nor the millionaires have overwhelmed them. They retain an ancient integrity as full of old-fashioned fault as old-fashioned charm. I personally am unable to resist either.

But they are not to be seen in summer. The houses where I rang bells resounded with my ringing, and only my ringing. Even the streets in the older sections of the town were empty. And there were no tourists, except me, in the western churchyard before St. Philip's. It was good for a little while to be alone there where all winter long the great dead and the dead good and the gay dead have so much company. I always go there when I am in Charleston to look at the impressive tomb of John C. Calhoun, not the great actor who played the tragedy of the old South to its final curtain which he never saw, but an unknown grandson who lived a historically insignificant life but sleeps at the end of it in a bigger tomb than that which the Southern statesman occupies. Behind the grandchild's mortuary pretensions the great John C.

329

sleeps undisturbed. Nowhere on earth, not excepting Westminster, is there a sweeter or nobler place for sleep.

Unless it is around the corner on Meeting Street in the churchyard of St. Michael's where James Louis Petigru is. Charleston grows from both of them and grows nobly, loving both, for as Calhoun led the South in an angrier arrogance toward war, Petigru walked Charleston's streets as war was made alone. He mistook the bells which rang so loud on December 20, 1860 for a fire alarm and when he was told that instead they announced secession, he cried: "I tell you there is a fire; they have this day set a blazing torch to the temple of constitutional liberty, and please God, we shall have no more peace forever." He was wrong. In three years a city in the midst of war honored its man of dissent at his burial. And when I went there to see in stone the epitaph, which Nell Battle Lewis of Raleigh had printed in her column in *The News and Observer,* St. Michael's was so hot and quiet that a humming bird broke its peace with its wings. And under the sun I read a man's epitaph and the best statement I know of the aristocratic ideal which remains as important as it has always been rare in the South as on the earth. It is not long. Indeed, never was so much engraved on so little stone. It is:

JAMES LOUIS PETIGRU

Born at

Abbeville May 10th, 1789

Died at Charleston March 9th, 1863

JURIST, ORATOR, STATESMAN, PATRIOT

Future times will hardly know how great a life
This simple stone commemorates
The tradition of his Eloquence, his
Wisdom and his Wit may fade;

Dut he lived for ends more durable than fame,
His Eloquence was the protection of the poor and wronged,
His Learning illuminated the principles of Law—
In the admiration of his Peers,
In the respect of his People,
In the affection of his Family,
His was the highest place;
The just meed
Of his kindness and forbearance,
His dignity and simplicity,
His brilliant genius and his unwearied industry,
Unawed by Opinion,
Unseduced by Flattery,
Undismayed by Disaster,
He confronted Life with antique Courage
And Death with Christian Hope.

In the great Civil War
He withstood his People for his Country,
But his People did homage to the Man
Who held his conscience higher than their praise;
And his Country
Heaped her honours on the grave of the Patriot,
To whom, living,
His own righteous self-respect sufficed
Alike for Motive and Reward.

I read the epitaph through. I read it again. Then slowly
I went out of the old churchyard and down Meeting Street.
I turned on Water Street to the Battery going past Dr. "Billy"
Ball's where one night we had talked late. I rang the bell at
the corner, but, though it sounded like muffled music inside
the door, no one came. So I went down the steps and across
the street to the sea wall. It was sticky and hot even here on
the water front. The sun burned on the water between me
and old Fort Sumter. And beyond Sumter somehow I looked

back to Calhoun and Petigru. Neither of them were native
to the Low Country. Both of them had come to Charleston
from the old Abbeville district in South Carolina, the up-
country of the Irish and Scotch-Irish where now spindles
turn, not far from Greenville where I had seen the little
man with his back against the high steel fence before the
huge mill, only a little way from Honea Path where men had
died in strike, only a little further from Cotswold where I
had seen in the commissary the girl huge with child. That
baby's suckling now, I thought. It may even have a brother
or a sister on the way. There may be milk in that girl's
breasts till she grows old or dies.

I turned and looked at the dignified houses along the
shore. Petigru and Calhoun might have been in a number
of them. The beds might stand—unsold—in which they had
slept. And yet they had been outlanders, highlanders even,
with Irish in them. Both of them had been pupils of that
famous teaching Irishman, one generation from County
Down, Moses Waddell. Yet somehow they above the others
—and there were others—gave content and weight to the
aristocratic tradition of the Low Country and Charleston. It
is an old custom, everywhere honored and not only in
Charleston, that they are soon among the well born who are
shrewd, strong or wise no matter where they began. It is a
custom which helps those on the way up, but those who are
already up, it helps more.

But in the houses along the Battery I knew there were
still, if no Calhouns or Petigrus, at least, which is much, men
of dignity and women of charm and grace, even of loveliness.
They lived as people, not as ghosts. Not all of them were rich,
not many of them were vastly wise. Perhaps too few of them
possessed the quality of flexibility which must go with continuity to make a great people. But nowhere on this earth
that I know are there any people with a clearer sense of the

tempo of good manners, of good living. And if the pleasant present people of Charleston do not possess the wisdom to lead the South to a civilization worthy of its pretensions and its past, even Calhoun led it into a war he did not live to see, and it would not follow Petigru the other way in peace. But in Charleston tradition is not merely secure; tradition is gay also and graceful, even warm. And the dead were not so solemn, if the living are not so wise.

But Charleston, they told me in the State capital, which is Columbia, is dying. Perhaps it is. But I would not swap its corpse for the capital. No, nor for half the other cities of the South which are proud either of their ancestry or their factories. Even in this so often so-called New South the epitaph above Petigru may mean more for the future than the stir of Atlanta or the sweat of Birmingham. It may even mean more than the progeny of such girls as that one in Conestee. And if Charleston serves to keep this in memory, while it eats its past, it may serve again a South which it has served— and sometimes a little recklessly ("he who dallies is a dastard; he who doubts is damned")—often before. Indeed, if Charleston could sell the Petigru epitaph to the Yankees along with the antiques and the plantations, the present Low Country generation might do more than once its grandfathers did when they began a Civil War and its grandmothers watched the beginning from housetops with ladylike excitement and ladylike applause. We are all Yankees at last, North and South, and there are none of us who do not need the memory of the pattern of Petigru. Certainly, the ideal ought not to be left to such a cold stone in a hot cemetery as I saw within the odor of little duchess roses on that empty day in July.

35

DIXIE DESTINATION

A TRAVELER comes to destinations. Or hopes to.

I remember when I was young and Admiral Robert E. Peary and Dr. Frederick Cook were quarreling (I was a great and small partisan of Dr. Cook) that I conceived of the North Pole as such a trimmed tree trunk as the Southern Bell Telephone Company or the Carolina Power & Light Company sometimes imbedded in the sidewalk before our house. I would not have been surprised, of course, had the North Pole been a little more ornate, and a trifle more impervious to heat and cold and bug and polar bear. But it provided a definite destination for explorer. And I think that the moment when loss of faith in Dr. Cook began to set in was when he failed to show a lantern slide of it in his illustrated lecture at the Academy of Music.

Certainly now at the end of my travels in discovery of the South I wish I had a definite destination to report—or a plan. Certainly a plan. For the South, the Philosophers at Chapel Hill tell me, will not escape without a plan or at least a planning. I agree.

All people are planners.

"I aim to plant lespedeza in that field if I ever get around to it. But it just seems natural somehow to put it in cotton."

All people are regionalists.

I discovered that when I was twelve. And I still believe that Dr. Howard W. Odum missed one of the best indices of the Southern region when he failed to determine a line on one side of which all nice children say, "No, ma'am" and "Yes, ma'am," to the teacher and on the other side of which they get laughed at for saying it by all including teacher. Such a line, I understand, no longer exists. At any rate, when I asked my daughter about it she said, "Hunh?"

But certainly all people are planners and regionalists. The plan may not extend beyond dinner time and the region may not reach beyond the creek. Indeed, in one section of North Carolina plan and region are combined.

"Well, I guess we'll do like the folks across the river do."

"How's that?"

"Do without."

In more ways than one that has been the regional plan of the American South, and I for one Southerner, speaking also without fear of contradiction for 25,000,000 others, am ready to find another.

This program was adopted shortly after the surrender at Appomattox and has been in force almost without interruption since. That was a grand war for the poets and the politicians, but I am beginning to wonder quite seriously whether the Civil War itself ever made any really profound difference in the life and history of the South. The war itself seems a detail almost insignificant between what went before and what came after. Mine, I suppose, was the last Southern generation reared in a combination of indignation and despair. Now, fortunately, save in a few groups devoted to a form of rebel yelling which is also a form of ancestor whooping, the Civil War as such plays little or no part in the life and thinking of the South. That means, I hope, escape from the old Do-Without Economy of the Southern States, for the chief injury inflicted upon us late Confederates by the war was the excuse which it gave us for giving up and sitting in the sun. The South was poor; the war caused it. The South was ignorant; the war made us too poor to educate. The

South was slow; well, after what the damyankees did it wasn't any use to stir. The war provided a satisfying, acceptable and even mildly exhilarating excuse for everything from Captain Seabrook's wooden leg to the quality of education dispensed at the Centennial School.

Unfortunately, like a great many simple explanations this one did not explain. The tariff did at least as much damage in Dixie as Sherman and Grant together in making the South poor and keeping it poor. Indeed, while Grant and Sherman have gone to whatever they had coming to them, the tariff remains. The process of selling the fertility of the land along with the cotton began a long time before the Civil War and had reduced Virginia gentlemen to the unpleasant business of breeding slaves for the Deep South markets. Even now men tremble over the possible loss of cotton markets; it is a trembling like that of the old slave fearful of losing his chains. The contempt for labor which everywhere and in all times has been an inevitable item of slavery was full grown before 1860. The hookworm was in the South but not discovered. Yellow fever, typhoid and malaria were there but not understood. Pellagra was seen as clay eating and was considered a perverse habit of the perverted po' whites. Most of the white people were desperately poor. Most of the Negroes had instinctively developed an apparently racial shiftlessness as a shrewd labor defense under slavery long before ladies and gentlemen on the Charleston housetops applauded the firing on Fort Sumter. And Reconstruction: Mississippi had defaulted on its bonds sometime in the 40's. The Rothschilds were involved, and, if Mississippi paid her debts, the Governor said, he was fearful that they might use the money to gain control of the sepulcher of Our Blessed Saviour. That would never do, so Mississippi defaulted, and there was not a Negro in the Legislature that did it.

The Civil War killed men and broke hearts and caused

a tremendous amount of private suffering. But war is too spectacular. All of the major faults and flaws in Southern economy were on the way to full growth before the war began. But it served as an alibi—a magnificent alibi—for them all, and for those that came after, too. In a false present, the South had begun the adoration of a fictitious past. It luxuriated in its tragedy. The South, like some ladies in it, enjoyed ill-health. Delicacy of constitution became a positive social virtue. And generally the fact was overlooked that as early after Appomattox as 1870 the South produced more cotton than it did in 1860 and got more for it, the most, indeed, that it had ever received.

The South's faults were many, but the South's faults were not alone. The war and Reconstruction were important as memory of them served as screen of emotionalism behind which moved, ever praising Lee, those unemotional gentlemen from the North who knew what they wanted and how much they would have to pay for it, which was not much. This second wave of carpetbaggers was received with honors and banquets and bands. They were the agents of the new and ever greater absentee ownership of the South. They came from the North with excellent financial connections to buy up broken down Southern railroads and other properties and they picked up some pretty bargains and some pretty Southerners. The town was properly impressed when Colonel Cadwallader entertained Mr. Prentiss, the Boston banker. (It continues impressed when his name is Manaccus and he is in the garment business.) The banks of those same gentlemen who bought up Southern railroads were also deeply interested in Northern railroads. It has even been suggested that while they were ever willing to make money they were also careful not to build up Southern traffic and industry at the expense of those older developed areas of the North and East through which their older lines ran. Freight rates certainly have not been shaped to aid the industrial development of the South; instead they still sit providing inland the protection which tariffs provide on coast and frontier. Some trade tacticians feel that freight rate and tariff together made a prettier pincher than that which Grant and Sherman applied on the Confederacy.

Of course, all ownership in this modern corporate civilization assumes the pattern of absentee ownership. Stockholders, South as North, are increasingly irresponsible and uncreative as individual capitalists. But the control of capital is in the North and East and it may be significant that the only industrial development which has taken place in the South since the industrial North overcame the country culture of the South has been in the widely dispersed manufacture of textiles and in the new big industry of the cigarette. Otherwise the South, devoted to the culture of cotton and tobacco, the prices of which are fixed in world markets, still buys from the protected factories of the North. Its new overseers, faithful to the absentee owners, beg and plead and promise for more absentee investment and control while simultaneously they cry to hysteria in condemnation of foreign agitators among nice native labor.

There is reason for both fear and elation. The new pincher movement upon the South has not been applied in recent years with the precision which Grant and Sherman exercised, or perhaps the body seized is a good deal less easily grasped than was the old half-dead Confederacy between Richmond and Atlanta. At any rate those capitalists, local and absentee, who are concerned for low wages in the South, and those who are concerned for sales in the South do not seem to be acting in perfect unity. The most profoundly disturbing foreign agitators in the region are the salesmen of Chevrolets and radios, gaudy machine-stitched dresses and other shining gadgets and gewgaws. Even the power companies, incited by TVA, are filling the tow-heads and the burr-heads with glittering dreams. Not only the spindle has come South, so also has the automobile. The worker and the mill have both become mobile. As whole mills may move from Massachusetts to Mississippi so may whole philosophies.

It is not the Communists who are coming but the advertisers. The cabins of the South are wall papered with the pages of newspapers and magazines and so much advertising has a practically permanent appeal. There may not come to the cabin in a year enough money to meet for a month the requirements of the persuasive suggestion that it is easy to own a Packard. But if all of those who see the walls cannot read them, all of them can desire. If they lack the money, they can wish for it. They can be dissatisfied with the old Do-Without Plan of the Southern regions of the United States. They are. And those new absentees who are coming South in a movement which New England Governors call "a threat from the South" should come warned: the South has much to offer, place and people and resources and power, but it does not honestly have docility to offer. Such as it possessed is disappearing before the building of desire. And the first problem of the South today is people. It is by no means limited to the South. Indeed, it is the newly exciting question of the possibility of democracy. In contemplation of it too many people have been looking at Italy and Spain and Russia and Germany, as well as at the old democracies of England and France. It is less disturbing to consider it over water, perhaps, but the seeing is clearer in the South. Contemplate the questions:

Are the Southern people capable of serving, governing and saving themselves?

Or must they depend for guidance in government and to

decency and adequacy in living upon an oligarchy of so-called aristocrats, a committee of experts, a ring of politicians? Upon plutocrat, demagogue or professor?

Is democracy possible in the South? (Is it possible anywhere?)

Surely, those questions are properly raised with regard to the folk of a region in which the sharp-eyed regional planners have found natural resources in superabundance, population in abundance, but a deficiency in science, skills, technology and organization, waste in its general economy and a richness, combined with immaturity and multiple handicaps, in its culture. The trends they discovered show hesitancy and relative regression in many aspects of culture. They found the lowest incomes and the poorest fed people in America in a region which should be a garden.

Beyond those findings, I pretend to no simple, certain answers to the questions. In the first place, of course, the Southern people will not show their capability or the lack of it in a vacuum. They must work in a realm not only patterned by their past and their prejudices, but also one definitely shaped by tariffs and freight rates fixed largely at the North for the benefit of the North. It is a region governed in important degree by absentee owners and one which has been stirred deeply more frequently by reflex response to exterior criticism than by agitators, native or foreign, at work within. It is a sensitive region, more romantic than idealistic, and one which is expiating for more sins than its own, though there are enough of them.

The answers like the questions go deep into the past. Important aspects of democracy grew in the South. Much of its philosophy was shaped at Monticello by Thomas Jefferson. But Jefferson in Virginia and John Adams in Massachusetts died on the same afternoon in 1826. And sometime thereafter, perhaps at the very time it began to become solidly

Democratic, the South discarded democracy. Or perhaps
more fairly stated, its democracy was destroyed. From the
beginning there were Southerners, big and rich, who held to
the faith that wisdom reposed only in the big and the rich
and that therefore the franchise should be restricted to them.
More and more democracy asserted itself against them. Requirements for voting and office were slowly but steadily
scaled down. And then after a long and passionate war, in the
South the electorate was enlarged, by force from without, by
thousands of Negroes and decreased by thousands of white
men who had formerly borne arms as Southerners and so as
Confederates and so as Rebels. The result was a condition
which seemed intolerable to the most faithful Democrats.
Perhaps at that time no entry of any sort by the Negroes into
the rights of citizenship would have been tolerable to the
South. Certainly, however, the Negroes were given no chance
to be absorbed. They were hurried from slavery into a power
which, in general, other men misused. Any unemotional
reader of history must recognize the similarity between the
Ku Klux of the South and the Brown Shirts of Germany and
the Black Shirts of Italy and the similarity of the conditions
which created them. They provided a rank and file violence.
But in the South they brought the Bourbons to power. And
the native Bourbon has steadily served the large propertied
classes, absentee or local, in the exploitation of the South.
Almost without exception the rout of the carpetbaggers, the
Negroes and the scallywags carried the old planter class and
a new promoter class to power also over the vast white mass
of little farmers and storekeepers, mechanics and laborers.
For them as for the Negroes to too great an extent democracy
was in the years afterwards effectually denied. But little men
stir: And men to lead them. There was, for instance, Ben-
jamin Ryan Tillman in South Carolina. And "Pitchfork
Ben" was by no means the only name applied to him. Low

341

Country aristocrats still snort to speak of him. After him there were others like him—and not like him. There will be more. They are Southern demagogues, some better and some worse, but all indicative of a Southern unwillingness to leave government entirely to the political gentlemen of the gentlemen of business—gentlemen who know exactly what they want and how much they will pay for it. It is only an alternative, when as in the case of such a man as Huey Long, he leaves as a political estate a power to plunder. Neither he nor his inheritors discovered that power. It always exists when the people are incapable of government or careless of government. And Southerners might be plundered by the very people who made them also for a time incapable of government. They were. And those who plundered them also saw sign of inferiority in the poverty that was left.

There are Southerners still who would more quickly deny the ability of the people of the South to manage the South than any people outside of it. They are the persisting and ineradicable Bourbons and Brigadiers who are devoted to a class before a region. That made them readier to serve as the agents of the new mastery. They still serve it and serving also themselves believe they serve the South. Their minds are still patterned in that master-slave concept which in sense of superiority applied not only to slaves but to white men lacking slaves. They apply it now to the cotton mill as well as to the plantation. Many aristocrats in the South—and that is the name for both the Coca-Cola bottler and the member of the Society of the Cincinnati—do not believe and never have believed that the people should—if they could—govern the South. Such a faith or faithlessness leads to the unincorporated mill village and the company union. Included under it are both the kindliest paternalism and the most vicious and careless exploitation.

This lack of faith by the few great in the many small

342

seems to me sad, but the saddest thing in the South is the fact that those at the top who do not believe in the intelligence of those at the bottom have not shown themselves capable of a leadership satisfactory to the people they assume to lead—nor, so far as I could discover, to anybody else. The market for stuffed shirts is glutted.

Finally, the people are not as disturbing as the patricians. The most encouraging thing is that the ordinary Southern whites, given fair chance and training, are showing themselves capable of performing the best types of work. This is so in the South. TVA discovered it and was surprised. Others are discovering it. And in the black and white migration to the North this generation of Southern immigrants has been able to compete with the workers already on the ground. The depression saw them shivering and jobless in every Northern city: by the thousands it sent them scurrying home again. Now they and more beside them move again. They are, of course, inadequately trained, inadequately skilled. Sometimes they are underfed. Sometimes they are sick. Sometimes they are criminal, feeble-minded, perverted, insane. But they move and they will move. They march to eat. They will not be stopped. They need not be feared unless they are resisted. But fear in the South has slandered both of them:

The Southern Negro is not an incurably ignorant ape.

The Southern white masses are not biologically degenerate.

Both are peoples capable of vastly more training than they possess. Both are peoples who may hang heavy on the national advance, or help to speed and sustain it. Both are peoples who could consume and produce more wealth. And they are capable of happy, productive, peaceful life, side by side. White men and black men have shared the South's too little for a long time and, though there is more than a casual connection between hunger and lynchings, they have shared

343

it in relative quiet, decency and peace. They would be able to build a South in terms of the South's potentiality, if together they had a chance to make and share plenty.

Increasingly the ancient and venerable Do-Without Plan is deserted. But what of a new plan for the South? The materials for its shaping have grown at the University of North Carolina in a huge, wise book, *Southern Regions of the United States*. But I believe that the new Southern plan will grow more directly from itching than from statistics. The South is awaking, scratching at new desires. A plan of course should provide the way to fulfillment and at the moment the South faces the prospect of plenty with more wish than way.

"Chile, yo' eyes is bigger'n yo' belly."

But the big-eyed stage is important. Once they were sleepy. Now they stir and are wide open at last. And a regional plan is a plot from seeing to getting, from needing to wanting, to possessing. Such an ordered program in the South must include expansions of facilities for public education in a region lacking skills, for public health in a region still plagued by preventable diseases, for public welfare in a country in which the private welfare of so many is so insecure. None of these are in any sense simply Southern. The children of the South —which is the land of children in America—are more and more the adults of tomorrow in other States and so they will be the criminals or the sick or the creative or the consumers or the burdens of other States soon, very soon.

Such a plan for a new, free, fed, housed, happy South must include not merely program at home for improvement but also program in the nation for the relinquishment of advantages elsewhere over the South. Perhaps those advantages are so deeply fixed as in freight rate and tariff that to change them to give the South a chance might do vast harm elsewhere, might cause much suffering in the areas which have grown rich on advantage, like that which wrings the hearts of Northerners when they see it in the South. Perhaps the South, as New England seems now fearing, may be able to escape its single-slavery to cotton and advance to a diverse industrial and agricultural development despite the imperial advantages which New England took as its loot after the Civil War. There was some sort of bargain then, now dimly seen. The Negroes were sold down the river again after emancipation, and the price paid was a fixed economic differentiation which left the whole South in slavery to New England instead of some of the South in slavery to other Southerners. But I mean to start no new war: the South is at last escaping from the economic occupation which succeeded the military occupation. The South is at last escaping from the more destructive Reconstruction which economically continued the South as captive. And New England is afraid: the terrible danger is that it is about to lose at last the slavery from which it profited long after Lincoln in a manner of speaking set the Negroes free. Of course everybody was free in the South, free to fight among themselves for the too little that was left when tribute was paid.

Cato the Elder was no more implacable than the Brahmans of Boston who came after the Abolitionists with considerably cooler heads. The South was not plowed up and planted with salt as Carthage was. If no more generous, Bostonians (citizens of a region and an attitude and not a town) were less wasteful. They recognized that the South kept in its place (a place in the nation geographically similar to that of the Negro in the South) might be useful and profitable. It was. And as Southerner at the end of discovery I ask now only that they recognize the poverty of the South as a part of the same civilization as Harvard and in a measure as the creation of the same people. Cato did not ride through Carthage on the train and blame its condition on the Carthaginians. That much only I ask of the Yankees.

A good deal more is necessary for the Southerners. Item one is escape from pretentiousness. The Southerner has deluded only himself. The boy who was brought in to Savannah from Bryan County with malaria, pellagra, hookworm and a pelvis pierced by his thigh bone as a result of malnutrition nevertheless insisted in the hospital that he was the best alligator catcher on the coast of Georgia. Perhaps he was. Maybe still one Reb can beat ten Yankees. It is irrelevant. But planning in the South must begin at the bottom where so many of its people are. There is no handle on its top by which it can be lifted. Tyranny, like that of Huey Long's, would be swifter. Government by an oligarchy of plutocrats might possibly provide a more orderly way, though it would be concerned with profits first and people only afterwards, not recognizing that there is a difference. But in the South the tyrants and the plutocrats and the poor all need teaching. One of them no more than the others. All are in the warm dark, and whether they like it or not—white man, black man, big man—they are in the dark together. None of them will ever get to day alone.